ANTI SEMITISM AND ZIONISM

Selected Marxist Writings

Edited by Daniel Rubin

INTERNATIONAL PUBLISHERS New York

© 1987 International Publishers Co., Inc.
1st printing, 1987
All rights reserved.

Manufactured in the United States of America

Library of Congress Cataloging-in-Publication Data

Anti-semitism and Zionism.

Includes index.
1. Antisemitism. 2. Zionism. 3. Jews—Politics
and government—1948–   2. 4. Israel. I. Rubin,
Daniel, 1931–
DS145.A632 1987   956.94′001   87-3123
ISBN 0-7178-0663-4 (pbk.)

CONTENTS

Our Contributors

Gus Hall

General Secretary of the Communist Party, USA since 1959. Author of many books, including *Fighting Racism* (1985), and *Working Class USA* (1987).

Henry Winston
(1911–1986)

National Chairman of the Communist Party, USA, 1966–1986. Author of *Strategy for a Black Agenda* (1973); *Class, Race and Black Liberation* (1977), and many articles.

Dr. Herbert Aptheker

Editor of *Jewish Affairs*. Marxist historian and educator. Author of numerous books on Afro-American history and other subjects. Editor of the complete works of Dr. W. E. B. Du Bois.

Dr. Hyman Lumer
(1909–1976)

Former editor of *Jewish Affairs*, and of *Political Affairs* (theoretical journal of the CPUSA). Author of two books extensively excerpted herein, and others.

Lewis Moroze

Managing editor of *Jewish Affairs*, and a member of the New Jewish Agenda. Was secretary of the New Jersey Committee to Free Angela Davis, and is a retired schoolteacher.

Daniel Rubin

Chair of the education department of the CPUSA; has been active for peace and economic justice, a former youth leader and the author of many articles.

ANTI SEMITISM AND ZIONISM

1

INTRODUCTION

DANIEL RUBIN

This selection of writings represents Marxist-Leninist thought on the struggle against anti-Semitism and on Zionism, beginning with V. I. Lenin in 1903. It also includes some complete articles as well as excerpts from books and articles written from 1973 through May 1987 by Gus Hall, Henry Winston, Herbert Aptheker, Hyman Lumer and Lewis Moroze.

Recent events confirm, under new conditions, the basic approach of Marxism-Leninism toward anti-Semitism and Zionism. Here is how Lenin spoke of anti-Semitism in July 1903 (*Collected Works [CW]* Vol. 6, p. 470):

Complete unity between the Jewish and non-Jewish proletariat is moreover especially necessary for a successful struggle against anti-Semitism, this despicable attempt of the government and the exploiting classes to exacerbate racial particularism and national enmity.

Again in March 1919, Lenin declared (CW 29:253):

Shame on accursed tsarism which tortured and persecuted the Jews. Shame on those who foment hatred towards the Jews, who foment

1

hatred towards other nations. Long live the fraternal alliance of the workers of all nations in the struggle to overthrow capital.

In the czarist Russia of 1913, Lenin considered, "the most oppressed and persecuted nationality—the Jews" (CW 20:26).

In different times and countries, anti-Semitism has always served the interest of the ruling class to divide working people and to divert attention from the real source of oppression of the popular masses. Today anti-Semitism in the United States and the rest of the capitalist world serves the interests of the most reactionary sections of the monopoly capitalists. It attempts to mislead workers and middle strata into believing, "Jews are the wealthy, own the banks, control the government" and Jews are, therefore, the cause of their problems.

This lie is a coverup that prevents working people from uniting and understanding who is the real source of homelessness, hunger, poverty, unemployment and job insecurity, farm foreclosures, the high price of necessities, high taxes, threats to democratic rights, foreign anti-popular aggressions and, in nuclear war—the threat to the very existence of humanity and nature. Only the monopoly capitalists benefit in direct terms of hundreds of billions in profits and in securing their domination, while they postpone the day when working people will replace the outmoded, anti-human capitalist system with socialism. These monopolies spawn, nurture and often finance reactionary, violent, anti-Semitic groups—particularly among urban and rural middle strata.

They use anti-Semitism along with even more pernicious racism toward Afro-Americans, peoples of darker color generally and all specially oppressed national minorities. These are the main weapons of reaction, used together with anti-Communism and male supremacy, to divide and divert the working majority from the common source of social evils—the transnational monopolies and the military industrial complex.

Anti-Semitism is not simply a religious prejudice against the Jewish religion. It is an ideology and practice that does not die out because it serves the vital interests of monopoly capitalism and its most reactionary sectors. As Lenin pointed out it is a matter of oppression against a nationality group that appears in a religious garb. Though Jewish people are not a distinct race, extreme anti-Semitism uses a theory of alleged "racial" qualities to denounce all Jews, religious or not.

The monopoly capitalists include Protestants, Catholics, some from other religions, a few atheists and· also some Jews. These monopoly capitalists are people from a number of ethnic backgrounds—English, German, French, Italian, Dutch, Japanese, etc. and some non-religious, secular Jewish-Americans. The vast majority from each of these ethnic backgrounds, including Jewish, are not monopoly capitalists, but are working people. The owners of the giant monopoly and transnational corporations are only a handful.

Marxism-Leninism has also viewed Zionism as an ideology and practice that serves the interests of monopoly capitalism. However, it presents itself as an answer for the Jewish people to anti-Semitism. In fact it serves not only those Jewish-Americans who are monopoly capitalists, like Goldman, Sachs, the Wall St. firm, and the monopoly capitalists who now dominate the economic and political life of Israel, but the interests of monopoly capital in general in the U.S. and in the rest of the capitalist world. Zionism serves the interests of world imperialism, which is monopoly capitalism on a world scale and is headed by U.S. imperialism.

When we speak of Zionism, we do not mean the attachment and special concern nearly all Jewish-Americans feel for what happens to Israel, similar to the concern Italian- and Greek-Americans feel for Italy and Greece. Large numbers of Jewish-Americans who consider themselves "Zionists" are in fact not Zionists. They may be influenced to some degree by Zionism because most major Jewish organizations and publications are still headed by Zionists. It would be wrong, however, to characterize them as Zionists because, as we shall see, in their majority, and a growing majority at that, they are moving away from the specific policies of Zionism.

Marxism-Leninism has long argued that the interests of the Jewish masses, working people who also experience anti-Semitism, lie in unity with the progressive forces in each country and worldwide—with the working class as a whole, the forces for peace, democracy, national equality and social progress. Marxist-Leninists predicted this would be the path of Jewish masses even if there were temporary zigs and zags. Lenin pointed out on January 9, 1917 (CW 23:250):

> The Jews furnished a particularly high percentage (compared with the total Jewish population) of leaders of the revolutionary movement. And now, too, it should be noted to the credit of the Jews, they furnish a relatively high percentage of internationalists, compared with other nationalities.

Jewish-Americans had long been considered one of the most progressive ethnic-religious groups in helping to build the labor movement, the old Socialist Party, the International Workers Order, the American Labor Party, etc. and had one of the largest percentage memberships in the Communist Party, USA. But during the height of the Cold War with its virulent anti-Sovietism and anti-Communism, and later with a wave of Zionist national chauvinism connected to the early Israeli aggressive wars of expansion (1956, 1967, 1973), considerable numbers of Jews moved away from their progressive heritage.

Now the course of development—Reaganism and the far right danger, the bankruptcy of Israeli government policy, the role of the Soviet Union in leading the world fight against nuclear war, the socioeconomic crises of U.S. capitalism—interrelated with a new framework of struggle by our multinational, multiracial, male-female working class (including Jewish workers) and by the Afro-American and Latino peoples and many other strata, and with the Communist Party, USA actively influencing such changes, all this has produced a new direction for the great bulk of Jewish-Americans.

Before we consider this change and what has given rise to it in greater detail, we will clarify the Marxist-Leninist view of what Zionism is. Zionism today is a particular, extreme form of Jewish bourgeois nationalism. It is an ideology and practice that corresponds to the interests of the Jewish monopoly bourgeosie. Zionism poses as an answer to anti-Semitism through alliance with world imperialism. While there is an overall common ideology, there are sometimes tactical differences reflecting different national environments as among Israeli Zionists, Jewish-American Zionists, French, British or Dutch Zionists or South African Zionists. There are at times even tactical differences of some importance with U.S. imperialism, while the clear main tendency is mutual support.

Zionism is an extreme form of Jewish national chauvinism, a kind of racialism. It seeks to mislead Jewish masses by holding that the Jewish people are a superior, "chosen" people. In this view, Jewish people are more intelligent and enterprising and, therefore, inequality for "ignorant Arab terrorists" in Israel and the occupied territories is justified as a result of their alleged own actions (blaming the victim). Zionism attempts to use anti-Semitism (not openly, of course) to its advantage by arguing that Jewish working people can never trust other working people.

Historic anti-Semitism, plus this distrust of other, "morally inferior" peoples, are used to justify aggression and repression as "first strike" measures to "prevent" anti-Jewish acts that would otherwise "necessarily" take place. Thus Jewish working people should not and can not unite with non-Jewish working people against the monopoly capitalists in the U.S., Israel, South Africa, etc. but should unite with "their own" leaders who happen to be Jewish members of the monopoly capitalist ruling class.

Originally Zionism presented itself to Jewish masses as an answer to anti-Semitism, through world imperialism granting a Jewish homeland where all Jews would go and be safe, in return for favors to imperialism. Zionism feared mass struggle in alliance with other exploited and oppressed working people against ruling class promoted anti-Semitism because Zionism represented the Jewish bourgeoisie who might lose leadership in such a struggle to Jewish workers who were attracted to socialism and Marxism.

Now Zionism is an expression of a nationality section of world imperialism that even more fears mass struggle in alliance with other exploited and oppressed working people against anti-Semitism and against monopoly capital in individual countries and internationally. It identifies even more fully with imperialist interests, particularly with the most reactionary, military-industrial complex sector. It supports nuclear confrontation with the Soviet Union, opposes all steps toward disarmament agreement, opposes national liberation movements in general and that of the Arab peoples and the Palestinian Arab people in particular. It hates the Soviet Union, world socialism, Marxism-Leninism and the Communists (Communist Party, USA, the Communist Party of Israel, the Communist Party of the Soviet Union, etc.).

Within the United States, Zionism in the main has supported Reaganism, though some Zionists are identified with more conservative sections of the Democratic Party machine. Zionism is hostile to trade unionism and to full equality for the Afro-American and other specially oppressed peoples. It opposes affirmative action as "reverse discrimination."

Many Israeli Zionists still maintain the necessity for all Jews to move to Israel because they "can never completely escape anti-Semitism and never realize themselves fully as Jews elsewhere." The fact is many more Israeli Jews are moving to the U.S. to escape the catastrophic consequences of the Israeli Zionist policies, than are U.S. Jews moving to Israel. In order to continue their Zionist pro-expansionist policies in the Mideast, the policy of being imperialism's gendarme for the oil monopolies, the Israeli Zionists seek a larger Jewish population, whom they would seek to poison with extreme nationalism. At the same time, few U.S. Zionists today support the idea of all Jews moving to Israel but they support the basic Israeli policy in the Mideast and its resulting Israeli domestic policy.

Our thus characterizing Zionism today is not in contradiction with saying that the majority of U.S. Jews are not now Zionists and are moving away from its influence, though many are still influenced by it on particular questions. Working people of most nationality backgrounds in capitalist countries are to some degree influenced by the ideas of the monopoly bourgeoisie, especially nationalist ideas and moods, if not also by the forms of class collaboration. The overall process underway in the U.S. is for a lessening of these influences on all other working people as well as on those who are Jewish Americans.

Nor is it contradictory to recognize that the Labor Party of Israel, Mapai, is Zionist controlled or that small groups of "labor Zionists", even "left labor Zionists" exist in the U.S. It is necessary to note, however, big changes taking place. The policies of Zionism illustrated by the Labor Party governments and joint governments with the Likud Party, as well as the dominant Zionist groups in the U.S., have become so bankrupt that this contradiction in terms is in crisis and in the process of being resolved. One can not act in the interests of Israeli workers and simultaneously pursue the international terrorist, aggressive policies of the Israeli Government and U.S. imperialism. The result must also be anti-worker, anti-popular domestic policies. Because of these contradictions and various scandals flowing from them, the Labor Party leadership has lost much of its credibility and masses of workers are seeking a way out of the contradictions along a road of peace, equality, democracy and satisfying their social needs.

In the U.S., "labor Zionist" groups have become a shell because events have made much clearer the impossibility of combining Zionism with pro-worker policies internationally and domestically.

Current developments sharply uphold the basic Marxist-Leninist positions expressed in the writings selected for this volume. While there is a new worldwide people's sentiment for peace and nuclear disarmament, Zionists carried out anti-Soviet provocations in efforts to disrupt and block meaningful agreement at Geneva and Reykjavik.

When Soviet performing artists come to the U.S. to promote

peaceful relations under new cultural exchange agreements, the extreme Zionist groups plant bombs. Evidence was found in the home of a Jewish Defense League member that "Federal authorities said linked the group to 'recent bombings and other terrorist acts,' including two incidents at Lincoln Center last year while Soviet entertainers were performing" (*New York Times*, 4/2/87).

The military-industrial complex and its foremost spokesman, Secretary of Defense Caspar Weinberger, do everything possible to block any kind of new arms agreement and press on with Star Wars to gain U.S. military superiority. The hard-line frontmen in this struggle contain an unusually large number of Jewish people in the Administration who are extreme Reaganites and Zionists. These include Richard Perle, Assistant Secretary of Defense; Elliot Abrams, Assistant Secretary of State for Latin American Affairs; Kenneth Adelman, Director of the Disarmament Agency; John Lehman, the retiring Secretary of the Navy, etc. These Reaganites are joined by those outside the Administration who run interference for Reaganism like Norman Podhoretz, Editor of *Commentary*; Nathan Perlmutter, Executive Director of the Anti-Defamation League of B'Nai B'rith; Morris Abram, formerly on the Civil Rights Commission; and Albert Shanker, President of the American Federation of Teachers.

Polls show, however, that Jewish Americans want progress toward nuclear disarmament, and they oppose Star Wars at least as much as, if not more than, the population in general. Therefore, most are coming to see these actions as anti-peace and extreme Reaganite rather than as "in defense of Soviet Jews" as they are alleged to be. The hard-line Zionist Reaganites are seen more and more as an embarrassment rather than their presence in government being a source of pride for Jewish people.

Belief in the lie that the Soviet Union was persecuting Soviet Jews had been quite effective for some years in moving Jewish Americans in the wrong direction on many issues. Substantial numbers of Jews voted for Ronald Reagan in 1980. But this lie is wearing thin. Jewish Americans like most others have been impressed by the Soviet peace initiatives under Mikhail Gorbachev's leadership. They believe the Soviets want to prevent nuclear war and are genuinely seeking disarmament. Especially did the 18-month Soviet unilateral test moratorium make an impression. It became evident to many that military-industrial-complex forces in the Reagan Administration are the main obstacle to agreement.

Soviet moves to renew and speed up development of their economy, democratic rights, availability of truthful information and social justice have all made a positive impression, even though Jewish Americans are largely unaware of the details and history. They are unaware that socialism long ago eliminated all governmental and organized expression of anti-Semitism and all other forms of national oppression and that anti-Semitism is a crime in the Soviet Union. Lenin signed the "Resolution of the Council of People's Commissars On Uprooting of the Anti-Semitic Movement" on July 27, 1918. It reads in part,

> The Council of People's Commissars instructs all Soviet deputies to take uncompromising measures to tear the anti-Semitic movement out by the roots. Pogromists and pogrom-agitators are to be placed outside the law.

Nor are Jewish-Americans aware that Soviet Jews have achieved full economic, social and political equality, evidenced, for example, by the fact they have the highest percentage of all 110 Soviet nationalities among college students and among members of the Communist Party. About 14% of Soviet Jews are members of the CPSU (*People of the USSR: Facts & Figures,* Novosti, Moscow, 1986).

Jewish culture is made available in Yiddish, which flourishes there more than anywhere else in the world, as well as in Russian and many other languages. Those who wish to practice the Jewish religion have no difficulty in doing so.

Nor are U.S. Jews aware that the only Jewish population of Europe to survive World War II were two million Soviet Jews who were given preference in being moved to safer areas to the East during the terrible Nazi attack upon the USSR.

The question of Soviet Jewish emigration is discussed by Hyman Lumer later in this volume. Suffice it to point out here that the Soviet Union, like many other countries in the world, does not permit general emigration and has made a broader exception for Soviet Jews, especially in connection with reuniting families. It has done this despite political difficulties in permitting people to leave who say they are going to Israel (though most end up in the U.S.) while Israel seeks a larger Jewish population useful for its Zionist aggressive policies in the Mideast.

Recently the Soviet Union has made a number of changes that many Jewish-Americans have welcomed. Soviet authorities have indicated that the present 12–14,000 applicants to emigrate will leave within this year (Zionists claim that from "400,000" to "all" Soviet Jews wish to leave). A number of Soviet Jews who have violated specific Soviet laws, as well as non-Jews, have been released and are emigrating. Rabbi's can now be trained outside as well as within the Soviet Union.

Socialism has long been the most humane society in the world, having no unemployment, poverty, national and racial oppression or advocacy of nuclear war or military superiority, and possessing the widest democracy for working people. The Soviet Union is now restructuring socialism to speed up its development and perfection with the aim of achieving social justice wherever it is violated or does not exist. To do this it seeks active involvement of the whole population and is undergoing an all-embracing further democratization to achieve such involvement. It is attempting to reduce all restrictive laws and regulations that are not absolutely necessary so that anti-social behavior will first be combatted by ideological and political means and not by administrative measures. It considers that the ideas of Marxism and the socialist way of life are so firmly implanted among the tens of millions that government action to prevent or punish anti-social behavior can be replaced in many instances by more humanitarian means as part of the renewal process.

General Secretary Gorbachev, in his January 1987 Central Committee Report on democratization, also spoke of efforts to raise ideological understanding among the whole population on a number of questions so that backward ideas would no longer find any expression even in unofficial and private interpersonal relations. Among the questions he mentioned was vestiges of anti-Semitism.

From experience, many Jewish Americans know that Soviet Jews who have emigrated here very seldom complain of any kind of anti-Semitism in the Soviet Union. Many have no complaints at all about their homeland and come for other reasons, to reunite families, in expectation of a more affluent life, etc. Many have returned after experiencing the anti-Semitism, unemployment and general insecurity of capitalist life.

All these developments have contributed to a more open mind toward the Soviet Union by Jewish Americans and less willingness to believe the flagrant lies of the Zionists, the Conference on Soviet Jewry, etc. about the life of the Jewish people in the Soviet Union.

The Israeli Zionist Government has supported Reaganite international policies and is participating in Star Wars research. No matter how reactionary and embarrassing the task, even one the U.S. has found it politically difficult to carry out, Israel has acted as U.S. surrogate and for its own reactionary interests. These have included military training and other aid to such groups and regimes as the Contras, South Africa, Chile, Paraguay, El Salvador, Honduras—Guatemala and Haiti under the dictatorships—Iran, etc. For documentation, see among other sources the *New York Times* article of April 3, 1987, "Congress Gets Report on Israeli Military Aid to South Africa."

Supposedly Moslem Iran and Arab Saudi Arabia mortally threaten Israel. But Israel has been deeply involved in the Iran Contragate scandal, supplying arms to Iran to fuel the seven-year war with Iraq as well as internal repression, and has joined Saudi Arabia in supplying arms for the Contras. Again there is much evidence that the majority of Jewish-Americans are on the other side. They are against apartheid, aid to the Contras, to other fascist regimes like Chile, etc.

In the Mideast itself, the aims of Israeli Zionist policy have been (1) to expand Israel's borders permanently (2) to support the U.S. oil monopolies in their efforts to keep their Mideast oil profits safe (3) to prevent the Palestinian Arabs from exercising self-determination and gaining their own homeland alongside an Israel restored to its pre-1967 borders (4) to weaken the Arab national liberation movement and progressive regimes while strengthening reactionary ones that kowtow to U.S. imperialism (5) to establish an Israeli puppet regime on as much of Lebanese territory as possible.

These policies have become more and more clearly impossible of realization and ruinous for the Jewish and Arab people of Israel and for neighboring Arab peoples. They can be a basis only for a continuing state of war—no basis for peace and good neighborly relations. The invasion of Lebanon has proved a disaster not only for the Lebanese people but also for the Israeli people. Not only have they suffered heavy casualties but they have been compelled to withdraw from nearly all of Lebanon, with the progressive forces in Lebanon on the ascendancy and the fascist phalangists and Israeli puppets in near total disrepute. The cost economically, morally and politically has also been most heavy. There was the massacre in the Palestinian camps of Sabra and Shatla, the murder of Arab prisoners in custody of the Shin Beth (Israeli FBI) and other atrocities and coverups now exposed. Due to the aggression in Lebanon and its general policy, Israel's prosperity and economic growth has given way to one of the world's highest inflation rates; unemployment and stagnation; severe corrosion of democratic rights with increased discrimination, oppression and violence directed at Palestinian Arabs in the West Bank and other occupied areas, at Israeli Arabs and darker Sephardic Jews.

Most Israeli Jews now consider the Lebanese adventure a complete failure and the movement for a just peace has become massive. Worker strikes and other forms of opposition to the consequences of the Zionist policy are growing substantially.

The present government leaders from both Likud and Mapai Parties—Shamir, Perez, Rabin, Sharon—have become discredited. Much has been written on this subject. Typical is the column in the *New York Times*, (4/17/87) by Gideon Samet, columnist for the Israeli *Haaretz*, "A Dawning Revolution in Israeli Politics: Younger leaders are needed. Both Labor and Likud now stand discredited." They have lost their credibility not only because of the coverups mentioned, including Iran Contragate and the Pollard affair, but because the policies that led to these scandals are dead ends, leading only to more economic hardship, loss of life and domestic turmoil. They have also led to isolation of Israel on the world scene.

In the Pollard affair, the Israeli leadership got caught spying on its foremost ally, the U.S., rewarded those directly involved, covered-up official approval and ideologically justified trying to use Jewish Americans to spy in accordance with a "higher" Zionist loyalty. This led to further loss of credibility before the people of Israel and to a sharp reaction among Jewish Americans. Jewish American masses totally rejected these Israeli Government actions, became even more critical of Israeli policy and expressed concern that these Zionist actions would play into the hands of U.S. anti-Semitic groups and lead to even more anti-Semitic acts. Even U.S. Zionist leaders openly expressed differences with the Israeli leadership on this and some other questions. According to the *New York Times* (4/12/87), "Most American Jews say they believe the Jonathan Jay Pollard spy affair and Israel's involvement in the Iran arms scandal will increase anti-Semitism in the U.S., a NYT/CBS News Poll shows." In a *New York Times* article, "Jews In America Upset Over Israel" (4/8/87), Rabbi Alexander M. Schindler, President of the Union of American Hebrew Congregations, said, "American Jews, more than any other Jews, have an ideal conception of Israel. Somehow the reality of Israel as an arms merchant and as a spy clashes with the ideal of Israel."

The morass has become so deep that there is new worldwide pressure for an International Conference on the Mideast to seek a just peace on the basis of UN Resolutions 242 and 338, guaranteeing the existence of a Palestinian Arab state as well as Israel. Such a conference can take place and achieve such a purpose only if the Palestine Liberation Organization (PLO) represents the Palestinian Arab people, the five Security Council members, including the Soviet Union and U.S., participate along with Israel and other Arab governments. Divisions are taking place both in the Reagan Administration and in Israeli ruling circles over such a conference. Some have come to recognize that the present impasse of instability and hostility is counterproductive to everyone's interests and that there is no way out except through such a conference. Others still seek an imperialist-controlled conference and/or solution.

Among large and increasing numbers of U.S. Jews, the ideal view of Israel as a model democratic, egalitarian society that lives up to its high moral standards—of a poor little Israel that is surrounded and threatened by big, hostile, anti-Semitic Arab countries—has been drastically changed to something much closer to the reality.

From a sympathetic, open-minded attitude toward Reaganism in 1980, Jewish Americans have become more strongly anti-Reaganite. In 1980, President Carter received 45% of the Jewish vote, Ronald Reagan 39% and John B. Anderson 15%. By 1984 Walter Mondale received 67% of the Jewish vote. In a NYT/CBS poll April 5–8, 1987 white people in general gave Reagan a 53% to 37% favorable job performance rating, while Jews disapproved 61% to 29%. Jewish Americans were also more sympathetic than white people generally to affirmative action programs for Afro-Americans with 48% favorable, compared to 45% unfavorable, the *New York Times* reported on 4/12/87.

Perhaps most crucial in the shift has been Reagan's support for prayer in the public schools and close identification with the right-wing fundamentalist doctrine in the content of education—creationism instead of Darwin and natural selection, etc. For Jewish people this is a do-or-die issue; it is a matter of forced assimilation—of "Christianizing" their children, a form of anti-Semitism with which they are quite familiar. This issue relates closely to defense of the Constitution, democratic rights and equality for oppressed peoples.

When it became evident that the far right embraced Reaganism, the choice became clear. Historically the far right has been tinged with or was more openly anti-Semitic. It was one of the major ways the far right tried to win a mass base while hiding the monopoly source of the sharp social problems working people were experiencing. Initially the opposition to affirmative action as "reverse discrimination" and the promise to get "big government off your back" had wide appeal among Jewish Americans.

Then things began to fall into place. Reaganism and the far right, who were against affirmative action, were against equality itself. They were racist. They were for turning the clock back on civil rights. They were for "Christianizing" the Jews and were anti-Semitic. Their idea of ending big government was to drastically increase military spending for a mad race to annihilation based on rabid anti-Communism. To them, the Soviet Union was an "anti-Christian evil empire."

At the same time the Reaganites sought to end all social welfare programs, many of which benefited millions of Jews—medicaid and medicare, social security, aid to dependent children. Of the 2½ million Jews living in the New York City area, 300,000 live below the poverty line, as do 20,000 in South Miami Beach. A United Jewish Appeal report cited in the March/April 1982 issue of *Jewish Affairs* (p. 9), estimated that one in six Jewish Americans live below the poverty line.

The Reaganites want to destroy public education. Nor was the promised economic well-being from supply side economics materializing for the mass of Jewish people. Unemployment among white collar workers, the new scientific and technological layers of the working class, came on the scene. There are many Jewish Americans among them. The structural crisis and stagnation, and, an end to large scale upward mobility set in as the new generation could expect only to be poorer than its parents.

The large number of Jewish trade unionists in the Amalgamated Clothing and Textile Workers Union, United Food & Commercial Workers, AFSCME, American Federation of Government Employees, National Education Association and American Federation of Teachers (despite the Shankers) faced a hostile Reagan Administration and sharp struggle to hold on to gains and to advance their unions and defend them from destruction.

Reaganism and its policies against the "evil empire," against unions, against affirmative action and *for* lower living standards of all working people but especially Afro-American, Latino and other oppressed peoples, and for the fundamentalist religious right naturally gave rise to a growth of organized and spontaneous anti-Semitic and racist violence and vandalism. These things clearly go hand in hand. When there is a substantial increase in violence against the Afro-American people, there is also a substantial increase of synagogue defacings and violence of an anti-Semitic character.

The KKK and Aryan Nation groups that are organizing and perpetrating much of the violence declare their extreme anti-Black, anti-immigrant, anti-Semitic, anti-Communist and anti-labor views. The Aryan Nation groups have been found armed to the teeth and are accused of assassinating Alan Berg, the Denver Jewish newscaster who fought against their influence.

Long ago Georgi Dimitrov, the great Bulgarian Communist leader who played a leading role in fighting the fascism of the '30s and '40s pointed out the connection between general reaction and fascism. Reaction lays the basis for fascism and to fight fascism you must fight reaction. Reaganism laid the basis for the expansion of fascist violence by KKK and Aryan Nation groups against nationally and racially oppressed peoples and against Jewish-Americans.

The revelation that a White House basement junta had taken over running much of the Reagan Administration greatly intensified the feeling of Jewish Americans, as it did of the people generally, that democracy was in danger and that the danger to themselves from reaction and fascism was very real. At the same time the exposure of the junta has delivered another very heavy blow against Reaganism and the right, and stimulated the new mass thought patterns now spurring a general democratic upsurge.

This helps explain the more pronounced movement of the mass of Jewish-Americans in recent months against Reaganism and in support of peace, democracy, equality and social progress. One example was the Chicago reelection of progressive Black Mayor Harold Washington with increased white support—20%. Among Jewish Americans, 51% voted for Mayor Washington.

The large-scale participation of Jewish religious leaders and community groups in the April 25, 1987, Washington, D.C. action of 150,000 against Reagan's policy in Central America and South Africa is further evidence. For some time the New Jewish Agenda and publications like the *Chicago Sentinel* have moved in a progressive direction and seriously questioned Israeli Government policy. Now their ranks are growing with many new forms of expression, including the new national publication, *Tikkun*.

These developments fully confirm the Marxist-Leninist analysis of ongoing events and the theoretical and policy conclusions drawn, starting with Lenin's early writings. This book begins with a May 1987 article by Gus Hall that discusses the self-interest of Jewish Americans in opposing Zionism and participating in the main streams of struggles against Reaganism and for peace, democracy, equality, jobs and social progress.

We have included considerable sections from two books by Hyman Lumer: *Lenin on the Jewish Question* (1974), and *Zionism: Its Role in World Politics* (1973), to provide a relatively brief but comprehensive Marxist-Leninist theoretical foundation for the subsequent articles and speeches. These have been arranged chronologically to help the reader follow the Marxist analysis of events as they have developed since 1973.

Readers who are interested in further information on this subject should consult current and/or back issues of *Jewish Affairs* and *Political Affairs*. Both may be reached at 235 West 23rd Street, New York City 10011; (212) 989-4994.

2

NEW CURRENTS IN THE JEWISH COMMUNITY*

GUS HALL

Israel's role in the Iran-Contragate scandal is having serious political repercussions in both the U.S. Jewish community and in Israel.

In Israel, the government's arrogance and hypocrisy in responding to the scandals have created a volatile political situation that may end with the downfall of the Shamir-Peres-Rabin government. Opinion polls in Israel indicate the country's leaders have the lowest standing in its history.

Israel's role as an arms merchant for the most reactionary customers in the world is forcing many Jewish Americans to have second thoughts about the reactionary role Israel plays in many areas—about its imperialist alliance with the U.S., about its trade relations with South Africa, about questions of patriotism, dual loyalty and about Zionism in general.

We should take note, however, that it is important not to equate Zionism with the Jewish people, with their just aspirations and sentiments of national pride, and their support for an Israel at peace with its neighbors and the world. Understandably, Jewish people pay particular attention to developments in Israel. Progressive people worldwide supported the achievement of Israel's independence. But progressives must also support an independent state, with equal rights, for the inhabitants of the former Palestine.

Today many Jewish Americans are having second thoughts about giving mechanical, uncritical support to the policies of the Israeli government. On the other hand, it is understandable that many Jewish people support what is in the best interests of Israel. Especially

*People's Daily World, 5/7/87

16

today, among the Jewish people themselves, there are many who do not agree with the policies of the Israeli government. There is a strong and growing peace movement of the people, and a rejection of concepts of dual loyalty.

Another example is the reaction of the majority of Jewish Americans to the Pollard spy case. When the scandal broke, a delegation of Jewish American leaders went to Israel to demand answers. At an airport press conference, explaining why they were going to discuss the case with Israeli officials, they said: "American Jews have to live with the consequences."

The turmoil in the Jewish community was intensified when Pollard's wife stated, "As Jews, we have the right and the obligation to spy for Israel." She shamelessly proclaimed what Zionist leaders have taken such pains to deny, namely, that Zionism means dual loyalty and dual citizenship.

New questions are being raised in the Jewish community. Jewish leaders are asking how they should deal with an Israel that has become an arms merchant, an Israel that deals in arms with a country that supports terrorists and whose aim is to destroy Israel, and Israel that lied about its dealings with Iran and lied about the spy case.

In both Israel and the U.S., there are now serious questions about the direction and leadership of the Zionist movement. The scandals have created a political crisis in Zionism. They have wrecked the myth on which Zionism is based. Zionist leaders have played a duplicitous role in promoting conflict in the Middle East and confrontation with the Soviet Union. There is a new wave of disillusionment and even anger—disillusionment with Israel, but especially with Zionism.

This disillusionment takes the form of seriously questioning the basic Zionist concepts. That's one direction of developments. But there are also developments in the opposite direction. There is a growing mood against huge foreign aid subsidies to Israel, both in Congress and among the American people.

The same developments that are creating apprehension, disillusionment and anger among Jewish Americans are giving rise to anti-Semitism. The ultra-right is exploiting the actions of the Zionists in an effort to stir up anti-Semitic feelings. Anti-Semitism is a tool of the ultra-right. Today the anti-Semitic groups are using the developments to spread anti-Semitism. If there is not a counter movement, the anti-Semitism will increasingly turn into provocations. Already we are hearing of incidents like the one in Florida: a gang jumped a Jewish senior citizen, calling him names and beating him. In the same area a monument to the Jewish war dead was knocked over and defaced.

The use of an anti-Semitic campaign by ultra-right organizations in the farm belt in an attempt to blame the farm crisis on "Jewish bankers" is another example. The LaRouchites have used the same scapegoat to explain the drug trade. The *Wall Street Journal* keeps emphasizing the Jewish background of some of the Wall Street insiders. Even in Japan this tactic is being used and several best sellers are openly anti-Semitic, blaming Japan's economic problems on the "international Jewish economic conspiracy."

This presents two kinds of problems. One is the importance of exposing the Zionist organizations that fuel anti-Semitism. Two, we have to expose anti-Semitism as a tool of the right wing, as a method that diverts from the real class enemy, monopoly capital.

Together with new thinking on Israel and Zionism, the Jewish American community is also taking a more progressive position on Reagan and Reaganism. The last *New York Times*/CBS poll showed that 61% of Jewish Americans disapprove of Reagan, while only 29% approve. However, the actions of the Zionists pose a continuous threat to peace in the Middle East and the prospects of peaceful coexistence with the Soviet Union. At the same time, their actions are providing grist for the ultra-right mill of anti-Semitism. This must be simultaneously exposed.

The ultra-right, like the Zionists, are working on behalf of the transnational corporations and the military-industrial complex; these are the real source of the war danger. To be effective, the fight against Zionism must be linked to the fight against anti-Semitism.

Writing in the *Chicago Sentinel* (April 9, 1987), Rabbi David Polish said: "The hard and unavoidable issues deal with those of Israel's friends, Jews and gentiles, who are stunned by Israel's role and some of its leaders' evasions of responsibility." He concluded, "Nothing less than a thorough examination of Israel-American relations as well as the condition of Zionism, is required. Not a self-controlled whitewash, but a painful and objective scrutiny of all aspects of a collective debate. Do we have the vision to demand this?"

The new currents, recent events and discussions demonstrate that the U.S. Jewish community does, indeed, have the "vision" to give Israel the kind of healthy support that will result in a turnaround in Israeli policies in the Mideast, on the Soviet Union and in its relationship with both the Soviet Union and the United States.

*Lenin on the Jewish Question**

3

INTRODUCTION

HYMAN LUMER

Among V. I. Lenin's most outstanding theoretical contributions are his writings on the national question. That he dealt extensively with this subject is not surprising. In the "prisonhouse of nations" that was tsarist Russia, liberation of the oppressed nations and national minorities and unification of workers of diverse nationalities against their common oppressor were in the forefront of the problems faced by the revolutionary movement. Within this context the Jewish question occupies a prominent position, first, because the Jews were, as Lenin notes, the most oppressed of all nationalities in tsarist Russia, and second, because of the lengthy battle that had to be waged against the nationalist stand of the Jewish Bund (the General Jewish Workers' Union in Lithuania, Poland and Russia), which called for a separate political organization for Jewish workers and claimed the sole right to speak for them.

However, Lenin dealt with the Jewish question not in isolation but as an important component of the national question as a whole. He wrote no special treatises on the Jewish question as such. Rather, his references to it occur mainly within his writings on the national question in general and particularly in his numerous polemics against the Bund, whose separatism was an obstacle to the building of the Russian Social-Democratic Labor Party as a party of *all* workers in tsarist Russia. Indeed, many of Lenin's most important theoretical contributions are to be found in these polemics.

Consequently, a compilation of Lenin's writings on the Jewish question must of necessity include a substantial body of material on

*1974, International Publishers, New York

the national question as a whole, as well as considerable repetition of certain points to which Lenin had to return repeatedly in the fight against the nationalism of the Bund. What we have sought to do in this volume is to present a comprehensive selection of Lenin's writings on the subject within the context in which they were written, though without pretending to literal completeness. The selections are taken from the English edition of the *Collected Works*, issued by Progress Publishers in Moscow between 1960 and 1970, and are presented in the order in which they appear there. Appendix I and II present two important documents implementing Lenin's policies following the October Revolution.

* * *

Lenin's approach to the Jewish question, as to the national question in general, was a consistently class approach. Its point of departure was the need to unite workers of all nationalities against the tsarist autocracy and the capitalist class, which sought to divide them along national lines. In particular, he fought unceasingly for unity of Jewish and non-Jewish workers and against the anti-Semitism which was a prime weapon of the ruling class for splitting the workers and turning them against one another.

As early as 1903, on the occasion of the Second Congress of the RSDLP, he noted that "the fullest and closest unity of the militant proletariat is absolutely essential both for the purpose of achievement of its ultimate aim and in the interests of an unswerving political and economic struggle in conditions of the existing society." And he added that "in particular, complete unity between the Jewish and non-Jewish proletariat is moreover especially necessary for a successful struggle against anti-Semitism, this despicable attempt of the government and the exploiting classes to exacerbate racial particularism and national enmity." [See p. 41, this book-D.R.]

The theme of international working-class unity runs like a red thread through all of Lenin's writings. And he continually inveighs against bourgeois nationalism as an ideology which divides the working class. Thus, in 1913 he writes:

> The class-conscious workers combat *all* national oppression and *all* national privileges, but they do not confine themselves to that. They combat all, even the most refined nationalism and advocate not only the unity but also the *amalgamation* of the workers of all nationalities in the

struggle against reaction and against bourgeois nationalism in all its forms. Our task is not to segregate nations, but to unite the workers of all nations. Our banner does not carry the slogan "national culture" but *international* culture, which unites all the nations in a higher, socialist unity, and the way to which is already being paved by the international amalgamation of capital. (Lenin, *CW* 19:548.)

Unity and amalgamation. These concepts were fundamental in Lenin's thinking. And from this standpoint he fought tirelessly to unite the workers of the diverse nationalities in tsarist Russia, to bring them together in a single movement, a single working-class revolutionary party. He clashed uncompromisingly with nationalists of all stripes and the nationalism they preached, and in particular with the Bund.

This nationalist organization was formed as a separate revolutionary party for Jewish workers, independently determining its own policies and joining with the RSDLP on a basis of federation. It claimed for itself the status of sole representative of the Jewish revolutionary workers and insisted that within such a federated relationship as it proposed the RSDLP could address the Jewish workers only through its intermediacy.

To this proposal to isolate the Jewish workers from those of other nationalities and thus to weaken the whole struggle against tsarist autocracy and capitalist exploitation, Lenin counterposed the concept of a unitary working-class party based on the principle of democratic centralism. This "party of a new type" was a party with a single program and policy, democratically determined but binding, once agreed upon, on all subordinate bodies and individual members. As against federation, Lenin posed the concept of autonomy of party organizations representing specific groups of workers with regard to forms and methods of carrying out party policy within their particular fields of operation. Only such a united, disciplined party, Lenin contended, could effectively lead the struggles of the working class and the toiling masses. And indeed it was just such a party which led the workers and peasants to victory in the October Revolution.

The checkered career of the Bund—splitting from the RSDLP in 1903, rejoining it in 1906, later splitting again and ultimately sinking into Menshevism and counterrevolution—is amply set forth in Lenin's writings and the accompanying notes presented in this volume.

But the differences with the Bund were not purely on organizational questions. On the contrary, the organizational disputes stemmed from underlying ideological differences. The Bund's position was based not on proletarian internationalism but on Jewish nationalism. Though it declared itself to be opposed to Zionism it nevertheless borrowed from Zionist precepts. It grasped, said Lenin, "at the idea of a Jewish *'nation'* " (Lenin, *CW* 7:63). But, Lenin maintained, "this Zionist idea is absolutely false and essentially reactionary" *(Ibid.)*. Lacking even a common territory and a common language, the Jews could in no sense be considered a nation. He added: "Absolutely untenable scientifically, the idea that the Jews form a separate nation is reactionary politically." The Bund's position was helping "not to end but to increase and legitimize Jewish isolation, by propagating the idea of a Jewish 'nation' and a plan for federating Jewish and non-Jewish proletarians." *(Ibid.)* It served to perpetuate, not to end the tsarist ghettoization of Jews.

*   *   *

The legitimizing of Jewish isolation was fostered particularly by the Bund's advocacy of "cultural-national autonomy." This idea was a natural outgrowth of the notion that the Jews, though lacking a common territory, constitute a nation. It was noteworthy, Lenin pointed out, that its only exponents in Russia were the Jewish bourgeois parties and the Bund. In the absence of a common territory their separatism could only take the form of demands for *extraterritorial* autonomy.

According to this concept every individual, regardless of place of residence, would be permitted to register as a member of a given nation. More specifically any Jew, whether living in Moscow, Kiev, Vilna or Tbilisi, could register as a member of an extraterritorial Jewish "nation." Such a "nation" would constitute a legal entity with powers to tax, to elect a national parliament and to appoint ministers. But these would operate within the framework of the tsarist autocracy and their jurisdiction would be limited to cultural affairs.

Since education is a central aspect of cultural affairs, the essence of this scheme, said Lenin, is that it "ensures absolute precision and absolute consistency in segregating the schools according to nationality. [See p. 67.] Such segregation, he contended, could serve only to divide workers of different nationalities. In the case of the Jews, already confined to ghettos and denied access to Russian schools, it could only mean perpetuation of their isolation and the discrimination imposed on them. Separate schools for Jews was the slogan of the forces of tsarist reaction; it was with these forces, Lenin warned, that the Bund was allying itself.

The slogan of cultural-national autonomy is rooted, he said, in the bourgeois-nationalist concept of a nonclass "national culture." "The slogan of national culture," he wrote, "is a bourgeois (and often also a Black-Hundred and clerical) fraud. Our slogan is: the international culture of democracy and of the world working-class movement." (*CW* 20:23.) There are, he asserted, in every capitalist country *two* cultures:

> The *elements* of democratic and socialist culture are present, if only in rudimentary form, in *every* national culture, since in *every* nation there are toiling and exploited masses, whose conditions inevitably give rise to the ideology of democracy and socialism. But *every* nation also possesses a bourgeois culture (and most nations a reactionary and clerical culture as well) in the form, not merely of "elements," but of the *dominant* culture. Therefore the general "national culture" *is* the culture of the landlords, the clergy and the bourgeoisie. This fundamental and, for a Marxist, elementary truth, was in fact kept in the background by the Bundist. . . . *In fact,* the Bundist acted like a bourgeois, whose every interest requires the spreading of a belief in a non-class national culture. (*Ibid.* p. 24.)

But "international culture is not non-national." It is not a culture in which all national differences are obliterated. On the contrary, says Lenin: "In advancing the slogan of 'the international culture of democracy and of the working-class movement,' we take *from each* national culture *only* its democratic and socialist elements; we take them *only* and *absolutely* in opposition to the bourgeois culture and the bourgeois nationalism of *each* nation." (*Ibid.*) This approach serves to unite workers of different nationalities, whereas the slogan of "national culture" serves to divide them and to tie the workers of each nationality to its "own" bourgeoisie. Lenin adds:

> The same applies to the most oppressed and persecuted nation—the Jews. Jewish national culture is the slogan of the rabbis and the bourgeoisie, the slogan of our enemies. But there are other elements in Jewish culture and in Jewish history as a whole. Of the ten and a half million Jews in the world, somewhat over a half live in Galicia and Russia, backward and semi-barbarous countries, where the Jews are *forcibly* kept in the status of a caste. The other half lives in the civilized world, where the Jews do not live as a segregated caste. There the great world-progressive features of Jewish culture stand clearly revealed: its

internationalism, its identification with the advanced movements of the epoch (the percentage of Jews in the democratic and proletarian movements is everywhere higher than the percentage of Jews among the population). (*CW 20: 26*; [see also p. 71].)

In rejecting cultural-national autonomy, Lenin maintained that autonomy can only be *territorial* in character. That is, it can be exercised only where people of a given nationality inhabit a common territory. For nations, freedom from national oppression means exercise of the right of self-determination—the right to secede and form a separate state. But for national groups living within the territory of other nations it can mean only the attainment of consistent democracy, of full equality. "Social-democrats," wrote Lenin, "in upholding a consistently democratic state system, demand unconditional equality for all nationalities and struggle against absolutely all privileges for one or several nationalities." (*CW 19:245*; [see also pp. 57–58].)

But he never lost sight of the class context within which this demand is raised. In contrast to the bourgeoisie, he stressed, the basic concern of workers is not the preservation of national distinctions but rather the drawing together of the workers of all nationalities.

*   *   *

This brings us to the subject of Lenin's views on assimilation, which have been particularly subjected to distortion by bourgeois critics and by certain erstwhile Jewish Marxists infected with bourgeois nationalism.

Lenin, it is said, based himself on the since discredited writings of Karl Kautsky, who saw the distinctive features of Jews as the product of their persecution and isolation. With these ended they would simply be absorbed into the societies in which they lived and disappear as a distinct national group. And this, Kautsky argued, would be a desirable outcome since the Yiddish language and the culture based on it were only products of forced ghettoization. *

In accepting this idea, it is maintained, Lenin was wrong. As some

---

*Over a period of years Kautsky wrote a number of articles on the subject. His main work, the book *Rasse und Judentum* (*Race and Jewry*) appeared in 1914. A revised German edition was published in 1921 and this, with further updating, was published in English translation in 1926 by International Publishers, New York, under the title *Are the Jews a Race?*

put it, Lenin joined in the error of failing to recognize that other factors besides anti-Semitism and ghettoization were responsible for the continued existence of the Jews as a distinct nationality—religious, historical and cultural factors. And when Lenin posed the alternatives for the Jewish people as isolation or assimilation, they add, he failed to foresee that history would provide another alternative—that of integration.

Moreover, it is said, Lenin could not have foreseen such developments as the Hitlerite slaughter of Jews or the founding of the State of Israel, both of which have been powerful forces in perpetuating Jewish national consciousness. Had he lived longer, it is implied, he would have modified his views.

But this is a vulgarization of Lenin's ideas. True, he cites Kautsky on the assimilation of the Jewish people, but his views are no mere parroting of Kautsky. On the contrary, Lenin's own theoretical treatment of the question goes far beyond that of Kautsky. Unlike Kautsky's, Lenin's approach is a thoroughly dialectical one.

Lenin conceived of amalgamation in terms not merely of assimilation of national minorities but of the eventual fusion of *nations*. This, he contended, grows out of the very historical process that gave rise to nations in the first place. The modern nation arose with the development of capitalism, of a system of commodity production whose functioning demanded the amalgamation of the smaller feudal communities. But the growing economic interdependence which led to the emergence of nations and nation-states did not stop at national boundaries. The development of capitalism led to the rise of a world economy, marked by growing intercourse and interdependence between nations. And this brought with it the progressive breaking down of national barriers and national exclusiveness.

Thus, Lenin saw two historical tendencies in operation. In the much-quoted passage from his "Critical Remarks on the National Question" he says:

> Developing capitalism knows two historical tendencies in the national question. The first is the awakening of national life and national movements, the struggle against all national oppression and the creation of national states. The second is the development and the growing frequency of international intercourse in every form, the breakdown of national barriers, the creation of the international unity of capital, of economic life in general, of politics, science, etc.
>
> Both tendencies are a universal law of capitalism. The former pre-

dominates in the beginning of its development, the latter characterizes a mature capitalism that is moving towards its transformation into socialist society. (CW 20:27; [see also p. 72].)

Lenin asks: "Is there anything real left in the concept of assimilation, after all violence and all inequality are eliminated?" And he replies: "Yes, there undoubtedly is. What is left is capitalism's world-historical tendency to break down national barriers, obliterate national distinctions, and to *assimilate* nations—a tendency which manifests itself with every passing decade, and is one of the greatest driving forces transforming capitalism into socialism." (*Ibid.*, p. 28; [see also p. 73].)

Note that Lenin speaks of a "world-historical tendency" to "assimilate nations." More, he views this tendency not as coming into operation *after* the ending of national oppression but as existing *simultaneously* with the opposing tendency, that expressed in the striving for national freedom, national equality and national identity. He treats the two opposing tendencies as a dialectical unity of opposites and the contradiction between them as the motive force of national evolution. In this process, he says, it is the tendency toward assimilation that represents the future and must be recognized as a progressive tendency. It was in this light that he viewed the assimilation of national minorities and particularly that of the Jews.

For capitalism the two tendencies present an irreconcilable contradiction, since capitalism knows no relationship other then that based on exploitation and national oppression for the sake of capitalist profits. It is this aim which is served by the ideology of chauvinism and racism, including anti-Semitism. It is only in a socialist society, Lenin maintained, that such barriers to amalgamation can be fully removed. For him the fight against national oppression, though absolutely essential, was never one for the perpetuation of national distinctions; its goal was rather to pave the way for the free, voluntary union of peoples as equals.

He recognized the amalgamation of nations and national groups into broader communities as a feature of the socialist and communist future, as a development to be welcomed. The proletariat, he said, supports everything that helps to do away with national isolation, to create closer ties between nationalities, to merge nations, while at the same time he recognized that the basis of this process lies in uncompromising struggle against all forms of national oppression.

In the case of the Jewish people he notes:

. . . it is only Jewish reactionary philistines, who want to turn back the wheel of history, and make it proceed, not from the conditions prevailing in Russia and Galicia to those prevailing in Paris and New York, but in the reverse direction—only they can clamor against "assimilation."

The best Jews, those who are celebrated in world history, and have given the world foremost leaders of democracy and socialism, have never clamored against assimilation. It is only those who contemplate the "rear aspect" of Jewry with reverential awe that clamor against assimilation. (*Ibid.* p. 29; [see also pp. 73–4].)

· · ·

These words are no less true today than when Lenin wrote them. It is the Zionists—the purveyors of extreme Jewish nationalism and separatism—who lead the fight against assimilation and for the preservation of "Jewish identity." And in their view this means precisely what Lenin refers to as "the culture of the rabbis and the bourgeoisie." It means especially the preservation of the Jewish religion and in particular, among Soviet Jews, of Orthodox Judaism. To them the measure of "Jewish identity" in the Soviet Union is the number of synagogues, rabbis, prayer shawls and phylacteries. To them the dwindling number of practicing believers is a sign of cultural genocide.

Undoubtedly the day will ultimately come when there is not one synagogue (or church or mosque) left in the Soviet Union. Will this mean that the Soviet Jewish people have suffered cultural genocide? Not at all. What it *will* mean is that they, like other Soviet citizens, have advanced beyond adherence to religious superstition, that they no longer have any use for religious institutions and practices, that religious distinctions between Jews and non-Jews have vanished. But to Zionism, which equates "Jewish identity" with Judaism, this is a calamity.

Similarly, the day will come when Yiddish will have disappeared as a spoken language. Will this, too, mean that Soviet Jews have suffered cultural genocide? Not at all. Languages have their own process of historical evolution. It will simply mean that, living as equals among other people and freely intermingling with them, they will no longer have need of a separate language and least of all will they have need of segregated schools taught in that language. But the Zionists (who themselves for the most part do not speak Yiddish, and in Israel regard Hebrew as the language of the Jewish people) clamor for the preservation of Yiddish—in the Soviet Union—as the essence of Jewish culture and the hallmark of "Jewish identity." In this respect, too, they look toward the past, not the future.

Lenin wrote that "those Jewish Marxists who mingle with the Russian, Lithuanian, Ukrainian and other workers in international Marxist organizations, and make their contribution (both in Russian and in Yiddish) towards creating the international culture of the working-class movement—those Jews, despite the separatism of the Bund, uphold the best traditions of Jewry by fighting the slogan of 'national culture.'" (*CW* 20:26.)

This concept of "creating the international culture of the working-class movement" is central in the historical development of the USSR, where the abolition of national discrimination has given birth to a new kind of historical community, the *Soviet* people, embracing the myriad nations and nationalities within the Soviet state. In the words of Leonid Brezhnev, [then] general secretary of the CPSU Central Committee:

A new historical community of people, the Soviet people, took shape in our country during the years of socialist construction. New, harmonious relations, relations of friendship and cooperation, were formed between the classes and social groups, nations and nationalities in joint labor, in the struggle for socialism, and in the battles fought in defense of socialism. Our people are welded together by a common Marxist-Leninist ideology and the lofty aims of building communism. (*Report of the CPSU Central Committee to the 24th Congress of the CPSU*, Novosti Press Agency Publishing House, Moscow, 1971, p. 90.)

The Soviet Jews are an intimate part of this new historical community. Though offered the opportunity to establish a separate Jewish Autonomous Region in Birobidjan, few of them chose this path. The removal of all restrictions on Jews after the October Revolution led them not to Birobidjan but to Moscow, Leningrad, Kiev and other urban centers where they took advantage of the opportunity to enter industry and the professions. The overwhelming majority of Soviet Jews have, in fact, come to look upon themselves simply as Soviet citizens, as an integral part of the Soviet people.

There are, it is true, some negative influences of the past, expressed in part in the migration of a certain number of Soviet Jews to Israel. But such influences affect only a small minority. Soviet Jews on the whole emphatically reject them.

They are an intimate part of the unification of peoples and cultures taking place in the Soviet Union today, a development possible only in a socialist society in which the class and national antagonisms generated by capitalist exploitation and oppression have been abolished and in which there is a harmony of the interests of all the people. Of this the well-known Soviet scholar, Professor Iosef Braginsky, editor-in-chief of *Narody Azii i Afriki* (*Peoples of Asia and Africa*), himself Jewish, writes:

> The Marxist cannot view Jewish assimilation from the narrow angle of "dos pintele yid" [the Jewish spark]. One has to realize that assimilation is a natural, historical process. In the USSR assimilation is taking place in conditions of friendship among the peoples and national equality. National consolidation and international integration represent two sides of the development of one Soviet nation, which is inspired by feelings of Soviet national pride. (*Once Again About Assimilation*, Novosti Press Agency, Moscow, October 1964.)

Here we witness in actual process the "amalgamation of nations" of which Lenin wrote. What is envisaged is that with the full flowering of communism will come the full unity of all Soviet peoples. In the words of the *Program of the CPSU*:

> Full-scale communist construction constitutes a new stage in the development of national relations in the USSR in which the nations will draw still closer together until complete unity is achieved. The building of the material and technical basis of communism leads to still greater unity of the Soviet peoples. The exchange of material and spiritual values between nations becomes more and more intensive, and the contribution of each republic to the common cause of communist construction increases. Obliteration of distinctions between classes and the development of communist social relations make for a still greater social homogeneity of nations and contribute to the development of common communist traits in their culture, morals and way of living, to a further strengthening of their mutual trust and friendship. (International Publishers, New York, 1963, p. 116.)

What is envisaged is that ultimately national distinctions, like class distinctions, will vanish. The full realization of this, as Lenin makes clear, is seen as a matter of the as yet distant future. But the process leading toward that outcome is taking place now and its effects are already clearly visible.

Moreover, Lenin's concept of assimilation is not one of the simple absorption of one nationality by another, of the literal disappearance of national groups. On the contrary, as we have already noted, he stresses that the international culture of the working class which he advocates is not non-national but brings together what is progressive and democratic in each national culture. And in the case of the Jews he writes that "in the civilized world, where the Jews do not live as a segregated caste . . . the great world-progressive features of Jewish culture stand revealed: its internationalism, its identification with the advanced movements of the epoch. . . ."

National consciousness and national pride are not obliterated. Rather there develop mutual respect and friendship, and with this a growing intermingling of cultures. Such is Lenin's dialectical approach to the question of assimilation, whose validity the experience of the Soviet Union is bearing out. [See Appendix III for the relevant excerpt from the new edition of the Program of the CPSU by the 27th Congress, 1986.]

Lenin was an indefatigable opponent of anti-Semitism. The Jews, he said, were the most oppressed of all peoples in tsarist Russia. And they were the chief victims of the efforts of the tsarist autocracy to divert the wrath of the people from itself by turning one group against another through the stirring up of racial and national animosity. These efforts were intensified with the rise of the revolutionary movement and were expressed in a wave of pogroms beginning in 1903. He saw clearly the class roots of this persecution. He said:

> It is not the Jews who are the enemies of the working people. The enemies of the workers are the capitalists of all countries. Among the Jews there are working people, and they form the majority. They are our brothers, who, like us, are oppressed by capital; they are our comrades in the struggle for socialism. Among the Jews there are kulaks, exploiters and capitalists, just as there are among Russians, and the rich of all countries, are in alliance to oppress, crush, rob and disunite the workers. [See pp. 80–81.]

In characterizing anti-Semitism as the instrument of the ruling class to divide the workers, Lenin clashed from the outset with the Bund, which viewed it as rooted in the masses of non-Jewish workers as well as in the bourgeoisie and the tsarist autocracy. In its stand, he charged, the Bund acted to blunt the class consciousness of the Jewish workers and to encourage the Zionist fable that anti-Semitism is eternal [see pp. 38–40].

In the fight for national equality, Lenin gave first place to combatting the oppression of the Jewish people. Thus, a bill introduced in the Duma on this question in 1914 is entitled "A Bill for the Abolition of All Disabilities of the Jews and of All Restrictions on the Grounds of Origin or Nationality" [see p. 75]. The reason for putting it this way, said Lenin, was obvious: no nationality was so oppressed as the Jews, and anti-Semitism played a special role in the efforts of the ruling class to split the workers.

On the very heels of the October Revolution came the Declaration of the Rights of the Nationalities of Russia, reprinted as Appendix I of this volume, which proclaimed the equality, sovereignty and right of self-determination of all nations of Russia and called for the abolition of all national privilege and discrimination. For the Jews this meant the almost overnight removal of the scores of anti-Semitic restrictions which had plagued them and the establishment of full freedom and equality. This was a truly remarkable achievement, comparable in magnitude and significance to what would be achieved in the United States if all racist practices and all forms of discrimination against the Black and other oppressed peoples were totally abolished. It is a glowing tribute to Lenin's grasp of the national question and an important component of the resolution of the national question in the socialist Soviet Union, one of its most outstanding achievements.

In the period of civil war which followed the October Revolution it was the counterrevolutionary forces (whom the Zionists and Bundists generally supported) that resorted to pogroms and other anti-Semitic acts. These were energetically fought by the revolutionary forces as the Resolution of the Council of People's Commissars on the Uprooting of the Anti-Semitic Movement indicates. This resolution was the outcome of a report to Lenin by the newly established Commissar for Jewish Affairs, Shimen Dimanshtein, who wrote that when he informed Lenin of these anti-Semitic manifestations the latter was furious and called at once for the sharpest countermeasures. Such were Lenin's reactions to the crime of anti-Semitism at all times [see Appendix II].

The result of Lenin's policy on the Jewish question was, as is well known, a flourishing of Jewish culture in the years following the revolution. Schools, newspapers, magazines, books and theaters in the Yiddish language multiplied. In addition, Birobidjan in eastern Siberia was declared a Jewish Autonomous Region for those Jews who might wish to establish a community of their own.

But the liberation of the Russian Jews led to precisely what Lenin had predicted: a rapid development of the process of assimilation. Freed from confinement to the poverty-stricken ghetto villages, they poured into the large cities where they found employment in industry and other occupations. No longer excluded from Russian schools they flocked into them as the gateway to the learned professions.

In his *Pictorial History of the Jewish People*, Nathan Ausubel writes, after describing Yiddish cultural activities in the Soviet Union in the twenties and thirties:

> Yet, for all this unprecedented, large-scale Yiddish cultural activity, its decline was already in evidence at the very time of its flowering. Although hundreds of thousands of Soviet Jewish youth had been raised in Yiddish-language schools, the political and cultural pressures from without proved well-nigh irresistible. . . .
>
> In time, there was a sharp decline in the attendance of the Yiddish-language schools . . . the youth turned more and more to reading Russian newspapers, periodicals and books. In a late census, before the nazi attack on Russia, more Jews claimed Russian than Yiddish as their mother tongue. (Crown, New York, 1958, p. 253.)

This process was distorted for a time by the arbitrary closing down of Jewish cultural institutions by the Stalin regime and by the inclusion of many leading Jewish cultural figures among the victims of Stalin's crimes. But it has nevertheless taken its inexorable course. In the latest census [early 1970s—D.R.] only some 17 percent of Soviet Jews claimed Yiddish as their mother tongue. . . . There remains, to be sure, an appreciable though declining interest in Yiddish language culture. This is attested to by the existence of the monthly literary magazine *Sovetish Heimland* with a circulation of 25,000, by the existence of a number of Yiddish theatrical groups, by Yiddish music concerts, by the continuing publication of books in Yiddish and by the publication of the newspaper *Birobidjaner Shtern*, which appears four times a week. But it must be stressed that this is a limited and declining interest.

Does this mean that Jewish culture is disappearing? Not at all. On the contrary, the best of it is becoming a part of the total Soviet cultural heritage. The works of the Yiddish classicists Sholem Aleichem, Y. L. Peretz and Mendele Mocher Sforim are published in voluminous editions in Russian and other languages and are widely read. The same is true of other leading Jewish novelists and poets.

Jewish culture is becoming part of the over-all cultural life of the Soviet people.

To be sure, the Yiddish language and Yiddish-language culture will endure for some time to come and the distinctive existence of the Jews for a much longer period. But the basic historical trend, as Lenin defined it, is unmistakable. There is no third alternative of "integration" as some maintain, unless one wishes merely to substitute this term for assimilation.

The present-day nationalist correctors of Lenin contend that historical developments since World War I have basically altered the process. The past several decades, they say, have witnessed a flowering of nations and a growth of national consciousness, national pride and national cultures rather than a process of national diminution and amalgamation. And this is evident among the Jewish people, the Soviet Jews included, no less than among others.

Had Lenin lived longer, they maintain, he would have modified his views accordingly; indeed, after the October Revolution he had already begun to do so. The principal evidence for this contention is the following quotation from his *"Left-Wing" Communism:*

> . . . As long as national and state distinctions exist among peoples and countries—and these will continue to exist for a long time to come, even after the dictatorship of the proletariat has been established on a world-wide scale—the unity of the international tactics of the Communist working-class movement in all countries demands, not the elimination of variety or the suppression of national distinctions (which is a pipe dream at present), but the application of the *fundamental* principles of Communism (Soviet power and the dictatorship of the proletariat), which *correctly modify* these principles in certain *particulars*, correctly adapt and apply them to national and national-state distinctions. (*CW 31:92.*)

This is often accompanied by reference to Lenin's strictures on the need for extreme sensitivity to the feelings of oppressed peoples. But as we have shown above, these later statements by Lenin represent no change in his basic ideas; rather they represent a further elaboration of them in certain specific contexts.

Nor was the establishment of Jewish cultural institutions on a wide scale a repudiation of his earlier views on assimilation. On the contrary he had always stressed the fact that the path to voluntary amalgamation lay only through the fullest achievement of national rights in all their aspects.

To be sure, the present historical period has witnessed a great national upsurge, as the Soviet writer Alexander Sobolev states in these words:

> Ours is an epoch of the growth, self-assertion and rapid development of nations, of the growth of national cultures, national awareness and national pride. Influenced by the ideas and power of socialism, this process is historically of world-wide significance, for it is changing the character of humanity. The development of nations will continue in the foreseeable future, fostering as it does national patriotic consciousness. (*To Strengthen the Unity of the Communist Movement*, Novosti Press Agency Publishing House, Moscow, 1973.)

But it would be wrong to conclude from this that the historical trend is now toward growing national distinctness, not toward amalgamation. The process which Sobolev describes is in the main the fruit of the victories of the national liberation struggles, especially in Africa. However, these very victories are creating the conditions, which Lenin noted, for the voluntary coming together of nations and nationalities. More, national development entails the building of a modern industrial economy, which colonialism had held back, and which leads to growing economic interdependence and cultural intercourse. This is already reflected, for example, in the formation of the Organization of African Unity.

In short, the basic tendency remains that defined by Lenin even before World War I. Certainly, nothing has happened to reverse the process of assimilation of national minorities such as in the Soviet Union.

* * *

Lenin wrote little on the subject of Zionism, though it is clear, as we have noted, that he was totally opposed to it as a most reactionary manifestation of bourgeois nationalism. Recognizing the class roots of anti-Semitism, he proposed to combat it by fighting all forms of discrimination against Jews. And he saw its solution in the abolition of its class roots—in the victory of socialism. This approach has always been rejected by Zionism, which has contended that socialism not only is incapable of doing away with anti-Semitism but in fact promotes it.

Anti-Semitism, it is asserted by contemporary Zionist spokesmen, is historically a feature of the socialist movement. Thus, Marie Syrkin, a leading figure in the U.S. Zionist movement, maintains "that the non-Jewish radicals have often proven to be openly anti-Semitic and that Communist movements, as in Eastern Europe, have spewed out their zealous Jewish disciples." She speaks of "the socialist doctrinaire hostility to Jews, be it Marx's notorious essay on the Jewish question, in which he states that the essence of Judaism is the profit motive, or Proudhon's view that the Jews are the spirit of finance, or the statements of such German Social Democrats as Franz Mehring or Wilhelm Liebknecht." She adds other examples: the Austrian Social-Democratic Party and the anarchist Russian Narodnaya Volya, the latter of which regarded anti-Semitism, even pogroms, as having revolutionary potential. In her view there is an inherent connection between anti-Semitism and the Left. (*Congress Bi-Weekly,* March 30, 1973.)

Similarly, the U.S. sociologist Seymour Martin Lipset asserts that the Left has historically been afflicted by anti-Semitism in various forms. And he adds, apparently in reference to Lenin among others, that where the Left *has* supported Jewish political and social rights, it has assumed that "one of the payments the Jews would make to the Left for having liberated them would be to disappear—i.e., to become assimilated." ("Anti-Semitism of the Old Left and the New Left," *Encounter,* December 1969.)

These and numerous similar allegations, it should be noted, indiscriminately lump together under the term "Left" all sorts of trends and ideologies. The term is even more loosely used in the charge by Zionist sources that today "anti-Semitism of the Left" has grown to monstrous proportions and has become the chief threat to the Jewish people. Here the "Left" ranges from the Soviet Union and the Arab countries to the New Left, major sections of the Black liberation movement and the Communist Party of the United States.

This is, it must be said, a gross slander. Communists in particular have been the most resolute fighters against all national and racial discrimination and oppression.

This alleged monster is created by the simple device of equating anti-Zionism with anti-Semitism. Israel's foreign minister Abba Eban makes this plain when he states: "Let there be no mistake: the New Left is the author and the progenitor of the new anti-Semitism. One of the chief tasks of any dialogue with the Gentile world is to prove that the distinction between anti-Semitism and anti-Zionism is no distinction at all. Anti-Zionism is merely the new anti-Semitism." (*Congress Bi-Weekly*, March 30, 1973.)

At the heart of this "anti-Semitism of the Left" lies the spurious charge that the Soviet government follows an official policy of anti-Semitism, of cultural genocide for Soviet Jews, compounded by wholesale refusal of their right to migrate to Israel where they may "live as Jews." They are, it is alleged, being forcibly assimilated, being made "to disappear as Jews." Lenin was wrong, we are told; it is widely charged that the Soviet Union is guilty of brutal persecution of Jews, some of its accusers going so far as to compare it with Nazi Germany.

These slanderous allegations, it can readily be shown, have no basis in fact but are malicious concoctions of Right-wing reaction in concert with Zionism aimed at undermining the Soviet Union and promoting the migration of Soviet Jews to Israel. We cannot undertake to expose these falsehoods here; this has been done elsewhere.

Here we would only note that "anti-Semitism of the Left" and "Soviet anti-Semitism" are simply frauds designed to conceal the fact that socialism does indeed provide a solution to the Jewish question as it does to the national question generally—in fact, the only real solution. From a wretched, degraded, poverty-ridden ghetto existence Soviet Jews have risen to the status of Soviet citizens on a par with all others. This is truly a remarkable achievement, a tribute to the correctness of Lenin's views and actions on the Jewish question.

New York City   January 1974

Excerpts—
Lenin on the Jewish Question

DOES THE JEWISH PROLETARIAT NEED AN "INDEPENDENT POLITICAL PARTY"?

No. 105 of *Posledniye Izvestia*[1] (January 28/15, 1903), published by the Foreign Committee of the General Jewish Workers' Union of Lithuania, Poland, and Russia, carries a brief article entitled "Concerning a Certain Manifesto" (viz., the manifesto issued by the Ekaterinoslav Committee of the Russian Social-Democratic Labor Party) containing the following statement, which is as extraordinary as it is significant and indeed "fraught with consequences": "The Jewish proletariat has formed itself *(sic!)* into an independent *(sic!)* political party, the Bund."

We did not know this before. This is something new.

Hitherto the Bund[2] has been a constituent part of the Russian Social-Democratic Labor Party, and in No. 106 of *Posledniye Izvestia* we still (still!) find a statement of the Central Committee of the Bund, bearing the heading "Russian Social-Democratic Labor Party." It is true that at its latest congress, the Fourth, the Bund decided to change its name (without stipulating that it would like to hear the Russian comrades' opinion on the name a section of the Russian Social-Democratic Labor Party should bear) and to "introduce" new *federal* relations into the Rules of the Russian Party. The Bund's Foreign Committee has even "introduced" these relations, if that word can be used to describe the fact that it has withdrawn from the Union of Russian Social-Democrats Abroad and has concluded a federal agreement with the latter.

On the other hand, when *Iskra* polemized with the decisions of the Bund's Fourth Congress, the Bund itself stated very definitely that it only wanted to *secure the acceptance of its wishes* and *decisions* by the R.S.D.L.P.; in other words, it flatly and categorically acknowledged that until the R.S.D.L.P. adopted new Rules and settled new forms of its attitude towards the Bund, the latter would remain a section of the R.S.D.L.P.

But now, suddenly, we are told that the Jewish proletariat has already *formed itself* into an *independent* political party! We repeat— this is something new.

Equally new is the furious and foolish onslaught of the Bund's Foreign Committee upon the Ekaterinoslav Committee. We have at last *(though unfortunately after much delay)* received a copy of this manifesto, and we do not hesitate to say that in attacking a manifesto *like this* the Bund has *undoubtedly taken a serious political step.* [*] This step fully accords with the Bund's proclamation as an independent political party and throws much light on the physiogonomy and behavior of this new party.

We regret that lack of space prevents us from reprinting the Ekaterinoslav manifesto in full (it would take up about two columns in

---

[*]This is, of course, if the Bund's Foreign Committee expresses the views of the Bund as a whole on this question.

*Iskra**), and shall confine ourselves to remarking that this admirable manifesto excellently explains to the Jewish workers of the *city of Ekaterinoslav* (we shall presently explain why we have emphasized these words) the Social-Democratic attitude towards Zionism and anti-Semitism. Moreover, the manifesto treats the sentiments, moods, and desires of the Jewish workers so considerately, with such comradely consideration, that it specially refers to and emphasizes the necessity of fighting under the banner of the R.S.D.L.P. *"even for the preservation and further development of your* [the manifesto addresses the Jewish workers] *national culture," "even from the standpoint of purely national interests"* (underlined and italicized in the manifesto itself).

Nevertheless, the Bund's Foreign Committee (we almost said the new party's Central Committee) has fallen upon the manifesto for *making no mention of the Bund.* That is the manifesto's only crime, but one that is terrible and unpardonable. It is for this that the Ekaterinoslav Committee is accused of lacking in "political sense." The Ekaterinoslav comrades are chastized for not "yet having digested the idea of the necessity for a separate organization [a profound and significant idea!] of the forces [!!] of the Jewish proletariat," for "still harboring the absurd hope of somehow getting rid of it" (the Bund), for spreading the "no less dangerous fable" (no less dangerous than the Zionist fable) that anti-Semitism is connected with the bourgeois strata and with their interests, and not with those of the working class. That is why the Ekaterinoslav Committee is advised to "abandon the harmful habit of keeping silent about the independent Jewish working-class movement" and to "reconcile itself to the fact that the Bund exists."

Now, let us consider whether the Ekaterinoslav Committee is actually guilty of a crime, and whether it really should have mentioned the Bund without fail. Both questions can be answered only in the negative, for the simple reason that the manifesto is not addressed to the "Jewish workers" in general (as the Bund's Foreign Committee quite wrongly stated), but to "the Jewish workers *of the city of Ekaterinoslav*" (the Bund's Foreign Committee forgot to quote these last words!). *The Bund has no organization* in Ekaterinoslav. (And, in general, regarding the south of Russia the Fourth Congress of the Bund passed a resolution *not to organize separate committees of the Bund* in cities where the

---

**We intend to reprint in full the manifesto and the attack of the Bund's Foreign Committee in a pamphlet which we are preparing for the press.

Jewish organizations are included in the Party committees and where their needs can be fully satisfied without separation from the committees.) Since the Jewish workers in Ekaterinoslav are not organized in a separate committee, it follows that their movement (inseparably from the entire working-class movement in that area) is wholly guided by the Ekaterinoslav Committee, which subordinates them *directly* to the R.S.D.L.P., which *must* call upon them to work *for the whole Party*, and not for its individual sections. It is clear that under these circumstances the Ekaterinoslav Committee was not obliged to mention the Bund; on the contrary, if it had presumed to advocate "the necessity for a separate organization of the forces [it would rather and more probably have been an organization of *impotence**] of the Jewish proletariat" (which is what the Bundists want), it would have made a very grave error and committed a direct breach, not only of the Party Rules, but of the unity of the proletarian class struggle.

Further, the Ekaterinoslav Committee is accused of lack of "orientation" in the question of anti-Semitism. The Bund's Foreign Committee betrays truly infantile views on important social movements. The Ekaterinoslav Committee speaks of the *international* anti-Semitic movement of the *last decades* and remarks that "from Germany this movement spread to other countries and everywhere found adherents among the bourgeois, and not among the working-class sections of the population." "This is a no less dangerous fable" (than the Zionist fables), cries the thoroughly aroused Bund's Foreign Committee. Anti-Semitism "has struck roots in the mass of the workers," and to prove this the "well-oriented" Bund cites two facts: 1) workers' participation in a pogrom in Czestochowa and 2) the behaviour of 12 (*twelve!*) Christian workers in Zhitomir, who scabbed on the strikers and threatened to "kill off all the Yids." Very weighty proofs indeed, especially the latter! The editors of *Posledniye Izvestia* are so accustomed to dealing with big strikes involving five or ten workers that the behavior of twelve ignorant Zhitomir workers is dragged out as evidence of the link between international anti-Semitism and one

---

*It is this task of "organizing impotence" that the Bund serves when, for example, it uses such a phrase as "our comrades of the 'Christian working-class organizations.'" The phrase is as preposterous as is the whole attack on the Ekaterinoslav Committee. We have no knowledge of any "Christian" working-class organizations. Organizations belonging to the R.S.D.L.P. have never distinguished their members according to religion, never asked them about their religion and never *will*—even when the Bund will in *actual fact* "have formed itself into an independent political party."

"section" or another "of the population." This is, indeed, magnificent! If, instead of flying into a foolish and comical rage at the Ekaterinoslav Committee, the Bundists had pondered a bit over this question and had consulted, let us say, Kautsky's pamphlet on the social revolution,[3] a Yiddish edition of which they themselves published recently, they would have understood the link that *undoubtedly* exists between anti-Semitism and the interests of the bourgeois, and not of the working-class sections of the population. If they had given it a little more thought they might have realized that the social character of anti-Semitism today is not changed by the fact that dozens or even hundreds of unorganized workers, nine-tenths of whom are still quite ignorant, take part in a pogrom.

The Ekaterinoslav Committee has risen up (and rightly so) against the Zionist fable about anti-Semitism being eternal; by making its angry comment the Bund had only confused the issue and planted in the minds of the Jewish workers ideas which tend to *blunt* their class-consciousness.

From the viewpoint of the struggle for political liberty and for socialism being waged by the whole working class of Russia, the Bund's attack on the Ekaterinoslav Committee is the height of folly. From the viewpoint of the Bund as "an independent political party," this attack becomes understandable: don't dare anywhere organize "Jewish" workers together with, and inseparably from, "Christian" workers! If you would address the Jewish workers in the name of the Russian Social-Democratic Labor Party or its committees, don't dare do so directly, over our heads, ignoring the Bund or making no mention of it!

And this profoundly regrettable fact is not accidental. Having once demanded "federation" instead of autonomy in matters concerning the Jewish proletariat, you were *compelled* to proclaim the Bund an "independent political party" in order to carry out this principle of federation *at all costs*. However, your declaring the Bund an independent political party is just that reduction to an absurdity of your fundamental error in the national question which will inescapably and inevitably be the starting-point of a change in the views of the Jewish proletariat and of the Jewish Social-Democrats in general. "Autonomy" under the Rules adopted in 1898 provides the Jewish working-class movement with all it needs: propaganda and agitation in Yiddish, its own literature and congresses, the right to advance separate demands to supplement a single general Social-Democratic program and to satisfy local needs and requirements arising out of the special features of Jewish life. In everything else there must be complete fusion with the Russian proletariat, in the interests of the struggle waged by the entire proletariat of Russia. As for the fear of being "steam-rollered" in the event of such fusion, the very nature of the case makes it groundless, since it is autonomy that is a guarantee against all "steam-rollering" in matters pertaining specifically to the *Jewish* movement, while in matters pertaining to the struggle against the autocracy, the struggle against the bourgeoisie of Russia as a whole, we must act as a single and centralized militant organization, have behind us the whole of the proletariat, without distinction of language or nationality, a proletariat whose unity is cemented by the continued joint solution of problems of theory and practice, of tactics and organization; and we must not set up organizations that would march separately, each along its own track; we must not weaken the force of our offensive by breaking up into numerous independent political parties; we must not introduce estrangement and isolation and then have to heal an artificially implanted disease with the aid of these notorious "federation" plasters.

Iskra, No. 34
February 15, 1903
[Lenin, CW 6: 330–35]

Published according
to the Iskra text

SECOND CONGRESS OF THE R.S.D.L.P.
(July 17 (30)–August 10 (23), 1903 (Excerpts)

DRAFT RESOLUTION ON THE PLACE OF THE BUND IN THE PARTY

Taking into consideration that the fullest and closest unity of the militant proletariat is absolutely essential both for the purpose of the earliest achievement of its ultimate aim and in the interests of an unswerving political and economic struggle in conditions of the existing society;

that, in particular, complete unity between the Jewish and non-Jewish proletariat is moreover especially necessary for a successful struggle against anti-Semitism, this despicable attempt of the government and the exploiting classes to exacerbate racial particularism and national enmity;

that the complete amalgamation of the Social-Democratic organizations of the Jewish and non-Jewish proletariat can in no respect or manner restrict the independence of our Jewish comrades in conducting propaganda and agitation in one language or another, in publishing literature adapted to the needs of a given local or national movement, or in advancing such slogans for agitation and the direct political struggle that would be an application and development of the general program regarding full equality and full freedom of language, national culture, etc., etc.;

the Congress emphatically repudiates federation as the organizational principle of a Russian party and endorses the organizational principle adopted as the basis of the Rules of 1898, i.e., autonomy for the national Social-Democratic organizations in matters concerning. . . . [Here the manuscript breaks off.—*Ed.*]

Written in June–July, 1903   Published according
First published in 1927   to the manuscript
[Lenin, *CW* 6: 470]

PREFACE TO THE PAMPHLET
MEMORANDUM OF POLICE DEPARTMENT
SUPERINTENDENT LOPUKHIN (Excerpt)

. . . The springs of the police machinery have lost their snap; military force alone is now insufficient. One must stir up national hatred, race hatred; one must recruit "Black Hundreds"[4] from among the politically least developed sections of the urban (*and following that, naturally, the rural*) petty bourgeoisie; one must attempt to rally to the defense of the throne all reactionary elements among the population at large; one must turn the struggle of the police against study circles into a struggle of one part of the people against the other.

That is precisely what the government is now doing when it sets the Tatars against the Armenians in Baku; when it seeks to provoke new pogroms against the Zemstvo people, students, and rebellious Gymnasium youths; and when it appeals to the loyal nobles and to the conservative elements among the peasants. Ah, well! We Social-Democrats are surprised at these tactics of the autocracy; nor shall we be frightened by them. We know that it will no longer help the government to stir up racial animosity since the workers have begun to organize armed resistance to the pogrom-bandits; and by relying on the exploiting sections of the petty bourgeoisie the government will only antagonize still broader masses of real proletarians. We have never expected any political or social revolutions to come from "convincing" the powers that be, or from educated persons turning to the paths of "virtue." We have always taught that it is the class struggle, the struggle of the exploited part of the people against the exploiters, that lies at the bottom of political transformations and *in the final analysis* determines the fate of all such transformations. By admitting the complete failure of the pettifogging police methods and passing over to the direct organization of civil war, the government shows that *the final reckoning* is approaching. So much the better. It is launching the civil war. So much the better. We, too, are for the civil war. If there is any sphere in which we feel particularly confident, it is here, in the war of the vast masses of the oppressed and the downtrodden, of the toiling millions who keep the whole of society going, against a handful of privileged parasites. Of course, by fanning racial antagonism and tribal hatred, the government may for a time arrest the development of the class struggle, but only for a short time and at the cost of a still greater expansion of the field of the new struggle, at the cost of a more bitter feeling among the people against the autocracy. This is proved by the consequences of the Baku pogrom, which deepened tenfold the revolutionary mood of all sections against tsarism. The government thought to frighten the people by the sight of bloodshed and the vast toll of street battles; but actually it is *dispelling the people's* fear of bloodshed, of a direct armed encounter. Actually, the government is furthering our cause, with agitation of a scope wider and more impressive than we could ever have dreamed of. *Vive le son du canon!* say we in the words of the French revolutionary song: Hail the thunder of the cannon!" Hail the open revolution! Hail the open war of the people against the tsarist government and its adherents!

Written in February–March 1905
First published in 1905
in the pamphlet *Memorandum
of Police Department
Superintendent Lopukhin*
Published by *Vperyod*, Geneva
Signed: N. LENIN
[CW 8: 204–05]

Published according to
the text of the pamphlet

TO THE JEWISH WORKERS[5]

In publishing the Report on the Third Congress of the R.S.D.L.P. in Yiddish, the Editorial Board of the Party Central Organ considers it necessary to say a few words in connection with this publication.

The conditions under which the class-conscious proletariat of the whole world lives tend to create the closest bonds and increasing unity in the systematic Social-Democratic struggle of the workers of the various nationalities. The great slogan "Workers of all countries, unite!," which was proclaimed for the first time more than half a century ago, has now become more than the slogan of just the Social-Democratic parties of the different countries. This slogan is being increasingly embodied . . . among the proletarians of the various nationalities who are struggling under the yoke of one and the same despotic state for freedom and socialism.

In Russia the workers of all nationalities, especially those of non-Russian nationality, endure an economic and political oppression such as obtains in no other country. The Jewish workers, as a disfranchised nationality, not only suffer general economic and political oppression, but they also suffer under the yoke which deprives them of elementary civil rights. The heavier this yoke, the greater the need for the closest possible unity among the proletarians of the different nationalities; for without such unity a victorious struggle against the general oppression is impossible. The more the predatory tsarist autocracy strives to sow the seeds of discord, distrust and enmity among the nationalities it oppresses, the more abominable its policy of inciting the ignorant masses to savage pogroms becomes, the more does the duty devolve upon us, the Social Democrats, to rally . . . the different nationalities into a single Russian Social-Democratic Labour Party.

The First Congress of our Party, held in the spring of 1898, set itself the aim of establishing such unity. To dispel any idea of its being national in character, the Party called itself "*Rossiiskaya*" and not "*Russkaya*."* The organization of Jewish workers—the Bund—affiliated with the Party as an autonomous section. Unfortunately, from that moment the unity of the Jewish and non-Jewish Social-Democrats within the single party was destroyed. Nationalist ideas began to spread among the leading members of the Bund, ideas which are in sharp contradiction to the entire world view of Social-Democracy.

*The adjective *Russkaya* (Russian) pertains to nationality, *Rosiiskaya* (Russian) pertains to Russia as a country.—*Ed.*

Instead of trying to draw the Jewish and the non-Jewish workers closer together, the Bund embarked upon a policy of weaning the former away from the latter; at its congresses it claimed a separate existence for the Jews as a nation. Instead of carrying on the work begun by the First Congress of the Russian Social-Democratic Party towards still closer unity between the Bund and the Party, the Bund moved a step away from the Party. First, it withdrew from the united organization of the R.S.D.L.P. abroad and set up an independent organization abroad; later, it withdrew from the R.S.D.L.P. as well, when the Second Congress of our Party in 1903 refused by a considerable majority to recognize the Bund as sole representative of the Jewish proletariat. The Bund held to its position, claiming not only that it was the sole representative of the Jewish proletariat, but that no territorial limits were set to its activities. Naturally, the Second Congress of the R.S.D.L.P. could not accept such conditions, since in a number of regions, as, for instance, in South Russia, the organized Jewish proletariat constitutes part of the general Party organization. Ignoring that stand, the Bund withdrew from the Party and thereby broke the unity of the Social-Democratic proletariat, despite the work that had been carried out in common at the Second Congress, and despite the Party Program and Rules.

At its Second and Third Congresses the Russian Social-Democratic Labor Party expressed its firm conviction that the Bund's withdrawal from the Party was a grave and deplorable mistake on its part. The Bund's mistake is a result of its groundless claim to be the sole, monopolistic representative of the Jewish proletariat, from which the federalist principle of organization necessarily derives; the result of its long-standing policy of keeping aloof and separate from the Party. We are convinced that this mistake must be rectified and that it will be rectified as the movement continues to grow. We consider ourselves ideologically at one with the Jewish Social-Democratic proletariat. After the Second Congress our Central Committee pursued a non-nationalist policy; it took pains that such committees should be set up (Polesye, North-Western) as would unite all the local workers, Jewish as well as non-Jewish, into a single whole. At the Third Congress of the R.S.D.L.P. a resolution was adopted providing for the publication of literature in Yiddish. In fulfilment of that resolution we are now issuing a complete translation into Yiddish of the Report on the Third Congress of the R.S.D.L.P., which has appeared in Russian. The Report will show the Jewish workers—both those who are now in our

Party and those who are temporarily out of it—how our Party is progressing. The Report will show the Jewish workers that our Party is already emerging from the internal crisis from which it has been suffering since the Second Congress. It will show them what the actual aspirations of our Party are and what its attitude is towards the Social-Democratic parties and organizations of the other nationalities, as well as the attitude of the entire Party and its central body to its component parts. Finally, it will show them—and this is most important—the tactical directives that were drawn up by the Third Congress of the R.S.D.L.P. with regard to the policy of the entire class-conscious proletariat in the present revolutionary situation.

Comrades! The hour of political struggle against the tsarist autocracy is drawing near—the struggle of the proletariat for the freedom of all classes and peoples in Russia, for freedom of the proletarian drive towards socialism. Terrible trials are in store for us. The outcome of the revolution in Russia depends on our class-consciousness and preparedness, on our unity and determination. Let us set to work then with greater boldness and greater unity, let us do all in our power for the proletarians of the different nationalities to march to freedom under the leadership of a really united Russian Social-Democratic Labor Party.

Editorial Board of the Central Organ
of the Russian Social-Democratic Labor Party

Written at the end
of May (beginning of June) 1905

Published according to
the text of the pamphlet
translated from the Yiddish

First published in 1905 as a
preface to the pamphlet:
*Report on the Third Congress of the
R.S.D.L.P.*
(issued in Yiddish)
[CW 8: 495–98]

REACTION IS TAKING TO ARMS

The Social-Democratic press has long been pointing out that the vaunted "constitutionalism" in Russia is baseless and ephemeral. So long as the old authority remains and controls the whole vast machinery of state administration, it is useless talking seriously about the importance of popular representation and about satisfying the urgent needs of the vast masses of the people. No sooner had the State Duma begun its sittings—and liberal-bourgeois oratory about peaceful, constitutional evolution burst forth in a particularly turbulent flood—then there began an increasing number of attacks on peaceful demonstrators, cases of setting fire to halls where public meetings were proceeding, and lastly, downright pogroms—all organized by government agents.

Meanwhile the peasant movement is growing. Strikes among the workers are becoming more embittered, more frequent and more extensive. Unrest is growing among the most backward military units, the infantry in the provinces, and among the Cossacks.

Far too much inflammable material has accumulated in Russian social life. The struggle which ages of unprecedented violence, torment, torture, robbery and exploitation have paved the way for has become too widespread and cannot be confined within the limits of a struggle of a Duma for a particular Ministry. Even the most downtrodden and ignorant "subjects" can no longer be restrained from proclaiming the demands of awakening human and civic dignity. The old authority, which has always made the laws itself, which in fighting for its existence is resorting to the last, most desperate, savage and furious methods, cannot be restrained by appeals to abide by the law.

The pogrom in Belostok is a particularly striking indication that the government has taken to arms against the people. The old, but ever new story of Russian pogroms!—*ever*, until the people achieve victory, until the old authorities are completely swept away. Here are a few excerpts from a telegram received from a Belostok elector, Tsirin: "A *deliberately-organized* anti-Jewish pogrom has started." "In spite of rumors that have been circulated, *not a single order has been received* from the Ministry all day today!" "Vigorous agitation for the pogrom has been carried on for the past two weeks. In the streets, particularly at night, leaflets were distributed calling for the massacre, not only of Jews, but also of intellectuals. *The police simply turned a blind eye to all this.*"

The old familiar picture! The police organizes the pogrom beforehand. The police instigates it: leaflets are printed in government printing offices calling for a massacre of the Jews. When the pogrom begins, the police is inactive. The troops quietly look on at the exploits of the Black Hundreds. But later this very police goes through the farce of prosecution and trial of the pogromists. The investigations and trials conducted by the officials of the old authority always end in the same way: the cases drag on, none of the pogromists are found guilty, sometimes even the battered and mutilated Jews and intellectuals are dragged before the court, months pass—and the old, but ever new story is forgotten, until the next pogrom. Vile instigation, bribery, and fuddling with drink of the scum of our cursed capitalist "civilization," the brutal massacre of unarmed by armed people, and farcical trials conducted by the culprits themselves! And yet there are those who, seeing these phenomena of Russian social life, think, and say, that somebody or other is "recklessly" calling upon the people to resort to "extreme measures"! One must be, not reckless, but a poltroon, politically corrupt, to say such things in the face of events like the burning of the People's House at Vologda (at the time of the opening of the Duma) or the pogrom in Belostok (after the Duma had been in session a month). A single event like this will have more effect upon the people than millions of appeals. And to talk about "reckless" appeals is just as hopelessly pedantic and as much a sin of a deadened civic conscience, as to condemn the wild cry for revenge that is going up from the battlefields of Vologda and Belostok.

The Duma did the right thing by immediately discussing the interpellation on the Belostok pogrom, and sending some of its members to Belostok to investigate on the spot. But in reading this interpellation, and comparing it with the speeches of members of the Duma and the commonly-known facts about pogroms, one has a deep feeling of dissatisfaction, of indignation at the irresolute terms in which the interpellation is worded.

Judge for yourselves. The authors of the interpellation say: "The inhabitants *fear* that the local authorities and malicious agitators may try to make out the victims themselves to be responsible for the calamity that has befallen them." Yes, the downtrodden and tormented Jewish population is indeed apprehensive of this, and has *every* reason to be. This is true. But it is *not the whole truth*, gentlemen, members of the Duma, and authors of the interpellation! You, the people's deputies, who have not yet been assaulted and tormented, know perfectly well that this is not the whole truth. You know that the downtrodden inhabitants will *not dare* to name those who are *really responsible* for the pogrom. *You must name them.* That is what you are people's deputies for. That is why you enjoy even under Russian law— *complete* freedom of speech in the Duma. Then don't stand *between* the reaction and the people, at a time when the armed reaction is strangling, massacring, and mutilating unarmed people. Take your stand *openly and entirely* on the side of the people. Don't confine yourselves to conveying the fear of the townspeople that the vile instigators of the pogroms will say it is the murdered victims who are to blame. *Indict the culprits in unequivocal terms*—it is your direct *duty* to the people. Don't ask the government whether measures are being taken to protect the Jews and to prevent pogroms, but ask how long the government intends to shield the real culprits, who are members of the government. Ask the government whether it thinks that the people will long be in error as to who is really responsible for the pogroms. Indict the government openly and publicly; as the *only* means of protection against pogroms.

This is not in keeping with "parliamentary practice," you will say. Are you not ashamed to advance such an argument *even* at a time like this? Don't you realize that the people will condemn you if, even at a time like this, you do not give up playing at parliaments and do not dare to say straightforwardly, openly and loudly what *you really know and think?*

That you know the truth about the pogroms is evident from speeches delivered by members of the Duma. The Cadet Nabokov said: "We know that in many cases the administration has not succeeded in allaying the suspicion that the simultaneous outbreak of the pogroms is the result either of the Black-Hundred organizations operating *with the knowledge of the local authorities,* or, at best, of the latter's systematic inaction."

If you *know* that this is so, gentlemen of the Cadet Party, you should have said so in your interpellation. You should have written: We *know* such-and-such facts and therefore ask questions about them. And if you know what happens "at best," it is *unseemly* for people's deputies to keep silent about what happens at worst, about the deliberate organization of pogroms by the police on orders from St. Petersburg.

"Belostok is not an exceptional case," rightly said Levin. "It is one of the consequences of the system that you want to combat." Quite right, citizen Levin! But while in newspapers we can only speak of the "system," you in the Duma ought to speak out more plainly and sharply.

"Pogroms are part of a whole system. In the October days . . . the government . . . found no other means of combating the liberation movement . . . You know how that chapter of history ended. Now the same thing repeated. . . . This system is *perfidiously* prepared and thought out, and is being carried out *with equal perfidy.* In many cases we know very well who organizes these pogroms; we know very well that leaflets *are sent out by the gendarmerie departments.*"

Once again, quite right, citizen Levin! And therefore you should have said in your interpellation: does the government think that the Duma is not aware of the commonly-known fact that the gendarmes and police send out those leaflets?

Deputy Ryzhkov bluntly stated that the allegation that pogroms are due to racial enmity was a lie, and that the allegation that they were due to the impotence of the authorities was a malicious invention. Deputy Ryzhkov listed a number of facts which proved that there had been "collaboration" between the police, the pogromists and the Cossacks. "I live in a big industrial district," he said, "and I know that the pogrom in Lugansk, for example, did not assume ghastly dimensions *only because* [mark this, gentlemen: *only* because] the *unarmed workers* drove back the pogromists with their bare fists, at the risk of being shot by the police."

In *Rech,* this part of the report of the debate in the Duma is headed "The Government Is Indicted." This is a good heading, but it belongs in the *text* of the Duma *interpellation,* not in a newspaper report. Either draft these interpellations in such a way as to make them a passionate indictment of the government before the people, or in a way that they may arouse ironical taunts and jeers at the crying discrepancy between the monstrous facts and the bureaucratic evasions in bureaucratically-restrained interpellations. Only by adopting the first-mentioned method will the Duma teach the reactionaries not to jeer at it. As it is, the reactionaries are jeering, quite openly and frankly. Read today's *Novoye Vremya.* These lackeys of the pogromists are chuckling and making merry: "One cannot help observing with particular satisfaction [!!] the haste with which the Duma interpellated the Minister on the anti-Jewish pogrom in Belostok." You see: the pogromists are particularly pleased—the flunkey blurts out the truth. The reactionaries are pleased with the Belostok pogrom, and with the fact that they can now abusively call the Duma the "Jewish" Duma. The reactionaries jeer and say: "If as was stated in the Duma today, we must pardon the riots against property made by the peasants in the Russian gubernias, then we must also pardon the pogroms against Jewish property in the Western territory."

You see, gentlemen of the Duma, the reactionaries are more outspoken than you are. Their language is stronger than your Duma language. The reactionaries are not afraid to fight. They are not afraid to associate the Duma with the peasant's struggle for freedom. *Then don't you be afraid to associate the reactionary government with the pogromists!*

Written on June 3 (16), 1906
Published in *Vperyod*, No. 9,
June 4, 1906
[*CW 10*: 508–13]

Published according
to the newspaper text

UNION OF THE BUND WITH THE RUSSIAN SOCIAL-DEMOCRATIC LABOR PARTY

The Seventh Congress of the Bund, the organization of the Jewish Social-Democratic workers of Russia, has recently taken place. According to the reports of this Congress, the total number of members of the Bund amounts to 33,000 in 257 organizations. Representation at the Congress was organized on a democratic basis, with one delegate for each 300 members of the Party. About 23,000 members took part in the elections and they sent to the Congress 68 delegates with the right to speak and vote.

The chief question that the Congress had to decide was that of the union of the Bund with the Russian Social-Democratic Labor Party. As is known, the Unity Congress of the R.S.D.L.P. pronounced in favor of unification and laid down the conditions for it. The Seventh Congress of the Bund has now accepted these conditions. Union with the R.S.D.L.P. was adopted by 48 votes against 20. Thus, the Russian Social-Democratic Labor Party has at last become a truly all-Russian and united organization. The membership of our Party is now *over* 100,000: 31,000 were represented at the Unity Congress, and then there are about 26,000 Polish Social-Democrats, about 14,000 Lettish and 33,000 Jewish Social-Democrats.

Representatives of the Central Committee of the Bund joined the Central Committee of the R.S.D.L.P. The rather difficult work of unifying the local organizations of the Bund and those of the R.S.D.L.P. now lies ahead.

The second question discussed at the Bund Congress was that of the present political situation. In a detailed resolution, adopted by a large majority of votes, the Seventh Congress of the Bund accepted *the convocation of a constituent assembly* as a tactical slogan, and rejected all reservations tending to weaken this slogan, such as "through the Duma", etc. Boycott of the Duma was rejected conditionally, that is to say, the necessity of taking part in the elections was recognized provided that the party of the proletariat was in a position to carry out an independent election campaign.

The third question was that of "guerrilla actions," without any division of them into "expropriations" and terrorist acts. By an overwhelming majority, a resolution *against* guerrilla actions was adopted.

The last question concerned the organization of the Bund. Organizational rules were adopted.

We limit ourselves to this short note for the time being; we hope in the near future to acquaint our readers more fully with the decisions of the Seventh Congress of the Bund.

Written in September 1906
First published in 1937
[CW 11: 195–6]

Published according to
the manuscript

SEPARATISTS IN RUSSIA AND SEPARATISTS IN AUSTRIA

Among the various representatives of Marxism in Russia the Jewish Marxists, or, to be more exact, some of them—those known as the Bundists—are carrying out a policy of *separatism*. From the history of the working-class movement it is known that the Bundists *left the Party* in 1903, when the majority of the party of the working class refused to accept their demand to be recognized as the "sole" representatives of the Jewish proletariat.

This exit from the Party was a manifestation of separatism deeply harmful to the working-class movement. But, in fact, the Jewish workers have entered and continue to enter the Party everywhere in spite of the Bund. Side by side with the *separate* (isolated) organizations of the Bundists, there have *always* existed *general* organizations of the workers—Jewish, Russian, Polish, Lithuanian, Latvian, etc.

From this history of Marxism in Russia we know, furthermore, that when the Bund in 1906 again returned to the Party, the Party stipulated the condition that separatism should cease, i.e., that there should be local unity of *all* the Marxist workers of *whatever* nationality.

But this condition *was not* fulfilled by the Bundists, despite its *special* confirmation by a special decision of the Party in December 1908.[6]

That, shortly, is the history of Bundist separatism in Russia. Unfortunately, it is little known to the workers, and little thought is given to it. Those having the closest practical acquaintance with this history are the Polish, the Lithuanian (especially in Vilna in 1907) and the Latvian Marxists (at the same time, in Riga), and the Marxists of South and Western Russia. It is well known, incidentally, that the Caucasian Marxists, including *all* the Caucasian Mensheviks, have until quite recently maintained local *unity* and even fusion of the workers of all nationalities, and have condemned the separatism of the Bundists.

We should also note that the prominent Bundist, Medem, in the well-known book, *Forms of the National Movement* (St. Petersburg, 1910), admits that the Bundists have never implemented unity in the localities, i.e., they have always been separatists.

In the international working-class movement, the question of separatism came to the front most urgently in 1910, at the Copenhagen Congress. The *Czechs* came forward as separatists in Austria, and destroyed the unity that had existed previously between the Czech and German workers. The International Congress at Copenhagen *unanimously* condemned separatism, but the Czechs have unfortunately remained separatists right up to the present.

Feeling themselves isolated in the proletarian International, the Czech separatists spent a long time searching unsuccessfully for supporters. Only now have they found some—in the *Bundists and liquidators*. The *čechoslavische Sozialdemokrat*, the bit of a journal published by the separatists in German, printed an article in its issue No. 3 (Prague, April 15, 1913) under the title "A Turn for the Better." this "turn" that is supposed to be for the "better" (actually, towards separatism) the Czech separatists saw—where do you think, reader? In *Nasha Zarya*,[7] the liquidators' journal, in an article by the *Bundist* V. Kossovsky!

At last the Czech separatists are not alone in the proletarian International! Naturally they are glad to be able to rope in even liquidators, even Bundists. But all class-conscious workers in Russia should give this fact some thought: the Czech separatists, unanimously condemned by the International, are clinging to the coat-tails of liquidators and Bundists.

Only the complete unity (in every locality, and from top to bottom) of the workers of all nations, which has existed so long and so successfully in the Caucasus, corresponds to the interests and tasks of the workers' movement.

Pravda No, 104   Published according to
May 8, 1913   the *Pravda* text
[CW 19: 87–8]

THE WORKING CLASS AND
THE NATIONAL QUESTION

Russia is a motley country as far as her nationalities are concerned. Government policy, which is the policy of the landowners supported by the bourgeoisie, is steeped in Black-Hundred nationalism.

This policy is spearheaded against the *majority* of the peoples of Russia who constiture the *majority* of her population. And alongside this we have the bourgeois nationalism of other nations (Polish, Jewish, Ukranian, Georgian, etc.), raising its head and trying to *divert* the working class from its great world-wide tasks by a national struggle or a struggle for national culture.

The national question must be clearly considered and solved by all class-conscious workers.

When the bourgeoisie was fighting for freedom together with the people, together with all those who labor, it stood for full freedom and equal rights for the nations. Advanced countries, Switzerland, Belgium, Norway and others, provide us with an example of how free nations under a really democratic system live together in peace or separate peacefully from each other.

Today the bourgeoisie fears the workers and is seeking an alliance with the Purishkeviches, with the reactionaries, and is betraying democracy, advocating oppression or unequal rights among nations and corrupting the workers with *nationalist* slogans.

In our times the proletariat alone upholds the real freedom of nations and the unity of workers of all nations.

For different nations to live together in peace and freedom or to separate and form different states (if that is more convenient for them), a full democracy, upheld by the working class, is essential. No privileges for any nation or any one language! Not even the slightest degree of oppression or the slightest injustice in respect of a national minority—such are the principles of working-class democracy.

The capitalists and landowners want, at all costs, to keep the workers of different nations apart while the powers-that-be live splendidly together as shareholders in profitable concerns involving millions (such as the Lena Goldfields); Orthodox Christians and Jews, Russians and Germans, Poles and Ukrainians, everyone who possesses *capital*, exploit the workers of all nations in company.

Class-conscious workers stand for *full unity* among the workers of all nations in every educational, trade union, political, etc., workers' organization. Let the Cadet gentlemen disgrace themselves by denying or belittling the importance of equal rights for Ukrainians. Let the bourgeoisie of all nations find comfort in lying phrases about national culture, national tasks, etc., etc.

The workers will not allow themselves to be disunited by sugary speeches about national culture, or "national-cultural autonomy." The workers of all nations together, concertedly, uphold full freedom and complete equality of rights in organizations common to all—and that is the guarantee of genuine culture.

The workers of the whole world are building up their own internationalist culture, which the champions of freedom and the enemies of oppression have for long been preparing. To the old world, the world of national oppression, national bickering, and national isolation the workers counterpose a new world, a world of the unity of the working people of all nations, a world in which there is no place for any privileges or for the slightest degree of oppression of man by man.

Pravda No. 106,
May 10, 1913
[CW 19: 91–2]

Published according to
the *Pravda* text

THESES ON THE NATIONAL QUESTION[8]

1. The article of our program (on the self-determination of nations) cannot be interpreted to mean anything but *political* self-determination, i.e., the right to secede and form a separate state.

2. This article in the Social-Democratic program is *absolutely* essential to the Social-Democrats of Russia

a) for the sake of the basic principles of democracy in general;

b) also because there are, within the frontiers of Russia and, *what is more, in her frontier areas*, a number of nations with sharply distinctive economic, social and other conditions; furthermore, these nations (like all the nations of Russia except the Great Russians) are unbelievably oppressed by the tsarist monarchy;

c) lastly, also in view of the fact that throughout Eastern Europe (Austria and the Balkans) and in Asia—i.e., in countries bordering on Russia—the bourgeois-democratic reform of the state that has everywhere else in the world led, in varying degree, to the creation of independent national states or states with the closest, interrelated national composition, has either not been consummated or has only just begun;

d) at the present moment Russia is a country whose state system is more backward and reactionary than that of any of the contiguous countries, beginning—in the West—with Austria where the fundamentals of political liberty and a constitutional regime were consolidated in 1867, and where universal franchise has now been introduced, and ending—in the East—with republican China. In all their propaganda, therefore, the Social-Democrats of Russia must insist on the right of all nationalities to form separate states or to choose freely the state of which they wish to form part.

3. The Social-Democratic Party's recognition of the right of all nationalities to self-determination requires of Social-Democrats that they should

a) be unconditionally hostile to the use of force in any form whatsoever by the dominant nation (or the nation which constitutes the majority of the population) in respect of a nation that wishes to secede politically.

b) demand the settlement of the question of such secession only on the basis of a universal, direct and equal vote of the population of the given territory by secret ballot;

c) conduct an implacable struggle against both the Black-Hundred-Octobrist and the liberal-bourgeois (Progressist, Cadet, etc.) parties on every occasion when they defend or sanction national oppression in general or the denial of the right of nations to self-determination in particular.

4. The Social-Democratic Party's recognition of the right of all nationalities to self-determination most certainly does not mean that Social-Democrats reject an independent appraisal of the advisability of the state secession of any nation in each separate case. Social-Democracy should, on the contrary, give its independent appraisal, taking into consideration the conditions of capitalist development and the oppression of the proletarians of various nations by the united bourgeoisie of all nationalities, as well as the general tasks of democracy, first of all and most of all the interests of the proletarian class struggle for socialism.

From this point of view the following circumstance must be given special attention. There are two nations in Russia that are more civilized and more isolated by virtue of a number of historical and social conditions and that could most easily and most "naturally" put into effect their right to secession. They are the peoples of Finland and Poland. The experience of the Revolution of 1905 has shown that even in these two nations the ruling classes, the landowners and bourgeoisie, reject the revolutionary struggle for liberty and seek a *rapprochement* with the ruling classes of Russia and with the tsarist monarchy *because of their fear* of the revolutionary proletariat of Finland and Poland.

Social-Democracy, therefore, must give most emphatic warning to the proletariat and other working people of all nationalities against direct deception by the nationalistic slogans of "their own" bourgeoisie, who with their saccharine or fiery speeches about "our native land" try to divide the proletariat and *divert its attention* from their bourgeois intrigues while they enter into an economic and political alliance with the bourgeoisie of other nations and with the tsarist monarchy.

The proletariat cannot pursue its struggle for socialism and defend its everyday economic interests without the closest and fullest alliance of the workers of all nations in all working-class organizations without exception.

The proletariat cannot achieve freedom other than by revolutionary struggle for the overthrow of the tsarist monarchy and its replacement by a democratic republic. The tsarist monarchy *precludes* liberty and equal rights for nationalities, and is, furthermore, the bulwark of barbarity, brutality and reaction in both Europe and Asia. This monarchy can be overthrown only by the united proletariat of all the nations of Russia, which is giving the lead to consistently democratic elements capable of revolutionary struggle from among the working masses of all nations.

It follows, therefore, that workers who place political unity with "their own" bourgeoisie above complete unity with the proletariat of all nations, are acting against their own interests, against the interests of socialism and against the interests of democracy.

5. Social-Democrats, in upholding a consistently democratic state

system, demand unconditional equality for all nationalities and struggle against absolutely all privileges for one or several nationalities.

In particular, Social-Democrats reject a "state" language. It is particularly superfluous in Russia because more than seven-tenths of the population of Russia belong to related Slav nationalities who, given a free school and a free state, could easily achieve intercourse by virtue of the demands of the economic turnover without any "state" privileges for any one language.

Social-Democrats demand the abolition of the old administrative divisions of Russia established by the feudal landowners and the civil servants of the autocratic feudal state and their replacement by divisions based on the requirements of present-day economic life and in accordance, as far as possible, with the national composition of the population.

All areas of the state that are distinguished by social peculiarities or by the national composition of the population, must enjoy wide self-government and autonomy, with institutions organized on the basis of universal, equal and secret voting.

6. Social-Democrats demand the promulgation of a law, operative throughout the state, protecting the rights of every national minority in no matter what part of the state. This law should declare inoperative any measure by means of which the national majority might attempt to establish privileges for itself or restrict the right of a national minority (in the sphere of education, in the use of any specific language, in budget affairs, etc.), and forbid the implementation of any such measure by making it a punishable offense.

7. The Social-Democratic attitude to the slogan of "cultural-national" (or simply "national") "autonomy" or to plans for its implementation is a negative one, since this slogan (1) undoubtedly contradicts the internationalism of the class struggle of the proletariat, (2) makes it easier for the proletariat and the masses of working people to be drawn into the sphere of influence of bourgeois nationalism, and (3) is capable of distracting attention from the task of the consistent democratic transformation of the state as a whole, which transformation alone can ensure (to the extent that this can, in general, be ensured under capitalism) peace between nationalities.

In view of the special acuteness of the question of cultural-national autonomy among Social-Democrats, we give some explanation of the situation.

a) It is impermissible, from the standpoint of Social-Democracy, to issue the slogan of *national* culture either directly or indirectly. The slogan is incorrect because already under capitalism, all economic, political and spiritual life is becoming more and more international. Socialism will make it completely international. International culture, which is now already being systematically created by the proletariat of all countries, does not absorb "national culture" (no matter of what national group) as a whole, but accepts from *each* national culture *exclusively* those of its elements that are consistently democratic and socialist.

b) Probably the one example of an approximation, even though it is a timid one, to the slogan of national culture in Social-Democratic program is Article 3 of the Brünn Programme of the Austrian Social-Democrats. This Article 3 reads: "All self-governing regions of one and the same nation form a single-national alliance that has complete autonomy in deciding its national affairs."

This is a compromise slogan since it does not contain a shadow of extra-territorial (personal) national autonomy. But this slogan, too, is erroneous and harmful, for it is no business of the Social-Democrats of Russia to unite into one nation the Germans in Lodz, Riga, St. Petersburg and Saratov. Our business is to struggle for full democracy and the annulment of *all* national privileges and to unite the German workers in Russia with the workers of all other nations in upholding and developing the international culture of socialism.

Still more erroneous is the slogan of extra-territorial (personal) national autonomy with the setting up (according to a plan drawn up by the consistent supporters of this slogan) of national parliaments and national state secretaries (Otto Bauer and Karl Renner). Such institutions contradict the economic conditions of the capitalist countries, they have not been tested in any of the world's democratic states and are the opportunist dream of people who despair of setting up consistent democratic institutions and are seeking salvation from the national squabbles of the bourgeoisie in the artificial isolation of the proletariat and the bourgeoisie of each nation on a number of ("cultural") questions.

Circumstances occasionally compel Social-Democrats to submit for a time to some sort of compromise decisions, but from other countries we must borrow not compromise decisions, but consistently Social-Democratic decisions. It would be particularly unwise to adopt the unhappy Austrian compromise decision today, when it had been a complete failure in Austria and has led to the separatism and secession of the Czech Social-Democrats.

c) The history of the "cultural-national autonomy" slogan in Russia shows that it has been adopted by *all* Jewish bourgeois parties and *only* by Jewish bourgeois parties; and that they have been uncritically followed by the Bund, which has inconsistently rejected the national-Jewish parliament (sejm) and national-Jewish state secretaries. Incidentally, even those European Social-Democrats who accede to or defend the compromise slogan of cultural-national autonomy, admit that the slogan is quite unrealizable for the Jews (Otto Bauer and Karl Kautsky). "The Jews in Galicia and Russia are more of a caste than a nation, and attempts to constitute Jewry as a nation are attempts at preserving a caste" (Karl Kautsky).

d) In civilized countries we observe a fairly full (relatively) approximation to national peace under capitalism *only* in conditions of the *maximum* implementation of democracy throughout the state system and administration (Switzerland). The slogans of consistent democracy (the republic, a militia, civil servants elected by the people, etc.) unite the proletariat and the working people, and in general, all progressive elements in each nation in the name of the struggle for conditions that preclude even the slightest national privilege—while the slogan of "cultural-national autonomy" preaches the isolation of nations in educational affairs (or "cultural" affairs, in general), an isolation that is quite compatible with the retention of the grounds for all (including national) privileges.

The slogans of consistent democracy *unite* in a single whole the proletariat and the advanced democrats of all nations (elements that demand not isolation but the uniting of democratic elements of the nations in all matters, including educational affairs), while the slogan of cultural-national autonomy *divides* the proletariat of the different nations and links it up with the reactionary and bourgeois elements of the separate nations.

8. The sum-total of economic and political conditions in Russia therefore demands that Social-Democracy should *unite* unconditionally workers of all nationalities in *all* proletarian organizations without exception (political, trade union, co-operative, educational, etc., etc.). The Party should not be federative in structure and should not form national Social-Democratic groups but should unite the

proletarians of all nations in the given locality, conduct propaganda and agitation in *all* the languages of the local proletariat, promote the common struggle of the workers of all nations against every kind of national privilege and should recognize the autonomy of local and regional Party organizations.

9. More than ten years' experience gained by the R.S.D.L.P. confirms the correctness of the above thesis. The Party was founded in 1898 as a party of all Russia, that is, a party of the proletariat of all the nationalities of Russia. The Party remained "Russian" when the Bund seceded in 1903, after the Party Congress had rejected the demand to consider the Bund the *only* representative of the Jewish proletariat. In 1906 and 1907 events showed convincingly that there were no grounds for this demand, a large number of Jewish proletarians continued to co-operate in the common Social-Democratic work in many local organizations, and the Bund re-entered the Party. The Stockholm Congress (1906) brought into the Party the Polish and Latvian Social-Democrats, who favored *territorial* autonomy, and the Congress, furthermore, did *not* accept the principle of federation and demanded unity of Social-Democrats of all nationalities in each locality. This principle had been in operation in the Caucasus for many years, it is in operation in Warsaw (Polish workers and Russian soldiers), in Vilna (Polish, Lettish, Jewish and Lithuanian workers) and in Riga, and in the three last-named places it had been implemented *against* the separatist Bund. In December 1908, the R.S.D.L.P., through its conference, adopted a special resolution confirming the demand for the *unity* of workers of all nationalities, *on a principle other than* federation. The splitting activities of the Bund separatists in the fulfilling the Party decision led to the collapse of all that "federation of the worst type"[9] and brought about the *rapprochement* of the Bund and the Czech separatists and vice versa (see Kossovsky in *Nasha Zarya* and the organ of the Czech separatists, *Der čechoslavische Sozialdemokrat* No. 3, 1913, on Kossovsky), and, lastly, at the August (1912) Conference of the liquidators it led to an *undercover* attempt by the Bund separatists and liquidators and some of the Caucasian liquidators to insert "cultural-national autonomy" into the Party program *without any defense of its substance!*

Revolutionary worker Social-Democrats in Poland, in the Latvian Area and in the Caucasus still stand for territorial autonomy and the *unity* of worker Social-Democrats of *all* nations. The Bund-liquidator secession and the alliance of the Bund with non-Social-Democrats in Warsaw place the *entire* national question, both in its theoretical aspect and in the matter of Party structure, *on the order of the day* for all Social-Democrats.

Compromise decisions have been broken by the very people who introduced them against the will of the Party, and the demand for the unity of worker Social-Democrats of all nationalities is being made more loudly than ever.

10. The crudely militant and Black-Hundred-type nationalism of the tsarist monarchy, and also the revival of *bourgeois* nationalism—Great-Russian (Mr. Struve, *Russkaya Molva*, [10] the Progressists, etc.), the Ukrainian, and Polish (the anti-Semitism of Narodowa "Demokracja"[11]), and Georgian and Armenian, etc.—all this makes it particularly urgent for Social-Democratic organizations in all parts of Russia to devote greater attention than before to the national question and to work out consistently Marxist decisions on this subject in the spirit of consistent internationalism and unity of proletarians of all nations.

*　*　*

a*) The slogan of national culture is incorrect and expresses only the limited bourgeois understanding of the national question. International culture.

b*) The perpetuation of national divisions and the promoting of refined nationalism—unification, *rapprochement*, the mingling of nations and the expression of the principles of a *different*, international culture.

c*) The despair of the petty bourgeois (hopeless struggle against national bickering) and the fear of radical-democratic reforms and the socialist movement—only radical-democratic reforms can establish national peace in capitalist states and only socialism is able to terminate national bickering.

d*) National curias in educational affairs.[12]

e*) The Jews.

*These letters are in Greek in the manuscript.

Written in June 1913
First published in 1925
[CW 19:243–51]

Published according to
the manuscript

THE NATIONALIZATION OF JEWISH SCHOOLS

The politics of the government are soaked in the spirit of nationalism. Attempts are made to confer every kind of privilege upon the "ruling," i.e., the Great-Russian nation, even though the Great Russians represent a *minority* of the population of Russia, to be exact, only 43 per cent.

Attempts are made to cut down still further the rights of all the other nations inhabiting Russia, to segregate one from the other and stir up enmity among them.

The extreme expression of present-day nationalism is the scheme for the nationalization of Jewish schools. The scheme emanated from the educational officer of Odessa district, and has been sympathetically considered by the Ministry of Public "Education." What does this nationalization mean?

It means segregating the Jews into *special* Jewish schools (secondary schools). The doors of all other educational establishments—both private and state—are to be completely closed to the Jews. This "brilliant" plan is rounded off by the proposal to limit the number of pupils in the Jewish secondary schools to the notorious "quota"!

In all European countries such measures and laws against the Jews existed only in the dark centuries of the Middle Ages, with their Inquisition, the burning of heretics and similar delights. In Europe the Jews have long since been granted complete equality and are fusing more and more with the nations in whose midst they live.

The most harmful feature in our political life generally, and in the above scheme particularly, apart from the oppression and persecution of the Jews, is the striving to fan the flames of nationalism, to segregate the nationalities in the state one from another, to increase their estrangement, to separate their schools.

The interests of the working class—as well as the interests of political liberty generally—require, on the contrary, the fullest equality of all the nationalities in the state without exception, and the elimination of every kind of barrier between the nations, the bringing together of children of all nations in the same schools, etc. Only by casting off every savage and foolish national prejudice, only by uniting the workers of all nations into one association, can the working class become a force, offer resistance to capitalism, and achieve a serious improvement in its living conditions.

Look at the capitalists! They try to inflame national strife among the "common people," while they themselves manage their business affairs remarkably well—Russians, Ukranians, Poles, Jews, and Germans together in one and the same corporation. Against the workers the capitalists of all nations and religions are united but they strive to divide and weaken the workers by national strife!

This most harmful scheme for the nationalization of the Jewish schools shows, incidentally, how mistaken is the plan for so-called "cultural-national autonomy," i.e., the idea of taking education out of the hands of the state and handing it over to each nation separately. It is not this we should strive for, but for the unity of the workers of all nations in the struggle against *all* nationalism, in the struggle for a truly democratic *common* school and for political liberty generally. The example of the advanced countries of the world—say, Switzerland in Western Europe or Finland in Eastern Europe—shows us that only consistently-democratic state institutions ensure the most peaceable and human (not bestial) coexistence of various nationalities, *without* the artificial and harmful separation of education according to nationalities.

Severnaya Pravda No. 14
August 18, 1913
Signed: V. I.
[CW19:307–08]

Published according to
the *Severnaya Pravda* text

RESOLUTIONS OF THE SUMMER, 1913 JOINT CONFERENCE OF THE CENTRAL COMMITTEE OF THE R.S.D.L.P. AND PARTY OFFICIALS (Excerpt)[13]

RESOLUTION ON THE NATIONAL QUESTION

The orgy of Black-Hundred nationalism, the growth of nationalist tendencies among the liberal bourgeoisie and the growth of nationalist tendencies among the upper classes of the oppressed nationalities, give prominence at the present time to the national question.

The state of affairs in the Social-Democratic movement (the attempts of the Caucasian Social-Democrats, the Bund and the liquidators to annul the Party Program,[14] etc.) compels the Party to devote more attention than ever to this question.

This Conference, taking its stand on the Program of the R.S.D.L.P., and in order to organize correctly Social-Democratic agitation on the national question, advances the following propositions:

1. Insofar as national peace is in any way possible in a capitalist society based on exploitation, profit-making and strife, it is attainable only under a consistently and thoroughly democratic republican system of government which guarantees full equality of all nations and languages, which recognizes no compulsory official language, which provides the people with schools where instruction is given in all the native languages, and the constitution of which contains a fundamental law that prohibits any privileges whatsoever to any one nation and any encroachment whatsoever upon the rights of a national minority. This particularly calls for wide regional autonomy and fully democratic local self-government, with the boundaries of the self-governing and autonomous regions determined by the local inhabitants themselves on the basis of their economic and social conditions, national make-up of the population, etc.

2. The division of the educational affairs of a single state according to nationalities is undoubtedly harmful from the standpoint of democracy in general, and of the interest of the proletarian class struggle in particular. It is precisely this division that is implied in the plan for "cultural-national" autonomy, or for "the creation of institutions that will guarantee freedom for national development" adopted in Russia by all the Jewish bourgeois parties and by the petty-bourgeois, opportunist elements among the different nations.

3. The interest of the working class demand the amalgamation of the workers of all the nationalities in a given state in united proletarian organizations—political, trade union, cooperative, educational, etc. This amalgamation of the workers of different nationalities in single organizations will alone enable the proletariat to wage a victorious struggle against international capital and reaction, and combat the propaganda and aspirations of the landowners, clergy and bourgeois nationalists of all nations, who usually cover up their anti-proletarian aspirations with the slogan of "national culture." The world working-class movement is creating and daily developing more and more an international proletarian culture.

4. As regards the right of the nations oppressed by the tsarist monarchy to self-determination, i.e., the right to secede and form independent states, the Social-Democratic Party must unquestionably champion this right. This is dictated by the fundamental principles of international democracy in general, and specifically by the unprece-

dented national oppression of the majority of the inhabitants of Russia by the tsarist monarchy, which is a most reactionary and barbarous state compared with its neighboring states in Europe and Asia. Furthermore, this is dictated by the struggle of the Great-Russian inhabitants themselves for freedom, for it will be impossible for them to create a democratic state if they do not eradicate Black-Hundred, Great-Russian nationalism, which is backed by the traditions of a number of bloody suppressions of national movements and systematically fostered not only by the tsarist monarchy and all the reactionary parties, but also by the Great-Russian bourgeois liberals, who toady to the monarchy, particularly in the period of counter-revolution.

5. The right of nations to self-determination (i.e., the constitutional guarantee of an absolutely free and democratic method of deciding the question of secession) must under no circumstances be confused with the expediency of a given nation's secession. The Social-Democratic Party must decide the latter question exclusively on its merits in each particular case in conformity with the interests of social development as a whole and with the interests of the proletarian class struggle for socialism.

Social-Democrats must moreover bear in mind that the landowners, the clergy and the bourgeoisie of the oppressed nations often cover up with nationalist slogans their efforts to divide the workers and dupe them by doing deals behind their backs with the landowners and bourgeoisie of the ruling nation to the detriment of the masses of the working people of all nations.

* * *

This Conference places on the agenda of the Party congress the question of the national program. It invites the Central Committee, the Party press and the local organizations to discuss (in pamphlets, debates, etc.) the national question in fullest detail.

Written September 1913
Published in 1913 in the pamphlet
*Notification and Resolutions
of the Summer, 1913
Joint Conference of the Central
Committee of the R.S.D.L.P.
and Party Officials.*
Issued by the Central Committee
[CW 19:427–29]

Published according to
the text of the illegal
mimeographed edition
of the resolutions collated
with the text of the pamphlet

"CULTURAL-NATIONAL" AUTONOMY

The essence of the plan, or program, of what is called "cultural-national" autonomy (or: "the establishment of institutions that will guarantee freedom of national development") is *separate schools for each nationality.*

The more often all avowed and tacit nationalists (including the Bundists) attempt to obscure this fact the more we must insist on it.

Every nation, irrespective of place of domicile of its individual members (irrespective of territory, hence the term "extra-territorial" autonomy) is a united officially recognized association conducting national-cultural affairs. The most important of these affairs is education. The determination of the composition of the nations by allowing every citizen to register freely, irrespective of place of domicile, as belonging to any national association, ensures absolute precision and absolute consistency in segregating the schools according to nationality.

Is such a division, be it asked, permissible from the point of view of democracy in general, and from the point of view of the interests of the proletarian class struggle in particular?

A clear grasp of the essence of the "cultural-national autonomy" program is sufficient to enable one to reply without hesitation—it is absolutely impermissible.

As long as different nations live in a single state they are bound to one another by millions and thousands of millions of economic, legal and social bonds. How can education be extricated from these bonds? Can it be "taken out of the jurisdiction" of the state, to quote the Bund formula, classical in its striking absurdity? If the various nations living in a single state are bound by economic ties, then any attempt to divide them permanently in "cultural" and particularly educational matters would be absurd and reactionary. On the contrary, effort should be made to *unite* the nations in educational matters, so that the schools should be a preparation for what is actually done in real life. At the present time we see that the different nations are unequal in the rights they possess and in their level of development. Under these circumstances, segregating the schools according to nationality would *actually* and inevitably *worsen* the conditions of the more backward nations. In the southern, former slave states of America, Negro children are still segregated in separate schools, whereas in the North, white and Negro children attend the same schools. In Russia a plan was recently proposed for the "nationalization of Jewish schools," i.e., the segregation of Jewish children from the children of other nationalities in separate schools. It is needless to add that this plan originated in the most reactionary, Purishkevich circles.

One cannot be a democrat and at the same time advocate the principle of segregating the schools according to nationality. Note: we are arguing at present from the general democratic (i.e., bourgeois-democratic) point of view.

From the point of view of the proletarian class struggle we must oppose segregating the schools according to nationality far more emphatically. Who does not know that the capitalists of all the nations in a given state are most closely and intimately united in joint-stock companies, cartels and trusts, in manufacturers' associations, etc., which are directed *against* the workers irrespective of their nationality? Who does not know that in *any* capitalist undertaking—from huge works, mines and factories and commercial enterprises down to capitalist farms—we *always*, without exception, see a larger variety of nationalities among the workers than in remote, peaceful and sleepy villages? The urban workers, who are best acquainted with developed capitalism and perceive more profoundly the psychology of the class struggle—their whole life teaches them or they perhaps imbibe it with their mothers' milk—such workers instinctively and inevitably realize that segregating the schools according to nationality is not only a *harmful* scheme, but a downright fraudulent swindle on the part *of the capitalists*. The workers *can* be split up, divided and weakened by the advocacy of such an idea, and still more by the segregation of the ordinary peoples' schools according to nationality; while the capitalists, whose children are well provided with rich private schools and specially engaged tutors, *cannot in any way* be threatened by any division or weakening through "cultural-national autonomy."

As a matter of fact, "cultural-national autonomy," i.e., the absolutely pure and consistent segregating of education according to nationality, was invented not by the capitalists (*for the time being* they resort to cruder methods to divide the workers) but by the opportunist, philistine intelligentsia of Austria. There is *not a trace* of this brilliantly philistine and brilliantly nationalist idea in any of the democratic West-European countries with mixed populations. This idea of the despairing petty bourgeois could arise only in Eastern Europe, in backward, feudal, clerical, bureaucratic Austria, where *all* public and political life is hampered by wretched, petty squabbling (worse still: cursing and brawling) over the question of languages.

Since cat and dog can't agree, let us at least segregate all the nations once and for all absolutely clearly and consistently in "national curias" for educational purposes!—such is the psychology that engendered this foolish idea of "cultural-national autonomy." The proletariat, which is conscious of and cherishes its internationalism, will never accept this nonsense of refined nationalism.

It is no accident that in Russia this idea of "cultural-national autonomy" was accepted *only by all* the Jewish bourgeois parties, then (in 1907) by the conference of the *petty-bourgeois* Left-Narodnik parties of different nationalities, and lastly by the petty-bourgeois, opportunist elements of the *near-Marxist* groups, i.e., the Bundists and the liquidators (the latter were even too timid to do so straightforwardly and definitely). It is no accident that in the State Duma *only* the semiliquidator Chkhenkeli, who is infected with nationalism, and the petty bourgeois Kerensky, spoke in favor of "cultural-national autonomy."

In general, it is quite funny to read the liquidator and Bundist references to Austria on this question. First of all, why should the most backward of the multinational countries be taken as the *model?* Why not take the most advanced? This is very much in the style of the bad Russian liberals, the Cadets, who for models of a constitution turn mainly to such backward countries as Prussia and Austria, and not to advanced countries like France, Switzerland and America!

Secondly, after taking the Austrian model, the Russian nationalist philistines, i.e., the Bundists, liquidators, Left Narodniks, and so forth, have themselves changed it *for the worse.* In this country it is the Bundists (plus *all* the Jewish bourgeois parties, in whose wake the Bundists follow without always realizing it) that mainly and primarily use this plan for "cultural-national autonomy" in their propaganda and agitation; and yet in Austria, the country where this idea of "cultural-national autonomy" originated, Otto Bauer, the father of the idea, devoted a special chapter of his book to proving that "cultural-national autonomy" *cannot* be applied to the Jews!

This proves more conclusively than lengthy speeches how inconsistent Otto Bauer is and how little he believes in his own idea, for he excludes the *only* extra-territorial (not having its own territory) nation from his plan for extra-territorial national autonomy.

This shows how Bundists borrow *old-fashioned* plans from Europe, multiply the mistakes of Europe tenfold and "develop" them to the point of absurdity.

The fact is—and this is the third point—that at their congress in Brünn (in 1899) the Austrian Social-Democrats *rejected* the program of "cultural-national autonomy" that was proposed to them. They merely adopted a compromise in the form of a proposal for a union of the nationally delimited *regions* of the country. This compromise did *not* provide either for extra-territoriality or for segregating education according to nationality. In accordance with this compromise, in the most advanced (capitalistically) populated centers, towns, factory and mining districts, large country estates, etc., there are *no* separate schools for each nationality!

The Russian working class has been combating this reactionary, pernicious, petty-bourgeois nationalist idea of "cultural-national autonomy," and will continue to do so.

Za Paravdu No. 46,
November 28, 1913
[CW 19: 503–07]

Excerpts—Critical
Critical Remarks on the National Question

Those who seek to serve the proletariat must unite the workers of all nations, and unswervingly fight bourgeois nationalism, *domestic* and foreign. The place of those who advocate the slogan of national culture is among the nationalist petty bourgeois, not among the Marxists.

Take a concrete example. Can a Great-Russian Marxist accept the slogan of national, Great-Russian, culture? No, he cannot. Anyone who does that should stand in the ranks of the nationalists, not of the Marxists. Our task is to fight the dominant, Black-Hundred and bourgeois national culture of the Great Russians, and to develop, exclusively in the internationalist spirit and in the closest alliance with the workers of other countries, the rudiments also existing in the history of our democratic and working-class movement. Fight your own Great-Russian landlords and bourgeoisie, fight their "culture" in the name of internationalism, and, in so fighting, "adapt" yourself to the special features of the Purishkeviches and Struves—that is your task, not preaching or tolerating the slogan of national culture.

The same applies to the most oppressed and persecuted nation—the Jews. Jewish national culture is the slogan of the rabbis and the bourgeoisie, the slogan of our enemies. But there are other elements in Jewish culture and in Jewish history as a whole. Of the ten and a half million Jews in the world, somewhat over half live in Galicia and Russia, backward and semi-barbarous countries, where the Jews are *forcibly* kept in the status of a caste. The other half lives in the civilized world, and there the Jews do not live as a segregated caste. There the great world-progressive features of Jewish culture stand clearly revealed: its internationalism, its identification with the advanced movements of the epoch (the percentage of Jews in the democratic and proletarian movements is everywhere higher than the percentage of Jews among the population).

Whoever, directly or indirectly, puts forward the slogan of Jewish "national culture" is (whatever his good intentions may be) an enemy of the proletariat, a supporter of all that is *outmoded* and connected with *caste* among the Jewish people; he is an accomplice of the rabbis and the bourgeoisie. On the other hand, those Jewish Marxists who mingle with the Russian, Lithuanian, Ukrainian and other workers in international Marxist organizations, and make their contribution (both in Russian and in Yiddish) towards creating the international culture of the working-class movement—these Jews, despite the separatism of the Bund, uphold the best traditions of Jewry by fighting the slogan of "national culture."

Bourgeois nationalism and proletarian internationalism—these are the two irreconcilably hostile slogans that correspond to the two great class camps throughout the capitalist world, and express the *two* policies (nay, the two world outlooks) in the national question. In advocating the slogan of national culture and building up on it an entire plan and practical program of what they call "cultural-national autonomy," the Bundists are *in effect* instruments of bourgeois nationalism among the workers.

3. THE NATIONALIST BOGEY OF "ASSIMILATION"

The question of assimilation, i.e., of the shedding of national features, and absorption by another nation, strikingly illustrates the consequences of the nationalist vacillations of the Bundists and their fellow-thinkers.

Mr. Liebman, who faithfully conveys and repeats the stock arguments, or rather, tricks, of the Bundists, has qualified as "the *old assimilation story*" the demand for the unity and amalgamation of the workers of all nationalities in a given country in united workers' organizations (see the concluding part of the article in *Severnaya Pravda*).

"Consequently," says Mr. F. Liebman, commenting on the concluding part of the article in *Severnaya Pravda*, "if asked what nationality he belongs to, the worker must answer: I am a Social-Democrat."

Our Bundist considers this the acme of wit. As a matter of fact, he gives himself away completely by *such* witticisms and outcries about "assimilation," *levelled against* a consistently democratic and Marxist slogan.

Developing capitalism knows two historical tendencies in the national question. The first is the awakening of national oppression, and the creation of national states. The second is the development and growing frequency of international intercourse in every form, the breakdown of national barriers, the creation of the international unity of capital, of economic life in general, of politics, science, etc.

Both tendencies are a universal law of capitalism. The former predominates in the beginning of its development, the latter characterizes a mature capitalism that is moving towards its transformation into socialist society. The Marxists' national program takes both tendencies into account, and advocates, firstly, the equality of nations and languages and the impermissibility of all *privileges* in this respect (and also the right of nations to self-determination, with which we shall deal separately later); secondly, the principle of internationalism and uncompromising struggle against contamination of the proletariat with bourgeois nationalism, even of the most refined kind.

The question arises: what does our Bundist mean when he cries out to heaven against "assimilation"? He *could not* have meant the oppression of nations, or the *privileges* enjoyed by a particular nation, because the word "assimilation" here does not fit at all, because all Marxists, individually, and as an official, united whole, have quite definitely and unambiguously condemned the slightest violence against and oppression and inequality of nations, and finally because this general Marxist idea, which the Bundist has attacked, is expressed in the *Severnaya Pravda* article in the most emphatic manner.

No, evasion is impossible here. In condemning "assimilation" Mr. Liebman had in mind, *not* violence, *not* inequality, and *not* privileges. Is there anything real left in the concept of assimilation, after all violence and all inequality have been eliminated?

Yes, there undoubtedly is. What is left is capitalism's world-historical tendency to break down national barriers, obliterate national distinctions, and to *assimilate* nations—a tendency which manifests itself more and more powerfully with every passing decade, and is one of the greatest driving forces transforming capitalism into socialism.

Whoever does not recognize and champion the equality of nations and languages, and does not fight against all national oppression or inequality, is not a Marxist; he is not even a democrat. That is beyond doubt. But it is also beyond doubt that the pseudo-Marxist who heaps abuse upon a Marxist of another nation for being an "assimilator" is simply a *nationalist philistine.* In this unhandsome category of people are all the Bundists and (as we shall shortly see) Ukrainian nationalist-socialists such as L. Yurkevich, Donstov and Co.

To show concretely how reactionary the views held by these nationalist philistines are, we shall cite facts of three kinds.

It is the Jewish nationalists in Russia in general, and the Bundists in particular, who vociferate most about Russian orthodox Marxists being "assimilators." And yet, as the aforementioned figures show, out of the ten and a half million Jews all over the world, *about half* that number live in the *civilized* world, where conditions favoring "assimilation" are *strongest*, whereas the unhappy, downtrodden, disfranchised Jews in Russia and Galicia, who are crushed under the heel of the Purishkeviches (Russian and Polish), live where conditions for "assimilation" *least* prevail, where there is most segregation, and even a "Pale of Settlement",[15] a *numerus clausus*[16] and other charming features of the Purishkevich regime.

The Jews in the civilized world are not a nation, they have in the main become assimilated, say Karl Kautsky and Otto Bauer. The Jews in Galicia and in Russia are not a nation; unfortunately (through *no* fault of their own but through that of the Purishkeviches), they still a *caste* here. Such is the incontrovertible judgement of people who are undoubtedly familiar with the history of Jewry and take the above-cited facts into consideration.

What do these facts prove? It is that only Jewish reactionary philistines, who want to turn back the wheel of history, and make it proceed, not from the conditions prevailing in Russia and Galicia to those prevailing in Paris and New York, but in the reverse direction—only they can clamor against "assimilation."

The best Jews, those who are celebrated in world history, and have given the world foremost leaders of democracy and socialism, have never clamored against assimilation. It is only those who contemplate the "rear aspect" of Jewry with reverential awe that clamor against assimilation. . . .

[CW 20: 25–29]

THE NATIONAL EQUALITY BILL[17]

Comrades:

The Russian Social-Democratic Labor group in the Duma has decided to introduce in the Fourth Duma a Bill to abolish the disabilities of the Jews and other non-Russians. The text of this Bill you will find below.

The Bill aims at abolishing all national restrictions against all nations: Jews, Poles, and so forth. But it deals in particular detail with the restrictions against the Jews. The reason is obvious: no nationality in Russia is so oppressed and persecuted as the Jewish. Anti-Semitism is striking ever deeper root among the propertied classes. The Jewish workers are suffering under a double yoke, both as workers and as Jews. During the past few years, the persecution of the Jews has assumed incredible dimensions. It is sufficient to recall the anti-Jewish pogroms and the Beilis case.

In view of these circumstances, organized Marxists must devote proper attention to the Jewish question.

It goes without saying that the Jewish question can effectively be solved only together with the fundamental issues confronting Russia today. Obviously, we do not look to the nationalist-Purishkevich Fourth Duma to abolish the restrictions against the Jews and other non-Russians. But it is the duty of the working class to make its voice heard. And the voice of the *Russian* workers must be particularly loud in protest against national oppression.

In publishing the text of our Bill, we hope that the Jewish workers, the Polish workers, and the workers of the other oppressed nationalities will express their opinion of it and propose amendments, should they deem it necessary.

At the same time we hope that the Russian workers will give particularly strong support to our Bill by their declarations, etc.

In conformity with Article 4 we shall append to the Bill a special list of regulations and laws to be rescinded. This appendix will cover about a hundred such laws affecting the Jews alone.

A BILL FOR THE ABOLITION OF ALL DISABILITIES OF THE JEWS AND OF ALL RESTRICTIONS ON THE GROUNDS OF ORIGIN OR NATIONALITY

1. Citizens of all nationalities inhabiting Russia are equal before the law.

2. No citizen of Russia, regardless of sex and religion, may be restricted in political or in any other rights on the grounds of origin or nationality.

3. All and any laws, provisional regulations, riders to laws, and so forth, which impose restrictions upon Jews in any sphere of social and political life, are herewith abolished. Article 767, Vol. IX, which states that "Jews are subject to the general laws in all cases *where no special regulations affecting them have been issued*" is herewith repealed. All and any restrictions of the rights of Jews as regards residence and travel, the right to education, the right to state and public employment, electoral rights, military service, the right to purchase and rent real estate in towns, villages, etc., are herewith abolished, and all restrictions of the rights of Jews to engage in the liberal professions, etc., are herewith abolished.

4. To the present law is appended a list of the laws, orders, provisional regulations, etc., that limit the rights of the Jews, and which are subject to repeal.

Put Pravdy No. 48,
March 28, 1914
[CW 20: 172–73]

Published according to
the text in *Put Pravdy*

NATIONAL EQUALITY

In *Put Pravdy* No. 48 (for March 28), the Russian Social-Democratic Labor group in the Duma published the text of its Bill on national equality, or, to quote its official title, "Bill for Abolition of All Disabilities of the Jews and of All Restrictions on the Grounds of Origin or Nationality."

Amidst the alarms and turmoil of the struggle for existence, for a bare livelihood, the Russian workers cannot and must not forget the yoke of national oppression under which the tens and tens of millions of "subject peoples" inhabiting Russia are groaning. The ruling nation—the Great Russians—constitute about 45 percent of the total population of the Empire. Out of every 100 inhabitants, over 50 belong to "subject peoples."

And the conditions of life of this vast population are even harsher than those of the Russians.

The policy of oppressing nationalities is one of *dividing* nations. At the same time it is a policy of systematic *corruption* of the people's minds. The Black Hundreds' plans are designed to foment antagonism among the different nations, to poison the minds of the ignorant and downtrodden masses. Pick up any Black-Hundred newspaper and you will find that the persecution of non-Russians, the sowing of mutual distrust between the Russian peasant, the Russian petty bourgeois and the Russian artisan on the one hand, and the Jewish, Finnish, Polish, Georgian and Ukrainian peasants, petty bourgeois and artisans on the other, is meat and drink to the whole of this Black-Hundred gang.

But the working class needs *unity, not division.* It has no more bitter enemy than the savage prejudices and superstitions which its enemies sow among the ignorant masses. The oppression of "subject peoples" is a double-edged weapon. It cuts both ways—against the "subject peoples" and against the Russian people.

That is why the working class must protest most strongly against national oppression in any shape and form.

It must counter the agitation of the Black Hundreds, who try to divert its attention to the baiting of non-Russians, by asserting its conviction as to the need for complete equality, for the complete and final rejection of all privileges for any one nation.

The Black Hundreds carry on a particularly venomous hate-campaign against the Jews. The Purishkeviches try to make the Jewish people the scapegoat for all their own sins.

And that is why the R.S.D.L. group in the Duma did right in putting *Jewish* disabilities in the forefront of its Bill.

The schools, the press, the parliamentary rostrum—everything is being used to sow ignorant, savage, and vicious hatred of the Jews.

This dirty and despicable work is undertaken, not only by the scum of the Black Hundreds, but also by reactionary professors, scholars, journalists and members of the Duma. Millions and thousands of millions of rubles are spent on poisoning the minds of the people.

It is a point of honor for the *Russian* workers to have this Bill against national oppression backed by tens of thousands of proletarian signatures and declarations. . . . This will be the best means of consolidating *complete* unity, amalgamating all the workers of Russia, irrespective of nationality.

Put Pravdy No. 62,
April 16, 1914
[CW 20: 237–38]

Published according to
the text in *Put Pravdy*

CORRUPTING THE WORKERS WITH REFINED NATIONALISM

The more strongly the working-class movement develops the more frantic are the attempts by the bourgeoisie and the feudalists to suppress it or break it up. Both these methods—suppression by force and disintegration by bourgeois influence—are constantly employed all over the world, in all countries, and one or another of these methods is adopted alternately by the different parties of the ruling classes.

In Russia, particularly after 1905, when the more intelligent members of the bourgeoisie realized that brute force alone was ineffective, all sorts of "progressive" bourgeois parties and groups have been more and more often resorting to the method of *dividing* the workers by advocating different bourgeois ideas and doctrines designed to weaken the struggle of the working class.

One such idea is refined nationalism, which advocates the division and splitting up of the proletariat on the most plausible and specious pretexts, as for example, that of protecting the interests of "national culture," "national autonomy, or independence," and so on, and so forth.

The class-conscious workers fight hard against *every kind* of nationalism, both the crude, violent, Black-Hundred nationalism, and that most refined nationalism which preaches the equality of nations *together* with . . . the *splitting up* of the workers' cause, the workers' organizations and all the working-class movement *according to* nationality. Unlike all the varieties of the nationalist bourgeoisie, the class-conscious workers, carrying out the decisions of the recent (summer 1913) conference of the Marxists, stand, not only for the most complete, consistent and fully applied *equality* of nations and languages, but also for the *amalgamation* of the workers of the different nationalities in *united* proletarian organizations of every kind.

Here lies the fundamental distinction between the national program of Marxism and that of any bourgeoisie, be it the most "advanced."

Recognition of the equality of nations and languages is important to Marxists, not only because they are the most consistent democrats. The interests of proletarian solidarity and comradely unity in the workers' class struggle call for the fullest equality of nations with a view to removing every trace of national distrust, estrangement, suspicion and enmity. And full equality implies the recognition of the *right* of self-determination for all nations.

To the bourgeoisie, however, the demand for national equality very often amounts in practice to advocating national exclusiveness and chauvinism; they very often couple it with *advocacy* of the division and estrangement of nations. This is *absolutely* incompatible with pro-letarian *internationalism*, which advocates, not only *closer relations* between nations, but the *amalgamation* of the workers of all na-tionalities in a given state in the *united* proletarian organizations. That is why Marxists emphatically condemn so-called "cultural-national autonomy," i.e. the idea that educational affairs should be *taken out* of the hands of the state and transferred to the *respective* nationalities. This plan means that in questions of "national culture" educational affairs are to be split up in *national associations* according to the nationalities in the given state federation, each with it own *separate* Diet, educational budgets, school boards, and educational institu-tions.

This is a plan of refined nationalism, which corrupts and divides the working class. To this plan (of the Bundists, liquidators and Narod-niks, *i.e.*, of the various petty-bourgeois groups), the Marxists con-trapose the principle of complete equality of nations and languages and go to the extent of denying the necessity of an official language; at the same time they advocate the closest possible relations between the nations, uniform *state* institutions for all nations, uniform school boards, a uniform education policy (secular education!) and the unity of the workers of the different nations in the struggle against the *nationalism of every national bourgeoisie*, a nationalism which is pre-sented in the form of the slogan "national culture" for the purpose of deceiving simpletons.

Let the petty-bourgeois nationalists—the Bundists, the liquidators, the Narodniks and the writers for *Dzvin*—openly advocate their prin-ciple of refined bourgeois nationalism; that is their right. But they should not try to fool the workers, as Madam V. O.[18] does, for example, in issue No. 25 of *Severnaya Rabochaya Gazeta*, where she assures her readers that *Za Pravdu* is *opposed* to instruction in schools being given in the native languages!

That is gross slander. The Pravdists not only recognize this right, but are *more consistent* in recognizing it than anyone else. The Pravdists, who identified themselves with the conference of Marxists, which declared that *no compulsory official language was necessary*, were the *first* in Russia to recognize *fully* the right to use the native language!

It is crass ignorance to confuse instruction in the native language with "dividing educational affairs within a single state according to nationality," with "cultural-national autonomy," with "taking educational affairs out of the hands of the state."

Nowhere in the world are Marxists (or even democrats) opposed to instruction being conducted in the native language. And *nowhere in the world* have Marxists adopted the program of "cultural-national autonomy"; Austria is the *only* country in which it *was proposed.*

The example of Finland, as quoted by Madam V. O., is an argument against herself, for in that country the *equality of nations and languages* (which we recognize unreservedly and more consistently than anybody) is recognized and carried out, but *there is no question there about taking educational affairs out of the hands of the state,* about separate national associations to deal with all educational affairs, about partitioning up the school system of a country with national barriers, and so forth.

Put Pravdy No. 82,
May 10, 1914
Signed: V.I.
[*CW* 20: 289–91]

Published according to
the text in *Put Pravdy*

LECTURE ON THE 1905 REVOLUTION[19] (Excerpt)

Tsarism vented its hatred particularly upon the Jews. On the one hand, the Jews furnished a particularly high percentage (compared with the total Jewish population) of leaders of the revolutionary movement. And now, too, it should be noted to the credit of the Jews, they furnish a relatively high percentage of internationalists, compared with other nations. On the other hand, tsarism adroitly exploited the basest anti-Jewish prejudices of the most ignorant strata of the population in order to organize, if not to lead directly, *pogroms*—over 4,000 were killed and more than 10,000 mutilated in 100 towns. These atrocious massacres of peaceful Jews, their wives and children roused disgust throughout the civilized world. I have in mind, of course, the disgust of the truly democratic elements of the civilized world, and these are *exclusively* the socialist workers, the proletarians.

Written in German before
January 9 (22), 1917
First published in *Pravda*
No. 18, January 22, 1925
Signed: N. Lenin
[CW 23: 250]

Published according to
the manuscript
Translated from the German

SPEECHES ON GRAMOPHONE RECORDS[20]

ANTI-JEWISH POGROMS

Anti-Semitism means spreading enmity towards the Jews. When the accursed tsarist monarchy was living its last days it tried to incite ignorant workers and peasants against the Jews. The tsarist police, in alliance with the landowners and the capitalists, organized pogroms against the Jews. The landowners and capitalists tried to divert the hatred of the workers and peasants who were tortured by want against the Jews. In other countries, too, we often see the capitalists fomenting hatred against the Jews in order to blind the workers, to divert their attention from the real enemy of the working people, capital. Hatred towards the Jews persists only in those countries where slavery to the landowners and capitalists has created abysmal ignorance among the workers and peasants. Only the most ignorant and downtrodden people can believe the lies and slander that are spread about the Jews. This is a survival of ancient feudal times, when the priests burned heretics at the stake, when the peasants lived in slavery, and when the people were crushed and inarticulate. This ancient, feudal ignorance is passing away; the eyes of the people are being opened.

It is not the Jews who are the enemies of the working people. The enemies of the workers are the capitalists of all countries. Among the Jews there are working people, and they form the majority. They are our brothers, who, like us, are oppressed by capital; they are our comrades in the struggle for socialism. Among the Jews there are kulaks, exploiters and capitalists, just as there are among the Russians, and among people of all nations. The capitalists strive to sow and foment hatred between workers of different faiths, different nations and different races. Those who do not work are kept in power by the power and strength of capital. Rich Jews, like rich Russians, and the rich in all countries, are in alliance to oppress, crush, rob and disunite the workers.

Shame on accursed tsarism which tortured and persecuted the Jews. Shame on those who foment hatred towards the Jews, who foment hatred towards other nations.

Long live the fraternal trust and fighting alliance of the workers of all nations in the struggle to overthrow capital.

Recording made at the
end of March, 1919
[CW 29: 252]

Published according to
the gramaphone record

Zionism: Its Role in World Politics*

4

I. WHAT IS ZIONISM?

1. THE NATURE AND ROOTS OF ZIONISM

Origins of Political Zionism   **HYMAN LUMER**

The prolonged crisis in the Middle East, beginning with the events of May 1967 and the ensuing Israeli-Arab war, has brought the question of Zionism very sharply to the fore. It is Zionism which underlies the policies of the Israeli government, and which motivates the main body of its supporters in the United States and other capitalist countries. Hence, to understand fully the nature of the conflict between Israel and the Arab states, as well as the political and social orientation of the major Jewish organizations and spokesmen in this country, it is necessary to examine in some detail the nature of Zionism and its role in the present-day world.

Political Zionism, whose aim is the creation and perpetuation of a Jewish state, had its origins in the last decades of the 19th century, animated by the upsurge of anti-Semitism in Europe which accompanied the rise of modern imperialism. It is quite distinct from the older religious Zionism—the belief in an eventual return to the Holy Land upon the coming of the Messiah.

Its chief forerunner was Moses Hess, who for a number of years had been an associate of Karl Marx. But he later became an ardent Jewish nationalist, and in his book *Rome and Jerusalem,* published in 1862, he expounded such ideas as these: "We Jews shall always remain strangers among the nations. . . . Each and every Jew, whether he wishes it or not, is automatically, by virtue of his birth, bound in solidarity with his entire nation. . . . Each has the solidarity and responsibility for the rebirth of Israel." But at the time these ideas met with little

---

*Extensive excerpts. Published 1973; International Publishers, New York

82

response and nothing further came of them. The rise of political Zionism as a movement was to come somewhat later.

The two classical presentations of the Zionist doctrine are Leo Pinsker's *Auto-Emancipation* (1882) and Theodor Herzl's *The Jewish State* (1896).

Pinsker's book grew out of the sharply intensified persecution of the Jews in tsarist Russia in 1881, signalized by a wave of pogroms in Kishinev and other localities and by the imposition of a mass of discriminatory legislation, including confinement to ghettos. Shortly afterward, in 1884, there was launched in Odessa the Chovevei Zion (lovers of Zion), a society dedicated to the establishment of Jewish settlements in Palestine.

It is Herzl, however, who is considered the founder of modern political Zionism. An assimilated Austrian Jew, he was deeply shocked by the anti-Semitic frameup of Captain Alfred Dreyfus in France in 1894, which he covered as a journalist. It was this which led him to develop the doctrine of Zionism, entirely independently of Pinsker and other predecessors, and to devote himself to its fulfillment.

Thus the emergence of Zionism corresponds to a new upsurge of anti-Semitism, associated with the rise of modern imperialism and its extreme development of racism as an ideological instrument of oppression. It was a new type of anti-Semitism, not primarily rooted in religious bigotry as in the past, but essentially secular and racial in character. The historian S. M. Dubnow describes it as follows:

> The last quarter of the XIXth century saw a new anti-Jewish movement in Europe. It went by the name of "anti-Semitism" and resolved itself into an attempt to revive the old Jew-baiting practices of the Middle Ages under a new disguise. The rapid progress the Jews, once emancipated, had made in all fields of social and industrial activity had aroused the jealous fear of those sections of Christian society which still clung to the idea of the social inferiority of the Hebrew people. It was declared that the Jew, being a Semite on account of his racial characteristics, was not fitted to live side by side with the Aryan Christian. (*An Outline of Jewish History*, Vol. III, p. 316.)

But Zionism was not the only reaction to these developments. The masses of working-class Jews, especially in Russia, responded rather by joining the revolutionary movement and coming into irreconcilable conflict with Zionism.

Zionist Ideology

Political Zionism is a reactionary bourgeois-nationalist ideology based on two fundamental fallacies: (1) that the Jews throughout the world constitute a nation, and (2) that anti-Semitism is incurable and eternal.

That the Jews on a world scale, lacking a common territory, language, cultural and economic life, do not constitute a nation in any generally recognized (let alone Marxist) sense of the term hardly needs to be demonstrated. Zionism, however, looks upon the Jews as a nation only in a biological sense: that they are presumed to be the literal descendants of the Jews of ancient times; and in a spiritual sense: that they possess a common background (as some put it, the "same historic memory"), a common religion and, arising from this, the elements of a common culture. Indeed, Zionism sees the Jews as set apart by mystical bonds which non-Jews are incapable of understanding or sharing. Jacob Neusner, Professor of Religious Studies at Brown University, expresses it in these words:

> The inwardness of Zionism—its piety and spirituality—is not to be comprehended by the world, only by the Jew, for, like the Judaism it transformed and transcended, to the world it was worldly and political, stiffnecked and stubborn . . . but to the Jew it was something other, not to be comprehended by the gentile. ("Zionism and the 'Jewish Problem,'" *Midstream*, November 1969.)

Closely connected with such ideas of innate distinctness is the concept of the Jews as a "chosen people," destined to play a unique role in history, and thereby set apart from all other peoples.

In short, Zionism asserts the existence of an unbridgeable gulf between Jew and non-Jew. In its own way it upholds the racist doctrine of the anti-Semites that Jews are inherently different from other peoples and hence incapable of becoming integrated with them.

Directly related to this is the thesis that anti-Semitism is inherent in non-Jews and hence ineradicable. Pinsker regarded anti-Semitism as biological in nature. He wrote:

> Judeophobia is a variety of demonopathy with the distinction that it is not peculiar to particular races, but is common to the whole of mankind. . . . As a psychic aberration it is hereditary, and as a disease

transmitted for two thousand years it is incurable. (*Auto-Emancipation,* p. 9.)

Herzl, it is true, viewed the roots of anti-Semitism as social rather than biological. But he saw it as being none the less inevitable, since he regarded the social relationships between Jews and gentiles as essentially unchangeable. It was the Jews themselves, he maintained, who carried the seeds of anti-Semitism with them wherever they went. This idea was echoed 50 years later by Chaim Weizmann, then head of the World Zionist Organization, who said:

I believe the one fundamental cause of anti-Semitism . . . is that the Jew exists. We seem to carry anti-Semitism in our knapsacks wherever we go. The growth and intensity of anti-Semitism is proportional to the number of Jews or to the density of Jews in a given country. (*The Jewish Case Before the Anglo-American Committee on Palestine,* p. 7.)

Herzl wrote: "Above all I recognized the emptiness and futility of efforts to 'combat' anti-Semitism." (*The Diaries of Theodor Herzl,* p. 6.) He concluded, therefore, that the solution of the Jewish question lies not in fighting to end anti-Semitism and to achieve full equality for the Jewish people in all countries where they live, but in separating Jew from non-Jew—in establishing a Jewish state in which the Jewish nation, scattered in exile for some 2,000 years, could be reunited.

To Herzl and many of his followers the location of such a Jewish state was immaterial. Herzl regarded Palestine and Argentina as equally acceptable. And he fought for the acceptance of a British offer of territory in Uganda. But to others of his followers, chiefly those from Eastern Europe, a Jewish state could only mean Palestine, Weizmann writes in his autobiography:

Kishinev [the frightful pogrom of 1903—H. L.] had only intensified in the Jews of Russia the ineradicable longing for a Jewish home in Palestine—in Palestine and not elsewhere. Elsewhere meant for them only a continuation of the old historic rounds of refuge. They wanted Palestine because that meant restoration in every sense. (*Trial and Error,* p. 92.)

For David Ben-Gurion the basis of the Jewish state in Palestine is "the Messianic vision of the redemption of the Jewish people and all mankind." This is "the soul of prophetic Jewry, in all its forms and metamorphoses until this day, and it is the secret of the open and hidden devotion of world Jewry to the State of Israel." (Address to the 25th World Zionist Congress, December 28, 1960.)

Thus political Zionism becomes joined with the older religious Zionism with its "Messianic vision" of the return to the "promised land" of the Old Testament. But it was not an ancient longing to return to Zion that gave the impulse to political Zionism; this idea had long existed only as an ossified religious ritual. "Next year in Jerusalem" was uttered yearly by innumerable Jews who had not the faintest expectation—or desire—of returning to Jerusalem at any time. That impulse was provided rather by the rise of modern anti-Semitism of which we have already spoken, originally in the late 19th century and later, in its most hideous form, in the days of Hitlerism.

Zionism as an Organized Movement

Political Zionism is not only an ideology; it is also an organized world movement. The World Zionist Organization, launched through Herzl's initiative, held its First Congress in 1897. That Congress stated: "The aim of Zionism is to create for the Jewish people a home in Eretz Israel secured by public law." The 23rd Congress, held after the establishment of the State of Israel, revised this aim as follows: "The task of Zionism is the consolidation of the State of Israel, the ingathering of the exiles in Eretz Israel and the fostering of the unity of the Jewish people." Clearly, Israel is looked upon as the homeland of *all* Jews, to which the "world Jewish nation" scattered in exile is to be returned.

Zionism regards Jews as aliens in the lands in which they live. It seeks to withdraw them from the struggles for democracy and progress in their own countries as being of no consequence to them as Jews. It strives to build a wall between Jewish and non-Jewish workers, maintaining that the only real bond of Jewish workers is that with other Jews, including Jewish capitalists. It rejects socialism as an answer to anti-Semitism and is bitterly hostile to the socialist countries, insisting that anti-Semitism, being incurable, is no less rife in these than in the capitalist countries.

It stands at the very opposite pole from the ideology of working-class internationalism, which calls for the unity of workers of all countries against their common class enemy, world monopoly capitalism, and on this basis for a common struggle against all forms of national and racial oppression as being divisive and destructive of the interests of workers everywhere. In its extreme nationalism and separatism, in its capitulation to anti-Semitism, in its efforts to divide Jewish workers from other workers, Zionism serves the interests of the exploiters and oppressors of all workers and all peoples.

2. ZIONISM AND ISRAEL

How the State of Israel Was Born

The State of Israel had its origins in the UN resolution of November 29, 1947 which partitioned Palestine into two states, one Jewish and one Arab.

It was not, as is maintained in some quarters, a creation of Britain. To be sure, British imperialism encouraged Jewish settlement in Palestine through the Balfour Declaration of 1917. But it did so only to pit Jews and Arabs against one another in order to perpetuate British rule under the League of Nations Mandate. In the later years of the Mandate the British severely restricted Jewish immigration into Palestine, and at no time did they support the formation of an independent Jewish state.

The British ruling circles, though they had surrendered the Mandate in 1947 on the grounds that internal conflict made it impossible to exercise it, opposed the partition of Palestine. Their UN representatives abstained from voting on the partition resolution and on all related questions, and they announced that Britain would do nothing to implement the resolution if either the Jews or the Arabs objected to it. What they hoped was that partition would fail because of Jewish-Arab antagonisms and that in the ensuing chaos the UN would find no alternative other than continuation of British rule in one form or another.

Furthermore, it was British imperialism which instigated the Arab states to attack the new-born State of Israel in 1948. These Arab states were at that time governed by puppet rulers subservient to Britain and their armed forces were commanded by British officers taking orders from London. The war fought by Israel in 1948 was in fact a war against British imperialism. "The objective of this military action by

British imperialism," writes Bert Ramelson, "was to frustrate the implementing of the UN resolution, to hang on to the whole of Palestine, and by parcelling it out among Arab stooge rulers, to retain indirectly what Britain previously held directly as the mandatory power." (*The Middle East*, pp. 13–14.)

Nor did the Truman Administration in this country display any great enthusiasm for partition. On the contrary, motivated largely by pressures emanating from the oil interests, it maneuvered to modify or to circumvent the partition proposals.

The main initiative leading to the UN action came from the Soviet Union, supported by the other socialist countries. In a speech on May 14, 1947 Soviet UN representative Andrei Gromyko called for "the creation of a single Arab-Jewish state with equal rights for Jews and Arabs . . . as the solution most deserving attention, of this complicated problem." But should this prove unrealizable because of sharpened Jewish-Arab hostility, "then it would be necessary to consider an alternative solution which . . . consists of the division of Israel into two states—one, Jewish, and one, Arab."

Among the reasons given by Gromyko for his proposals was the need to find a haven for the many Jewish refugees who had been left stranded (thanks mainly to the refusal of the capitalist states to admit them). But he also presented a more cogent reason, namely, that there *already* existed a significant Jewish community in Palestine. He said:

> . . . We must bear in mind the incontestable fact that the population of Palestine consists of two peoples, Arabs and Jews. Each of these has its historical roots in Palestine. That country has become the native land of both these peoples, and both of them occupy an important place in the country economically and culturally. Neither history nor the conditions which have arisen in Palestine now can justify any unilateral solution of the Palestine problem, either in favor of the creation of an independent Arab state, ignoring the lawful rights of the Jewish people, or in favor of the creation of a Jewish state, ignoring the lawful rights of the Arab population. . . . A just settlement can be found only if account is taken in sufficient degree of the lawful interests of both peoples.

In 1946 there were in Palestine some 608,000 Jews, nearly one-third of the total population of 1,973,000. These constituted a substantial and distinct Jewish community. To be sure, they were in the main recent immigrants who had come during the war. The bulk of them came, however, not as Zionist usurpers of Arab land but rather, in the face of enormous difficulties, as refugees from the horrors of Nazism, and most of whom had literally nowhere else to go.

The Soviet Union has always been strongly opposed to the Zionist concept of a Jewish state. But that was not the issue here. Under the circumstances that prevailed in 1947, it would have been just as wrong to agree to complete Arab domination as to accede to the Zionist demand to make all of Palestine a Jewish homeland. The course proposed by the Soviet Union was therefore the only realistic and just one available.

Had the Jews and Arabs formed a common front against British imperialism at the end of World War II, the natural outcome of their victory in such a struggle would have been some form of binational state. In fact, it was such a possibility that the Soviet proposals envisaged. But this was not to be, and there remained in the end only the alternative of partition.

The basis for the coming into being of the State of Israel was not created by Zionism. Until the advent of Hitlerism with its monstrous crimes against the Jews, comparatively few Jews were induced by the Zionists to migrate to Palestine (in 1931 the Jewish population was about 175,000, a little more than one-fourth of the 1946 figure). It was the wave of immigration of refugees during and immediately after the war that first created a substantial Jewish community, and the new wave of immigration from Eastern Europe after 1948, stemming from the horrors of Hitlerism, that swelled the size of this community, doubling its numbers within a few years. But it was the Zionists who retained control and who fashioned the state according to their own design.

The validity of Israel's existence as a state derives from the UN partition resolution. However, the state envisioned by that resolution is not that conceived of and established by Zionism.

For Jews Exclusively

The Jewish state envisioned by Zionism was to be *exclusively* Jewish, for only in such a state, according to Zionist doctrine, would it be possible to escape anti-Semitism. That Palestine was also populated by Arabs was either ignored or regarded as an inconvenience to be removed or at best tolerated.

Herzl spoke of settlement in Palestine in terms of "a people without a land to a land without a people." For him the Palestinian Arabs simply did not exist as a people. And this attitude has continued to prevail up to the present time.

It was manifested in pronounced form by David Ben-Gurion, of whom the Israeli writer Aubrey Hodes says:

> Ben-Gurion had little time for the Arabs. . . . He despised the Arab way of life and warned publicly against the danger that Israel would become another Levantine country "like Saudi Arabia or Iraq." . . . It is significant that during his thirteen years as Prime Minister of Israel he did not pay a single official visit to the city of Nazareth, the largest Arab center in Israel. (*Dialogue With Ishmael*, p. 67.)

Michael Bar-Zohar, Ben-Gurion's biographer, gives the following picture of the latter's views at the time of the 1948 war:

> Ben-Gurion remained skeptical about any possibility of coexistence with the Arabs. The fewer there were living within the frontiers of the new Jewish state, the better he would like it. . . . (While this might be called racialism, the whole Zionist movement actually was based on the principle of a purely Jewish community in Palestine. When the various Zionist institutions appealed to the Arabs not to leave the Jewish state but to become an integral part of it, they were being hypocritical to some extent.) (*Ben-Gurion*, p. 103.)

Indeed, many were not thus hypocritical; they made no bones about wanting the Arabs out. The idea that Arabs do not really count as people remains widely prevalent in Israel today, as noted by another Israeli writer, Amos Oz, in these words:

> In time, Naomi Shemer [in her hit song "Jerusalem of Gold"] was to express this state of mind by describing East Jerusalem in terms of: "— the market place is empty/ And none goes down to the Dead Sea/ By way of Jericho"—meaning, of course: The market place is empty *of Jews* and no *Jew* goes down to the Dead Sea by way of Jericho. A remarkable revelation of a remarkably characteristic way of thinking. ("Meaning of Homeland," *New Outlook*, December 1967.)

In keeping with the Zionist concept, the establishment of Jewish settlements was from the outset based on displacement of Arabs by Jews. Uri Avnery, member of the Knesset and editor of the Israeli weekly *Ha'olam Hazeh*, writes in his book *Israel Without Zionists* of Hebrew Labor, Hebrew Land and Hebrew Defense as the three main themes of Zionism. He says:

> . . . Hebrew Labor meant, necessarily, no Arab Labor. The "redemption of the land" often meant, necessarily, "redeeming" it from the Arab *fellahin* who happened to be living on it. A Jewish plantation owner who employed Arabs in his orange grove was a traitor to the cause, a despicable reactionary who not only deprived a Jewish worker of work, but even more important, deprived the country of a Jewish worker. His grove had to be picketed, the Arabs had to be evicted by force. . . . This was the battle of Hebrew Labor, which continued for two generations, and relapses of which still trouble present-day Israel from time to time. . . .
>
> The struggle for the redemption of the land became, at times, as violent. The land was bought, often at exorbitant prices, with good money raised mostly by poor Jews abroad. In many cases, the Arab who sold it did not live on the land, but was a rich *effendi* whiling away his life in the casinos of Beirut or the French Riviera. He had no particular care for the fate of the poor *fellahin* tenants who made their meager living there. These were simply evicted when the land was redeemed by the Jewish National Fund to set up a *kibbutz*. If some of them later attacked the *kibbutz*, it only showed that an efficient system of armed defense was imperative. Thus the *Histadrut* became the sponsor and the patron of the *Haganah*, the underground army based on the *kibbutzim*, which became the forerunner of today's Israel Defense Army (p. 85).

There were some, notable among them the father of "spiritual Zionism," Ahad Ha'am, who spoke out strongly against such an approach to the Arabs, regarding it as a serious blunder. But this was no "mistake"; the fact is that such a racist attitude toward Arabs is inherent in Zionism.

Israeli Arabs: Second-Class Citizens

In accord with the Zionist concept, Israel has been established as a state in which any Jew anywhere in the world may claim citizenship and enjoy special ethnic and religious privileges. Until recently such citizenship had to be claimed by migrating to Israel, but now even this is not necessary. An amendment to the Israeli citizenship law, passed in May 1971, permits any Jew who "expresses a desire to settle in Israel" to become a citizen without budging one inch. *

On the other hand, Arabs whose ancestors have lived there for countless generations are merely tolerated as aliens, reduced to second-class citizenship and treated as a "fifth column" whose sympathies lie with Israel's enemies.

From the beginning, Israeli Arabs have been subjected to the emergency military regulations imposed by the British in 1945 on both Jews and Arabs in Palestine. With the founding of the State of Israel these regulations ceased to be applied to Jews but continued to be imposed on Arabs. Until very recently, Arabs were required to obtain military passes to travel from one part of the country to another. And under these regulations areas of land were closed off for "security" reasons and their inhabitants were forbidden to enter them. Through this device nearly half the land belonging to Israeli Arabs has been taken from them and turned over to kibbutzim. Many have been converted into "internal refugees," living in shacks in nearby villages and seeking work as agricultural laborers. Others have found their way into the cities and into already overcrowded slum ghettos, where they are often forced to live in condemned houses which have more than once collapsed, killing or seriously injuring their inhabitants.

According to official statistics, annual earnings of non-Jewish families in 1967 were less than 64 per cent of those of Jewish families, and this with 1.6 earners per family compared to 1.3 in Jewish families. (One looks in vain in the official statistics for data on Israeli Arabs as such.)

Only half of the Arab workers are members of Histradrut (the trade union organization) as against three-fourths of the Jewish workers. Only one-third are members of the Health Insurance Fund (Kupat Cholim) as against 72 per cent of Jewish workers. Moreover, the Fund has few clinics in Arab villages, so that the Arab members receive much poorer service than the Jewish.

In institutions of higher learning Arabs are only 1.5 per cent of the

---

*The chief motivation behind the amendment is the current drive to bring Soviet Jews to Israel, of which we shall have more to say later. By permitting Jews living in the Soviet Union to be granted Israeli citizenship, it becomes possible, at least for propaganda purposes, to charge that "Israeli citizens" are being prohibited by the Soviet government from going to their homeland.

student body, though they are 12 per cent of the population. And from certain fields of study they are excluded altogether as "security risks."

Arab farmers are discriminated against with regard to credits, irrigation, mechanization and other forms of government assistance. Most Arab villages lack labor councils or labor exchanges through which unemployed workers can seek work under union conditions, while these Histradrut institutions are the rule in Jewish communities.

No Arabs have occupied top level positions in government and the number in middle ranks has been insignificant. Only in 1971 was an Arab appointed, for the first time, to a minor cabinet post.

Illustrative of the whole pattern of discrimination is the city of Nazareth. Lower Nazareth, the old city dating back to Biblical times, has a population of some 30,000, all Arab. Upper Nazareth, located on the surrounding hills, with 22,000 residents, consists mostly of Jewish settlers. Lower Nazareth has almost no industry and many of its workers are forced to seek employment in other cities. On the other hand, Upper Nazareth boasts a Dodge assembly plant, a large textile mill and a number of other modern factories. In these factories few Arabs are employed, and these largely as janitors. Upper Nazareth also boasts a beautiful Histadrut vacation resort—for Jews only. The only Arabs there at the time I visited it in 1970 were two who were employed in the kitchen. Nor are Arabs able to rent apartments in the new apartment houses of Upper Nazareth.

I also encountered the "internal refugees" in Nazareth. On the outskirts of the city I came across a collection of galvanized iron shacks. These, I learned, were inhabited by the former population of the nearby village of Ma'lul, from which they had been expelled by the Israeli authorities not long after the 1948 war. I learned also that nearly one-third of the Arab residents of Nazareth are refugees from nearby villages. And these in turn are only part of a much larger body of such "internal refugees"—Arabs deprived of their homes and lands because they may have been temporarily absent from them during or immediately after the war, or for reasons of "security."

This situation was recently brought dramatically to a head by the former Arab residents of the towns of Biram and Iqrit, from which they had been expelled in 1948 on "security" grounds. At the time, they were told they would be permitted to return after a few weeks, but the promise was never honored and most of the property was turned over to Jewish settlements and kibbutzim—as *abandoned property!*

When, in early 1972, the military bars were lifted in the area, these expelled villagers, who had been living as refugees within Israel all these years, sought to return to what remained of their lands. They were refused and were beaten up by border guard policemen when they tried to enter them. The affair stirred up intense public feeling and led to unprecedented mass demonstrations in support of the villagers. But the Meir government was adamant. "Security" came first, the rights of Israeli Arabs second.

In all aspects of life, Israeli Arabs suffer severe discrimination and are treated like outsiders in their own country. And those who have been made refugees are not permitted to return to their homeland.

During the 1948 war some 750,000 Arabs either fled in panic or were driven from their homes, to become refugees living in wretched settlements of tents and shacks in the surrounding Arab countries, mainly in Jordan. As a result, cities and towns once wholly populated by Arabs are now either entirely Jewish or have small Arab minorities. Thus the formerly all-Arab city of Jaffa now has only 6,000 Arabs and formerly all-Arab towns like Beersheba and Ashkelon have none. The Israeli rulers seized more than half the territory allotted to the Palestinian Arab state in the UN partition resolution of 1947, and they proceeded to take over the property abandoned by the Arabs who had fled. Don Peretz writes in his book *Israel and the Palestine Arabs:*

> Abandoned property was one of the greatest contributions toward making Israel a viable state. . . . Of the 370 Jewish settlements established between 1948 and the beginning of 1953, 350 were on absentee property. . . . In 1954 more than one-third of Israel's Jewish population lived on absentee property and nearly a third of the new immigrants (250,000 people) settled in urban areas abandoned by Arabs. . . . Ten thousand shops, businesses and stores were left in Jewish hands. At the end of the Mandate, citrus holdings in the area of Israel totalled about 240,000 dunams, of which half were Arab-owned. Most of the Arab groves were taken over by the Israeli Custodian of Absentee Property (pp. 143, 165).

And despite a repeatedly reaffirmed UN resolution calling for either repatriation or compensation of the refugees, the Israeli authorities have rejected all responsibility for the refugees. Behind this policy lies the idea that the fewer Arabs remaining in Israel the better. *

---

*The only group in Israel which has waged a consistent, uncompromising struggle against anti-Arab oppression and for Jewish-Arab unity has been the Communist

Oriental Jews: An Oppressed Majority

Discrimination in Israel is not confined to Arabs. It is visited also on the darker-skinned Sephardic or Oriental Jews, coming mainly from Arab countries such as Yemen, Iraq and the North African states, and now comprising about 60 per cent of Israel's population. Much poorer and less educated than Jews of Western origin, these have been thrust down to the lowest rungs of the economic and social ladders. The recent demonstrations of the Israeli group calling itself the Black Panthers have forcefully brought their plight to public attention.

They are crowded into the most unskilled, lowest-paying jobs. According to a 1969 survey by Israel's Central Bureau of Statistics, in 1967 their average per capita yearly income was only 38.5 per cent of that of Western Jews and 42.6 per cent of that of Israeli-born Jews. In addition, they are packed into "old city" slum ghettos, with a housing density three to five times that of other groups.

They lag far behind in education. Whereas about 60 per cent of all children entering primary school are Sephardic, at the secondary school level the proportion falls to 25 per cent and at the university level to 10 per cent.

They are victims of discrimination and prejudice and are subjected to all sorts of insults and indignities. Robert Silverberg writes:

> . . . The Orientals are generally swarthy or dark-skinned. To a European Jew they look very much like Arabs, and the treatment accorded them is

---

Party of Israel, headed by Meir Vilner and Tawfiq Toubi. There have been, it is true, others who opposed the prevailing Zionist approach to the Arabs and who called for Jewish-Arab unity. The Ihud (Union) Movement for Jewish-Arab Rapprochement, headed by Dr. Judah L. Magnes and including among its leading figures the noted philosopher Martin Buber, called during the thirties and forties for bringing Jews and Arabs together and for a binational state in Palestine. But its approach, based on idealistic appeals to both sides and not on opposition to the chauvinistic Zionist doctrines, attracted few followers. At the time of Dr. Magnes' death in 1948 it was still a tiny minority and after that it folded up altogether. The Hashomer Hatzair Workers' Party, predecessor of the present Mapam, also called for a binational state. But this, too, represented only a small minority. Moreover, Mapam, like the other Zionist parties, opposed the ending of the British mandate and the establishment of an independent state until the Jews should become a majority of the population. Today there are groupings which purport to seek Jewish-Arab unity, but these, too, operate fully within the Zionist orbit and are, to say the least, ineffectual. The support of Israeli Arabs goes largely to the Communist Party, which in recent elections has received between 30 and 40 percent of the Arab vote.

not very sympathetic. As the American anthropologist Raphael Patai
. . . expressed it in his book *Israel Between East and West*, "In addition to
instability, emotionalism, impulsiveness, unreliability, and incompe-
tence, the Oriental Jew is accused [by European-born Israelis] of habitual
lying and cheating, laziness, uncontrolled temper, superstitiousness,
childishness, lack of cleanliness and in general, 'primitivity' and 'lack of
culture.';" (*If I Forget Thee O Jerusalem*, p. 480)

"'Cushi,' the Biblical term for Negro," according to *The New York
Times* (January 29, 1965), "has taken on the same pejorative meaning
in Israel as 'nigger' in the United States."

Illustrative of the attitude toward "Orientals" is an article by Yael
Dayan, daughter of Moshe Dayan and a well-known novelist, in the
Israeli newspaper *Yediot Aharonot* (March 22, 1968). She writes about
her difficulties in selling a house. "It's the neighborhood," the real
estate agent tells her. She explains:

> The house's only neighbors are "Orientals." It borders on a Yemenite
> quarter called Morashah, and actually forms the borderline between the
> respectable neighborhood of Naveh Magen, which boasts of Israeli army
> commanders, and the Yemenite quarter, with one-story houses and nice
> gardens whose sons serve in the army. . . . It was thus that ghettos were
> formed. Thus grew the Negro, the Puerto Rican and the Jewish slums.
> Would you want your daughter to marry a Negro? Would you want to
> have a Jew as your neighbor? . . .
> I don't know which is more insulting—the fact that the whole phe-
> nomenon exists, or the total lack of shame implicit in openly admitting
> it. "I would have paid 5,000 more for the house had it been in another
> neighborhood," a respectable lady told me. Five thousand Israeli pounds
> more so that Rabinovitz's children won't play with the children of this
> quarter. Five thousand pounds more so that they won't mix, God forbid,
> with those who have dark eyes and black hair.

Oriental Jews are grossly under-represented in the Israeli government. Of 120 seats in the Knesset, they occupy only some 20-odd. In
the Israeli Cabinet they hold only the Ministry of Posts and the
Ministry of Police. And even this minimal representation is mean-
ingless, since these officials were designated by the dominant Labor
Party and other parties completely controlled by Western Jews, primarily to provide a fig leaf for their policy of discrimination.

The fact is that Israel has been ruled since its birth by a group of
Zionists mainly of Eastern European origin, to whom a "Jewish state"

and "Jewishness" mean a state based on the culture of Eastern European Jewry. Nissim Rejwan, a prominent Oriental Jewish writer, says:

> When Israel's present East European Zionist Establishment and its spokesmen talk of the absolute necessity of preserving the country's Jewishness what they in fact then have in mind is little more than *their own brand* or Jewish culture. For them, this now thoroughly secularized culture of the Jews of the Pale of Settlement represents "Jewishness" pure and simple. ("Israel as an Open Society," *The Jewish Spectator,* December 1967.)

Correspondingly, the culture of the Middle Eastern Jews is rejected as not being "Jewish," and the dominant group of Western origin, though now decidedly in the minority, nevertheless seeks to impose its culture on a majority whose cultural traditions are quite different.

Underlying this is the Zionist conception of Israel as a "Western" society which is Middle Eastern only geographically. The Zionists' greatest fear is that Israel will become "Levantinized." And what greater source of such a danger is there than the already "Levantinized" Oriental Jews who are a majority of the population, not to speak of the added 12 per cent of the population which is Arab? Accordingly, every effort is made to downgrade and smother their culture—to "Westernize" them, to teach their children "Western" ways in the schools and to relegate them to a subordinate place in Israeli society. And every effort is made to promote immigration of Western Jews in order to offset the majority status of the Oriental Jews.

A Theocratic State

Finally, the Jewish state of the Zionists is a theocratic state in which Orthodox Judaism occupies a privileged position. Not even Conversative or Reform Judaism has any recognized standing. This is a natural outgrowth of Zionist ideology, which regards Judaism as central among the distinguishing features of the Jewish people, as that feature which confers upon them the special status of a "chosen people." And this means *Orthodox* Judaism, whose doctrines and practices have been built into the life the country.

A Jew is defined according to the Halakic code of Orthodox Judaism as one who is born of a Jewish mother or is converted to Judaism in accordance with the rigorous Orthodox procedures. And only recently this definition was reaffirmed by the Knesset, which overruled a decision of the Israeli Supreme Court abolishing it and defining a Jew as anyone who declared oneself as such.

A separate group of religious schools is maintained at government expense within the framework of the public school system, for the benefit of the religious parties. These parties, though commanding no more than 15 per cent of the vote, are able to exercise a power far beyond their numbers, since the dominant Labor Party and its predecessor, Mapai, have counted on coalition with them to provide a majority in the Knesset and have in turn acquiesced to their policies for this reason as well as on ideological grounds.

Consequently, there is to this day no such thing as civil marriage or divorce in Israel. A Jew can marry a non-Jew only by going out of the country to do so. And there are numerous other such religious restrictions to which all Israeli citizens are subjected.

I. F. Stone writes: "'It's Hard to be a Jew' was the title of Sholem Aleichem's most famous story." But in Israel, he notes, it's hard to be a non-Jew, and especially an Arab non-Jew. ("Holy War," *The New York Review of Books*, August 3, 1967.)

Such is the Zionist conception of a Jewish state. It is a racist conception, based on the fallacy that freedom from one's own oppression can be attained by oppressing others. And it has made of Israel a country permeated by narrow Jewish nationalism and chauvinism. Small wonder that it arouses such intense hostility among Arabs.

3. "Socialist" Zionism

"Socialist" Trends: Anti-Marxist and "Marxist"

Almost from the very inception of the Zionist movement there emerged within it trends seeking to unite the idea of Zionism with that of socialism. As early as 1900 one such trend began to take organized form as the Poale Zion (Workers of Zion), whose first groups appeared in tsarist Russia. These varied greatly in their ideological positions, but there soon crystallized a movement based on the concept of a socialist Jewish state in Palestine. In 1905 a Poale Zion Party was formed in the United States, in the city of Baltimore, which stated in its declaration of principles:

> Since the development of mankind expresses itself through the develop-ment of individual nations, since the normal socio-economic, political and cultural development of every people requires a majority status in some land, and since such a development can only be realized in the historical homeland of a given people, we attest our belief in Zionism which strives for an openly secured homeland for the Jewish people in Palestine.
>
> Since we consider a society based on private ownership as a society in which a minority owns the means of production and lives on the labor of the majority, we will strive to alter unjust forms and to introduce a socialist society. . . .
>
> We want the future Jewish state to be established insofar as possible on socialist principles. . . . (*Yiddisher Kemfer* 1906. Quoted by Nachman Syrkin, "Beginnings of Socialist Zionism," in Gendzier, A *Middle East Reader*, p. 112.)

The leading ideologist of this trend, which took an openly anti-Marxist direction, was Nachman Syrkin (1868–1924). On the other hand there arose a trend, led by Ber Borochov (1881–1917), which sought to merge Zionism with Marxism. Borochov wrote:

> . . . the class struggle can take place only where the worker toils, i.e., where he has already occupied a certain workplace. The weaker his status at this position, the less ground he has for a systematic struggle. As long as the worker does not occupy a definite position, he can wage no struggle. It is therefore in his own interests to protect his position.
>
> From whatever angle we may approach the national question to determine the scope of its existence for the proletariat . . . we must always arrive finally at its material basis, i.e., at the question of the place of employment and the strategic base of struggle which the territory represents for the proletariat. ("The National Question and the Class Struggle," in Hertzberg, *The Zionist Idea*, p. 368.)

Jewish workers, said Borochov, are removed from the basic branches of industry; they are at the periphery of production. This renders their economic life stagnant, their culture at a low ebb and their political life insecure. (*Selected Essays in Socialist-Zionism*.) Hence, lacking its own territorial base the Jewish working class cannot carry on the class struggle under normal conditions. Only within the framework of a

Jewish state can it normalize the conditions of struggle and successfully pursue the fight for socialism. Moreover, as an oppressed group, Jewish workers can achieve their liberation only through their own activity. They cannot rely, writes Daniel Ben Nachum, "on external forces: on general revolutionary changes that would bring salvation to them, too, although of necessity their part in these changes would be only limited and marginal." ("The Abiding and Transitory Elements in Borochovism," *Israel Horizons*, March 1971.) And this, again, means that they must have their own territorial base.

Both varieties of "socialist" Zionism—the anti-Marxist and the pseudo-Marxist—find expression today, in this country as well as in Israel. Among the Zionist organizations in the United States is Poale Zion—United Labor Zionist Organization of America—whose statement of purposes includes the building of Israel as a "cooperative commonwealth." In Israel the dominant Labor Party professes to be socialist and is affiliated with the Socialist International. The United Workers Party (Mapam) has since 1948 had among its purposes "the creation of a classless society" and has professed an adherence to Marxism. Its affiliate in this country, Americans for Progressive Israel-Hashomer Hatzair, describes its program as "Socialist-Zionist."

But all these organizations and parties are firmly wedded to Zionist separatism—to a nationalism which is totally incompatible with the proletarian internationalism that forms the cornerstone of genuine Marxism. Despite its claims to be Marxist, Borochovism tends, no less than any other variant of Zionism, to isolate the Jewish workers from the rest of the working class in their own countries instead of uniting them against their common exploiters.

Illustrative of this approach is a declaration issued by the Russian Poale Zion in the midst of the revolutionary upheaval in 1905. It states:

> Since we do not expect from the revolution any radical solution of the Jewish question and since we have a separate historic mission, we cannot occupy ourselves with the preparatory work for the revolution. . . . We Jews come forward as an independent social group only where it is a question of defending specific Jewish interests. (*The Jewish Worker*, Moscow, 1925, Vol. II, p. 401; quoted in Magil, *Israel in Crisis*, p. 124.)

Thus did these "socialists" preach abandonment of the struggle, in the face of the fact that the future of the Russian Jewish workers clearly lay in uniting with the workers of all other nationalities for the overthrow of the brutally oppressive, pogromist tsarist regime. Today, too, their successors manifest a concern about socialism not in their own countries, but only in Israel.

The claim of these elements to speak as Marxists is patently fraudulent. Hence it is not surprising that they have been repudiated by the world socialist movement, from the early days of Zionism up to the present. The noted British Marxist R. Palme Dutt has written:

> When the Zionist movement, alongside its close ties with the moneybags, sought also to develop sections which called themselves "socialist" and applied on this basis to the old Socialist International, the International Socialist Bureau, representing at that time all sections of the socialist movement from the Fabians to the Bolsheviks, turned them down. ("The Middle East—Explosion or Solution?," *Labour Monthly*, February 1970.)

And in 1920, when a majority at the Fifth World Congress of Poale Zion voted to join the Communist International, its application was flatly rejected. Today the Israeli Labor Party is affiliated with the so-called Socialist International and participates actively in its congresses, but this body is no more "socialist" than is the Israeli Labor Party.

"Socialism" in Israel

The "socialist" Zionists maintain that Israel, in keeping with their ideas, has developed as a socialist country. Shlomo Avneri, Chairman of the Department of Political Science at Hebrew University in Jerusalem, contends that Zionist policy "resulted in a *conscious* creation of a Jewish peasantry and a Jewish working class. . . ." He adds:

> It was the same conceptual framework which placed the kibbutzim and moshavim in such socially strategic positions in Israel society, created the Histadrut not as a mere trade union organization but as a Society of Laborers (Hevrat Ovdim), owning industries, banks and cooperatives and trying to coordinate a vision of social reconstruction with political aims and manipulation.
>
> In other words, Socialism and Zionism became inseparable. The socialistically-oriented structure became pivotal to the establishment of

a Jewish society. ("The Sources of Israeli Socialism," *Israel Horizons*, March 1971.)

He concludes that "the commanding heights of the Israeli economy are very much under public control." Others, on the grounds that a major share of Israeli enterprises—agricultural, industrial, financial and commercial—are cooperatively or publicly owned, assert that Israel is essentially socialist or is definitely moving toward socialism.

But this is confusing form with substance. The existence of public and cooperative sectors of the economy, however extensive, does not in itself mean the existence of socialism. A socialist society is one in which political power is in the hands of the working class and its allies, in which the exploitation of wage labor for private profit has been effectively abolished, and in which production is planned and is designed to serve the needs of the people. In Israel none of these features is present, as even a limited examination will show.

Let us look at the public sector. As of 1960, according to a study by Chaim Barkai, it accounted for 21.1 per cent of the net domestic product.* This includes enterprises owned by the central government, local governments and Zionist institutions, chiefly the Jewish Agency, which is involved in virtually every branch of the economy. What is the nature of the government investment? Chaim Bermont described it as follows:

> The government itself is a heavy investor, not for doctrinal reasons, but because of the paucity of private capital and the non-commercial nature of many of the projects which the government is anxious to promote. In general, public money goes where private enterprise and the Histadrut fear to tread, like the Timna Copper Mines. Where the government can find a private buyer for its holdings, it will dispose of them. Thus Israel has in recent years witnessed a process of denationalization, and the Haifa oil refineries, 65 per cent of the stock of Palestine Potash (which owns the Dead Sea works) and numerous public assets, have been sold to private buyers. (*Israel*, p. 166.)

Thus, government investment is limited to operations of a state capitalist character and is no more "socialist" than, say, government ownership of oil- and steel-producing facilities in Brazil. Moreover, the

*Chaim Barkai, "The Public, Histadrut, and Private Sectors in the Israeli Economy," *Sixth Report 1961–1963* (Jerusalem: Falk Project, 1964), p. 26. Cited by Halevi and Klinov-Malul, *The Economic Development of Israel*, p. 113.

trend is clearly toward reducing government holdings, not expanding them. Since 1967 this process has accelerated, and to Bermont's list may be added such enterprises as the ZIM steamship line and the Timna Copper Mines. And the lion's share of these assets has been sold to *foreign* capital—an aspect which will be dealt with below.

Then there is the Histradut sector of the economy which, according to Barkai, accounted for 20.4 per cent of the net domestic product in 1960.

In the field of agriculture this includes first of all the kibbutzim, communal enterprises whose members, in return for their labor, are provided with the necessities of life and receive little or no monetary remuneration. The kibbutzim have been held forth as Israel's most shining example of socialist development. But their membership embraces less than five per cent of Israel's population. Moreover, operating as they do within the larger framework of capitalist production, they are not immune from the economic afflictions characteristic of agriculture under capitalism. Their agricultural earnings are in the main not sufficient to sustain them and they are in part dependent on regular subsidies from the Jewish Agency.

In addition, to augment the income from agriculture, the kibbutzim have turned increasingly to the establishment of factories operated mainly with wage labor brought in from outside. The income from manufacturing is today at least equal to that from agriculture. Thus, more and more the kibbutzim are themselves becoming exploiters of wage labor. According to Ya'acov Goldschmidt, director of an inter-kibbutz advisory unit in Tel Aviv, "The kibbutz is a capitalist enterprise. Each enterprise must be large-scale. We have to get the most per unit of labor. We have to get the most for the capital invested." (*The New York Times*, November 21, 1971.)

The Histadrut sector also includes the moshavim, agricultural settlements in which each family farms its own plot of land, with cooperative marketing and purchasing. These are of relatively little significance as an economic factor. Their only claim to being "socialist" is that they do not employ wage labor.

A much more important part of the Histadrut sector is the complex of industrial, commercial and financial enterprises owned by the Hevrat Ovdim. The executive body of Histadrut is also the governing body of Hevrat Ovdim, and each member of the former is nominally the owner of a "share" in the latter, though he receives directly no share in its income. The Histadrut is presently the largest single employer in Israel, at the same time that it purports to represent the interests of the workers in its employ. Furthermore, a large and growing share of the stock in the Hevrat Ovdim enterprises is now privately owned, a significant part of it by foreign capital.

Finally, the Histadrut sector also includes a number of producer cooperatives. In the sector as a whole the boundaries between cooperative and private ownership and control are, to put it charitably, at best fuzzy. On this point Halevi and Klinov-Malul state:

> The four parts of the sector are not equally subject to central Histadrut control, and there is a wide range of motives among the various enterprises. Nevertheless there are grounds for separating the Histadrut from the private sector: in undertaking an activity, Histadrut enterprises retain the idea that they are supposed to serve a national or class interest. The Histadrut sector therefore holds a position somewhere between the public and private sectors (p. 46).

But even if we grant the validity of this conclusion, the fact remains that the *major* share of the net domestic product is accounted for by the private sector—according to Barkai's figures 58.5 per cent. And undoubtedly the proportion is substantially higher today than it was in 1960, thanks to the growing inroads of private capital into the other sectors. In addition, the private holdings are increasingly in the hands of foreign monopoly capital, as will be shown in a later chapter.

The simple fact is that Israel is a *capitalist* country, whose economy is predominantly in the hands of a capitalist class and whose government actively and energetically courts growing investment by foreign capital. It is marked by a sharp class struggle, with the workers engaging in frequent and at times bitter strikes—ironically, most often against the Histadrut itself. It is marked by oppression and super-exploitation of Israeli Arabs and Oriental Jews. And it is marked by the maintenance of ties not with the socialist world but with the imperialist powers—with the chief enemies of socialism.

If socialism is truly to be established in Israel, this will come about only through the struggles of a united Israeli working class—Jew and Arab—against both the Israeli capitalist class and the foreign monopolies which dominate the economy. To be successful, these struggles will require unity with the workers and peasants of the Arab countries and with the world working-class movement, particularly with the socialist countries.

To all this a prime obstacle is the influence of Zionist ideology among Israeli workers. Hence to fight for socialism is to fight against Zionism.

II. IN THE SERVICE OF IMPERIALISM

1. ZIONISM'S QUEST FOR IMPERIALIST SUPPORT

The Roles of Herzl and Weizmann

Clearly, the establishment of an exclusively Jewish state, in the heart of a territory already populated by Arabs, could be pursued only at the expense of and in opposition to the Arab people, and only in league with their oppressors. Indeed, from the very outset the Zionists based their hopes of success on the support of one or another imperialist power, offering in return a Jewish state which would serve imperialist interests in the Middle East.

It is well known that Herzl sought the backing of the rulers of tsarist Russia, France, Germany and Turkey. He even tried to sell his idea to the pogromist Russian Minister of the Interior von Plehve, whose hands still dripped with blood from the slaughter of Jews in Kishinev, as an antidote to the mounting revolutionary movement in Russia.

In *The Jewish State* he wrote: "Supposing His Majesty the Sultan were to give us Palestine, we could in return undertake to regulate the whole finances of Turkey. We should there form an outpost of civilization as opposed to barbarism" (p. 30). The barbarism he referred to was the rising tide of Arab revolt against the brutal Turkish role. Max Nordau, one of the top Zionist leaders, spelled this out in his speech at the 7th World Zionist Congress in 1905. He said:

The movement which has taken hold of a great part of the Arab people may easily take a direction which may cause harm in Palestine. . . . The Turkish government may feel itself compelled to defend its reign in Palestine, in Syria, against its subjects by armed power. . . . In such a position, Turkey might become convinced that it may be important for her to have, in Palestine and Syria, a strong and well organized people which, with all respect to the rights of the people living there, will resist any attack on the authority of the Sultan and defend this authority with all its might.

Later, during World War I, Weizmann similarly made overtures to British imperialism. In a letter to C. P. Scott, editor of the *Manchester Guardian*, written in November 1914, he stated:

> we can reasonably say that should Palestine fall within the British sphere of influence, and should Britain encourage a Jewish settlement there, as a British dependency, we could have in twenty to thirty years a million Jews out there, perhaps more; they would develop the country, bring back civilization to it and form a very effective guard for the Suez Canal. (*Trial and Error*, p. 149.)

This idea was repeatedly stressed during Weizmann's efforts, which culminated in the Balfour Declaration in 1917.

It is important to note that Weizmann conceived of the Jewish settlement not as an independent state but as a dependency of Britain—of a "benevolent imperialism." He wrote:

> What we wanted was . . . a British Protectorate. Jews all over the world trusted England. They knew that law and order would be established by British rule, and that under it Jewish colonizing activities and cultural development would not be interfered with. We could therefore look forward to a time when we would be strong enough to claim a measure of self-government (*ibid.*, p. 191).

Herzl had similarly conceived of the Jewish state in Palestine as a subject state under Turkish rule. The reason for this is obvious: the Jews would continue for a considerable length of time to be a minority in Palestine, hence the protection of a ruling power was needed for the establishment of a steadily growing Jewish settlement in the face of the opposition of the Arab majority.

The Goal: All of Palestine

Moreover, the Jewish state which Zionism envisioned as coming ultimately into being with the aid of British imperialism was to embrace *all* of Palestine—more, all of the Biblical Land of Israel.*
This idea was implicit in the Balfour Declaration, issued on November 2, 1917, which states:

*The territory included in "Eretz Yisrael"—the Biblical Land of Israel—is variously defined. In the account of God's Covenant with Abraham (Genesis, Chapters 15–17) God says: "Unto thy seed I have given this land, from the river of Egypt unto the great

His Majesty's Government view with favor the establishment in Palestine of a National Home for the Jewish People, and will use their best endeavors to facilitate the achievement of this object, it being clearly understood that nothing shall be done which may prejudice the civil and religious rights of the non-Jewish communities in Palestine or the rights and political status enjoyed by Jews in any other country.

Note that the Declaration speaks of "civil and religious rights" of the non-Jewish communities but says nothing of *national* rights. That is, these are treated as communities *within* a Jewish National Home.

That this is how it was understood at the time was made clear by David Lloyd George in his memoirs, in which he writes that "it was contemplated that when the time arrived for according representative institutions to Palestine, if the Jews had responded to the opportunity afforded them and had become a definite majority of the inhabitants, then Palestine would become a Jewish Commonwealth." (Cited in *Trial and Error*, p. 212.) Later, when Transjordan was cut off from Palestine by the British and set up as a separate state, Weizmann and other Zionist leaders were greatly disturbed at the removal of this area from the orbit of Jewish settlement.

Within the Zionist movement, as time went on, the idea of a Jewish state embracing all of Palestine was pressed with increasing insistence. In the United States, in May 1942, a conference called by the American Emergency Committee for Zionist Affairs adopted what came to be known as the Biltmore Program, which demanded "that Palestine be established as a Jewish Commonwealth." The 1944 convention of the Zionist Organization of America also adopted a resolution calling for a Jewish Commonwealth which "shall embrace the whole of Palestine, undivided and undiminished." The same stand was adopted by the World Zionist Conference held in London in 1945. If subsequently the Zionists agreed to partition of Palestine as called for by the 1947 UN resolution, this was motivated purely by expediency, with the anticipation that eventually the Jewish state *would* embrace all of Palestine.

That this is in fact the Zionist outlook has been repeatedly indicated. Thus, in the words of Yigal Allon, currently Deputy Prime Minister of Israel: "Our duty to populate 'Greater Israel' is no less

---

river, the river Euphrates. . . ." This claim the ancient Hebrews never made good. What is today referred to is rather the territory of Palestine as initially defined in the British Mandate, including Transjordan. Currently, the reference is primarily to the occupied territories, whose retention the Israeli ruling class seeks to justify.

important than in the past, when it was a mandate to populate the valley of the Jordan and the valley of Beisan; he who doubts this truth doubts the entire Zionist conception." (*Jerusalem Post*, April 18, 1968.)

More recently, the 28th World Zionist Congress, in January 1972, adopted a resolution stating: "Congress declares that the right of the Jewish people to Eretz Yisrael is inalienable." And the Israeli Knesset itself has endorsed this position. A resolution adopted on March 16, 1972 asserts: "The Knesset states that the historical right of the Jewish people to Eretz Yisrael is indisputable." These claims to all of Palestine (and more) violate the national rights of the Palestinian Arab people. They fly in the face of the UN Charter and the basis on which the State of Israel was established by the UN.

Small wonder that the Arabs met the Balfour Declaration with extreme hostility and that they viewed it as creating a bastion of imperialism in their midst. Nor did the Zionists do anything to dispel this hostility. During the period of the Mandate (1922–1948), when confronted with the duplicity of the British imperialists and their efforts to pit Jews and Arabs against one another, they rejected any idea of allying the Jewish settlers with the Arab peasants and workers in common struggle against British oppression—an alliance which might have led to the eventual emergence of a binational state. Instead, they pursued a policy of antagonism toward the Arabs and persisted to the end in their efforts to make Palestine a Jewish state with the aid of British imperialism. Thereby they drove the Arab peasantry into the arms of the reactionary Arab ruling class, the landowning effendis, who were for their own reasons opposed to British rule. Throughout the Mandate, Zionism served as a buffer between British imperialism and the striving of the Palestinian Arabs for their freedom from imperialist domination.

2. AN EXPANSIONIST POLICY

The Road to War: 1956 and 1967

Virtually from the very birth of the State of Israel its rulers have undeviatingly pursued a policy of aggressive expansionism in relation to the Arab states. And toward this end they have consistently based themselves on seeking the support of the imperialist powers, in return giving support to imperialist policies in the Middle East. In the relentless struggle between the oil-hungry forces of imperialism and the Arab forces of national liberation, the Israeli ruling circles have without exception placed themselves on the side of the former.

In its early years, in return for the supply of armaments by France, Israel supported French imperialism against the struggle of the Algerian people for independence, voting consistently on the side of the imperialist forces in the United Nations.

In 1956 Israel joined with Britain and France in the invasion of Egypt. To the Israeli people the Sinai invasion was presented as an act of self-defense, necessitated because (a) the border raids on Israel by the terrorist fedayeen had become intolerable and had to be stopped, and (b) Egypt, having received substantial supplies of arms from Czechoslovakia, was preparing to attack Israel. If there were simultaneous attacks by British and French forces, this was simply a happy coincidence of which Israel could take advantage.

But the facts were quite otherwise. Though they were completely concealed at the time, they have since come fully to light, particularly with the publication in 1967 of Anthony Nutting's book *No End of a Lesson*. Nutting, then Minister of State for Foreign Affairs under Anthony Eden, was privy to the whole unsavory business and resigned from his post because of his revulsion against it. In his book he exposes the intimate details of the plot, one of the most callous in the whole sordid history of imperialism, to overthrow Nasser, who had committed the unforgivable crime of supporting the National Liberation Front in Algeria and had capped this with the even more unforgivable crime of nationalizing the Suez Canal. Nutting describes the final unfolding of the conspiracy in the following passage:

> That day the Cabinet met in full to take the fateful decision. It proved impossible to get a final conclusion at one session, and the matter was held over until the following day. But this did not prevent the dispatch to Paris of a senior Foreign Office official with further assurances to pass on to the Israelis that we were determined to see the French plan carried out and would do all that the Israelis required in the way of air strikes against Egyptian airfields to forestall the bombing of their cities.
>
> These assurances turned the scale, and on Thursday, October 25th, Eden learned that the Israelis had decided finally to play their part in the

Sinai campaign. That afternoon the Cabinet came to its final, and for some at least probably unpalatable, decision. When [Selwyn] Lloyd returned to the Foreign Office from No. 10, I did not have to ask how it had gone. It showed in his face and, though he made a brave attempt to be light-hearted, I had never seen him more grim-faced and tormented with doubts.

"When is it to happen?" I asked.

"October 29; next Monday," Lloyd answered. "Israel will attack through Sinai that evening and the following morning we and the French will issue our ultimatum to her and Egypt to clear the Canal Zone for us to move our troops in. Egypt will presumably, refuse, and directly she does so we shall start bombing Egyptian airfields" (pp. 104–05).

As we know, the plot failed, thanks to the opposition of U.S. imperialism for its own reasons and thanks even more to the threat of the Soviet Union to enter the conflict on Egypt's side. France and England were forced to withdraw, and Israel was eventually compelled to abandon its Sinai conquest.

But its leaders did not abandon their policy of collusion with imperialism against the Arab peoples. Now they proceeded to ally themselves with the machinations of U.S. imperialism for the over-throw of the anti-imperialist governments in both the UAR and Syria, and U.S. imperialism became the Israeli government's chief backer. This was developed as a deliberate policy by Ben-Gurion in 1957. Michael Bar-Zohar records:

. . . The experiences of the Sinai campaign had convinced him that without the support or at least the good wishes of the Americans he would not again be able to act boldly. Fortunately, there existed a means of drawing the United States closer to Israel—by playing on the Communist danger. So Ben-Gurion endeavored to become the Middle East champion of anti-Communism in the eyes of Washington. "I feel sure," Dulles wrote to Ben-Gurion in August 1957, "that you share our consternation over recent developments in Syria. We are studying the problem closely, and we should like to proceed to an exchange of views with your Government on this subject in the near future."

Ben-Gurion jumped at the opportunity. "The transforming of Syria into a base for international Communism is one of the most dangerous events that the free world has to face up to. . . . I should like to draw your attention to the disastrous consequences if international Communism should succeed in establishing itself in the heart of the Middle East. I believe the free world ought not to accept this situation. Everything depends on the firm and determined line taken by the United States as a leading Power in the free world. . . ." (*Ben-Gurion*, pp. 241–42.)

It could hardly be put more plainly. And the Ben-Gurion government proceeded at once in this direction. It greeted the Baghdad Pact and the Eisenhower Doctrine, twin instruments of U.S. imperialist domination. In 1958, when an anti-imperialist regime took power in Iraq, Israel supported the landing of U.S. and British troops in Lebanon and Jordan on the pretext that they had been asked for as protection against the threat of Iraqi attack. Here we have the beginnings of the collusion which culminated in the Israeli aggression in 1967, just as the previous collusion with British and French imperialism had led to the Sinai invasion in 1956.

This period was marked also by the establishment of close ties with the revanchist Bonn regime in West Germany. Starting with the absolution of Nazi crimes through the payment of reparations, these involved West German investments in Israel and secret arms deals between Ben-Gurion and Konrad Adenauer. These relations have in large measure been retained since then.

In 1966, following a victory of the progressive forces in Syria, the U.S.-hatched plot to overthrow the governments of the UAR and Syria was greatly stepped up. Jordanian troops were massed on the Syrian border and in September an abortive military coup took place, whose leaders fled to Jordan when it failed. And there appeared growing signs of Israel's involvement in these machinations.

In the spring of 1966 the United States sold Israel a number of Skyhawk attack bombers. This was the first time that such offensive weapons had been sold directly to Israel, and official Israeli circles rejoiced. But it became quickly evident that this was no act of magnanimity. *The New York Times* correspondent, James Feron, reported on June 11, 1966 on some conversations with Israeli officials. The following excerpt is highly instructive:

> This is the way a Foreign Office official put it: The United States has come to the conclusion that it can no longer respond to every incident around the world, that it must rely on a local power—the deterrent of a friendly power—as a first line to stave off America's direct involvement.
> In the Israeli view, Defense Secretary Robert S. McNamara outlined this approach last month just a few days before the Skyhawk deal was

announced. In a major address in Montreal, one that attracted considerable attention in high circles here, Mr. McNamara reviewed American
commitments around the world and said:

"It is the policy of the United States to encourage and achieve a more
effective partnership with those nations who can, and should, share
international peacekeeping responsibilities."

Israel feels that she fits this definition and the impression that has
been conveyed by some Government officials is that Foreign Minister
Abba Eban and Mr. McNamara conferred over Skyhawk details in the
context of this concept when the Israeli diplomat was in Washington last
February.

The *quid pro quo* was clear. And it became even clearer in the events
that followed. Border raids from Syria and Jordan were met with acts of
massive retaliation far out of proportion to these raids—acts which
were strongly condemned by the UN Security Council. Of one such
attack, on the village of Es Samu in Jordan, even U.S. Ambassador
Arthur J. Goldberg was impelled to state that "deplorable as these
preceding incidents were . . . this deliberate governmental decision
must be judged as the conscious act of responsible leaders of a member
state and therefore on an entirely different level from the earlier
incidents. . . ." (*The New York Times*, November 20, 1966.)

The raids were accompanied by mounting threats of military invasion of Syria. There was growing talk in official circles about the need
for a "new Sinai." In an Independence Day interview, the London
Jewish Chronicle of May 19, 1967 reports, Prime Minister Levi Eshkol
stated that the only deterrent available to Israel against Syria was a
powerful lightning military strike—powerful enough to produce a
change of heart or even a change of government in Damascus and swift
enough to prevent any other countries from rallying to Syria's support.
So vehement did these threats become that UN Secretary General U
Thant, in a report to the Security Council on May 19, 1967, was led
to state:

Intemperate and bellicose utterances . . . are unfortunately more or less
routine on both sides of the lines in the Near East. In recent weeks,
however, reports emanating from Israel have attributed to some high
officials in that state statements so threatening as to be particularly
inflammatory in the sense that they could only heighten emotions and
thereby increase tensions on the other side of the lines.

In short, a groundwork was being laid for aggressive action just as it had been in 1956.

This chain of events culminated in the actions taken by Nasser in May 1967—the removal of the UN Emergency Force troops from the Egyptian-Israeli border, the blockade of the Straits of Tiran and the mobilization of Egyptian military forces. The purpose of these actions, he declared, was to come to the aid of Syria in the event of Israeli attack. The response of the Israeli leaders was the invasion of Egypt, Jordan and Syria in the June "six-day war."

It is not possible here to present a detailed refutation of the false contention that this was a war of self-defense and not an act of deliberate aggression in pursuit of Israeli expansionism and U.S. imperialist aims. There is ample evidence that Egypt was not planning to invade Israel and that the Israeli ruling circles knew it. Some of it is summed up by Fred J. Khouri in his extensive study, *The Arab-Israeli Dilemma*, in these words:

> . . . The very competent and highly respected Israeli military intelligence was well aware that (1) Israel continued to hold a substantial military lead over the Arabs; (2) the Arab military forces were far from sufficiently trained and organized for successful offensive operations against her; and (3) in June the UAR was not seriously preparing or planning to invade Israel, a fact which Western correspondents in Cairo readily observed and reported to their newspapers. Not only had American, as well as Israeli, intelligence been predicting before June 5 that Israel could win a war against the Arabs without great difficulty, but both the American and French governments had assured Israel that they would come to her aid if it became absolutely necessary. . . .
>
> Furthermore, if the Israeli leaders had really believed that an invasion was imminent and Israel's survival was at stake, they could easily have precluded any Arab attack by accepting U Thant's suggestion that UNEF be allowed to take up positions in their territory. . . . By firmly and unhesitatingly rejecting U Thant's proposals, Israel indicated that she was less interested in thwarting an Egyptian attack than she was in making sure that a UN presence did not frustrate her own ability to strike at the UAR at the time of her own choosing (pp. 281–82).

More recently, Israeli spokesmen themselves have begun to admit that Israel stood in no danger of annihilation, and that the government and the military were fully aware of this. Colonel Matatyahu

Peled, who had been Quartermaster-General in the Israeli army in 1967, spells it out in these words:

> I am convinced that the government never heard from the General Staff that the Egyptian military threat was dangerous to Israel, or that it did not lie in the power of Israel to defeat the Egyptian army, which was exposing itself with astounding stupidity to the crushing blow of the Israeli army.* All this talk was made only a few months after the war; it had no part in the complex of considerations of those days—this talk about the horrible danger in which Israel found itself, because of its narrow frontiers. When the Israeli army mobilized its full power, which surpassed that of the Egyptians several times, there was no person possessing any sense who believed that all this force was necessary in order to "defend" ourselves from the Egyptian threat. This force was necessary for dealing the Egyptians a crushing defeat on the battlefield, and to their Russian patrons in the political field. The claim that the Egyptian force which was concentrated on our southern border was capable of threatening Israel's existence is not only an insult to the intelligence of anyone who is capable of evaluating such matters. It is first of all an insult to the Israeli army. (*Ha'aretz*, March 19, 1972.)

Evidence that the Israeli invasion was a deliberate act of aggression in collusion with U.S. imperialism for the purpose of overthrowing the Egyptian and Syrian governments as well as territorial conquest does not come so readily to hand. Conspiracies are, after all, not carried on in broad daylight, and many of the facts of this one have yet to be brought to light. But there are definite indications of it. For example, there is the history of Israeli foreign policy which we outlined above, going back to Ben-Gurion's overtures to Dulles. Further, the U.S. assurance of support to Israel clearly implies the existence of a *quid pro quo* understanding. Then there are such items as the fact that the United States and Britain, despite a U.S.-British-French agreement which obligated them to defend Egypt, not only did nothing to halt

*Peled is referring here to the following statement in the Israel cabinet's resolution of June 4, 1967: "After hearing a report on the military and political situation from the Prime Minister, the Foreign Minister, the Defense Minister, the Chief of Staff, and the head of military intelligence, the Government ascertained that the armies of Egypt, Syria and Jordan are deployed for immediate multi-front aggression, threatening the very existence of the State."

the aggression but sabotaged UN efforts to do so. In fact, they prevented a cease-fire until Israel had achieved her military objectives.

Little by little the remaining facts will come out, and we have no doubt that they will disclose a no less sordid deal than that of 1956. And they will show further that, as in 1956, a plot to overthrow anti-imperialist Arab governments has failed.

Expansionism Since 1967

The annexationist character of the war is further evidenced by Israeli policy since 1967. In brief outline, its main points are as follows:

1. The Israeli leaders have persistently blocked efforts to find a political resolution of the conflict. Specifically, though claiming to accept it, they have rejected UN Security Council Resolution 242 of November 22, 1967 as the basis for arriving at a settlement.* In particular, they have refused to commit themselves to withdraw from the occupied territories even in the face of the offer of a peace treaty by Egypt, though they had long declared that such a treaty was their foremost desire.

2. While the Israeli Government has taken no formal stand on withdrawal from the occupied territories other than to declare that it desires no annexations, Golda Meir and other leading government spokesmen have made it clear that extensive areas are to be retained in

---

*This resolution, after "emphasizing the inadmissability of the acquisition of territory by war and the need to work for a just and lasting peace in which every State in the area can live in security," calls for:

"a) Withdrawal of Israeli armed forces from territories occupied in the recent conflict;

"b) Termination of all claims or states of belligerency and respect for and acknowledgement of the sovereignty, territorial integrity and political independence of every State in the area and their right to live in peace within secure and recognized boundaries free from any acts of force."

On the basis of acceptance by both sides of both these principles, the resolution calls for settlement of all outstanding differences. A special UN representative is to be designated to work with both sides to implement its provisions. (Dr. Gunnar Jarring has functioned in that capacity.) The governments of Egypt, Jordan, Syria and Lebanon have stated their acceptance of the resolution *in toto*; the Israeli government has never done so.

the name of "secure and defensible" borders. East Jerusalem is "not negotiable." Also to be kept are the Golan Heights, the Gaza Strip and Sharm el-Sheikh with a connecting corridor. The Jordan River is to become a "security border," which means that even if the West Bank is returned to Jordan, Israeli troops are to be stationed along the river while Jordanian troops are to be forbidden access to the West Bank. In short, the Israeli rulers propose to keep possession of a large part of the occupied territory and to retain at least partial control over other areas.

3. While stalling off negotiations endlessly, the Israeli government is carrying out an undeclared policy of *de facto* annexation of the occupied territories through a succession of accomplished facts. East Jerusalem has been annexed outright and is being converted as rapidly as possible into a Jewish city. A string of Israeli settlements has been built along the Jordan River, and numerous others in the Golan Heights, on the northern shore of the Sinai Peninsula, at Sharm el-Sheikh, at Hebron and other localities in the West Bank. The number is steadily growing. In the Gaza Strip a brutal process of displacing the Arab population is under way, supposedly on "security" grounds, but actually with the thinly veiled intention of settling the vacated lands with Jews. The Sinai oil wells have been taken over and are supplying all of Israel's oil requirements. And the economy of the occupied areas is being integrated into that of Israel along semi-colonial lines, providing Israel with profitable markets and a source of cheap labor.

4. In violation of the Geneva Convention, the inhabitants of the occupied territories have been subjected to brutal and repressive treatment including administrative arrest, collective punishment in the form of blowing up of houses, interminable curfews, etc., forcible deportations and torture of prisoners. The UN General Assembly has on more than one occasion called for an end to such practices.

Clearly, the aim is to annex most or all of the conquered territories.

These policies have increasingly isolated Israel in the eyes of world opinion. They have made its future increasingly dependent on U.S. arms and backing, and in return have subordinated Israel in growing measure to the interests of U.S. imperialism. They have imposed huge arms budgets on Israel which are bankrupting the country financially. And they have led to growing Arab hostility and the ever-present danger of new outbreaks of war.

Such is the disastrous course on which the Zionist ruling circles have placed the Israeli people.

3. ISRAEL AND AFRICA

A Pro-Imperialist Policy

Israeli spokesmen have made much of Israel's role as a supposed benefactor of the developing countries. But the Israeli government's policy in relation to these countries is likewise designed to serve the interests of world imperialism. Their penetration by Israel began in earnest after the ill-fated Sinai campaign of 1956. It represented an attempt to break out of the isolation resulting from that debacle and to establish an international base in the regions beyond the immediately surrounding Arab countries.

These aims were viewed as tied directly to those of the imperialist powers and as dependent on their assistance. Harvard professor Nadav Safran writes: "If there is any 'realistic' motive in Israel's program of foreign aid, it is probably to be found in the hope that it will draw tangible rewards from the United States by serving . . . the same objects that that country seeks to promote through its aid program." (*The United States and Israel*, p. 267.)

According to Leopold Laufer (*Israel and the Developing Countries*, p. 18), between 1958 and 1966 ties were established with 38 countries in Africa, 23 in Latin America, 11 in Asia and eight in the Mediterranean area. These relations have included Israeli financial and military aid, loans, investments in joint enterprises and training of personnel. The main area of concentration has been Africa. The number of Israeli experts sent to African countries has grown from 25 in 1958 to 406 in 1966 and some 2,000 today. Of some 14,000 foreign students trained in Israel between 1958 and 1971, about half have been Africans.

In monetary terms Israeli aid to African countries is insignificant (less than half of one per cent of the total aid received). But its strategic impact has been far greater. This impact lies primarily in the ability of Israeli ruling circles to present Israel as a moderate, "third force" form of socialism compatible with "free world" interests, and as a small country which is not an imperialist power. And this has made it possible for the Israeli rulers to act as intermediaries for imperialism, a function which they have extensively performed.

This is evident, first of all, in the character of the countries singled out for attention. In the main, these are countries ruled by neocolonialist regimes which see in Israel a means of helping to perpetuate the dominance of leaders oriented toward one or another imperialist power. Moreover, they include the Portuguese colonies, Rhodesia, West Africa and—not least—South Africa, countries constituting the remaining base of colonial and racial oppression in Africa.

The aid which Israel gives to these countries is primarily military or paramilitary in character. The Israeli government has become highly proficient in training elite military forces along the patterns which prevail in Israel itself today. Even in the field of agriculture, much of the aid has been in the establishment of paramilitary youth organizations and settlements, patterned after the *gadna* and *nahal* forms in Israel. The former is a battalion of youth aged 14–18 which engages in sports, camping, hiking, crafts and cultural activities, together with physical labor and paramilitary training. The latter is an agricultural settlement of young men and women of military age, established in dangerous border areas and including military training. Between 1960 and 1966, formations of these types were set up in Cameroon, the Central African Republic, Chad, Dahomey, Ivory Coast, Malawi and Togo.

This is in addition to the direct training of military forces. In Chad, Israel has trained troops for action against the guerrilla forces of the National Liberation Front of Chad. In the case of the Congo (Kinshasa)—now called Zaire—Israel has trained paratroops, both within that country and in Israel. In 1963, 243 paratroops sent to Israel for training included General Joseph Mobutu, now President of Zaire. In Ethiopia, Israel has trained troops to fight the guerrillas on the Eritrean border and in return has been granted military bases on islands off the Eritrean coast.

In the Ivory Coast, in Kenya, in Sierra Leone, Israel has been involved in providing arms or military training. In Ghana the Israeli presence goes back to 1956 and has continued up to the present. Questions have been raised of its possible involvement in the counter-revolutionary overthrow of the Nkrumah government. Israel currently sells some $20 million worth of arms a year, most of it to African countries.*

In Uganda, where Israel assumed all military training in 1956 and in

*These data are taken mainly from Sanford Silverburg, *Israel Military and Paramilitary Assistance to Sub-Saharan Africa: A Harbinger for the Military in Developing States,* Master's Thesis, American University, 1968, as cited in: Africa Research Group, *David and Goliath Collaborate in Africa,* Cambridge, 1969.

addition supplied a number of planes, former President Milton Obote has charged Israel with complicity in the overthrow of his government by Major General Idi Amin. It was Amin, reports Winston Berry, editor of the weekly newsletter *United Nations Report*, who sought Israeli aid. Berry writes:

> While the Uganda Government in the United Nations and elsewhere followed the Organization of African Unity in its policies toward the Middle East conflict (policies calling for Israeli withdrawal from the occupied territories—H.L.), Amin insisted that his junior officers be trained in Israel. He insisted that the Israeli instructors and advisers be retained by the army and airforce. (*People's World*, February 13, 1971.)*

Israeli instructors and advisers have been involved in anti-guerrilla fighting in the Portuguese colony of Angola. Servicemen from Portugal and its colonies have gone to Israel for training. Israel has also supplied much of the arms used by the colonialist forces. Thus, a captured punitive detachment in Angola was found to be armed with UZI submachine guns.

In Nigeria the Israeli government identified itself with the oil imperialism-inspired secession in Biafra. Audrey C. Smock, research associate of the Institute of African Studies of Columbia University, writes:

> Up to July 1969, Israel had sent £250,000 of official aid for Biafran relief and dispatched several medical teams. Foreign Minister Abba Eban, speaking in the Israeli Parliament, stated on July 9 that the Israeli Government had "the duty" to send maximum aid to Biafrà. A broadcast on Radio Kaduna (Northern Nigeria) later that month accused Israel of sending tanks, artillery and rockets to Biafra in the guise of relief supplies and of training Biafrans in guerrilla warfare techniques. . . . The *Daily Times* (Lagos) denounced Israel's stand as a "clear case of double-dealing" which violated Nigerian friendship and good will. ("Israel and Biafra: A Comparison," *Midstream*, January 1970.)

*Subsequently the situation was sharply reversed. In February 1972 Amin set in motion a process of severing all ties with Israel, charging that Israeli contractors were "milking Uganda dry." In the following month he made the break complete by refusing to renew all existing agreements between the two countries. The entire corps of Israeli diplomats, military advisers and technicians, numbering some 470 together with their dependents, was expelled. Amin has since distinguished himself by applauding Hitler's slaughter of six million Jews. But this only serves further to show the kind of elements with which Israel's rulers are prepared to ally themselves.

From the foregoing the pattern is clear. The Israeli ruling circles are to be found on the side of the forces of colonialism and neo-colonialism, of imperialist machinations against the struggles for national liberation. Today U.S. imperialism, in its quest for strategic raw materials, is injecting itself increasingly into the African scene, allying itself with the racist regimes in South Africa and Rhodesia and with the Portuguese colonialists against the forces of national liberation. In the pursuit of its imperialist aims, it is assisted in no small measure by the policies of the Israeli ruling circles.

Aside from military involvement, Israeli investments in African countries take the form of partnerships with local investors in which the Israeli share is a minority and is limited to five years, after which the local stockholders are required to buy out the Israeli interest. This approach, says Laufer, has "enabled Israeli companies to enter new markets with relatively small capital investment and under the benevolent protection of the governments of developing countries" (p. 148). It has served as a means of getting around competition from other sources.

The Israeli investors are not private firms but quasi-public corporations mainly under the aegis of the Histadrut's economic arm, Hevrat Ovdim. The chief of these is the construction firm Solel Boneh, whose African projects include, according to Laufer: "Public buildings in Sierra Leone and Eastern Nigeria, the international airport in Accra, luxury hotels in Eastern Nigeria, university buildings and 800 miles of roads in Western Nigeria, and military installations in the Ivory Coast" (*ibid.*). These, it may be noted, are scarcely top priorities in relation to the needs of the poverty-stricken populations of these countries.

The amount of direct investment is small and is intended to serve largely as an opening for the development of trade. But more important, in these enterprises the Israeli ruling class serves as a "middleman" for U.S. and other imperialist forces in their efforts to penetrate and control the economies of the African countries. The Israeli leaders lend themselves to such schemes since they can pose as being "socialist" yet anti-Communist and hence as being "more acceptable" than the imperialist states themselves. It is in this capacity, also, that the Israeli government has sought to develop ties with the Common Market.

The Israeli insistence on a minority interest in joint ventures also opens the door to U.S. and other imperialist investment. The Soviet writer Y. Kashin notes that

> Israel's commitment to provide only 40 or 50 per cent of project costs makes it much easier for American and international banks to get a foothold in Africa, for by means of loans these banks can "indirectly secure most of the majority interest, nominally owned by local governments." (*Jeune Afrique*, No. 485, 1970.) There we discover Israel's secret neocolonialist mission in Africa. ("Israeli Designs in Africa," *International Affairs*, February 1972.)

Characteristic of this role are the operations of the Afro-Asian Institute for Labor Studies and Cooperation, located in Tel Aviv and sponsored by the Histadrut. Its purpose is to provide an intensive, short-term training program for as many African trade union leaders as possible. Launched in 1960 with a $60,000 grant from the AFL-CIO, between 1960 and 1962 it received more than $300,000 in grants and scholarships from the AFL-CIO and affiliated unions, and additional sums from British and other labor organizations. It is well known that these activities of the AFL-CIO were financed by the CIA and were regarded as an integral part of its strategy. Yet today the AFL-CIO continues to be a major financial supporter of the Institute. Its contributions are listed regularly in its convention financial reports.

What is taught in such a school, obviously, is the pro-imperialist and anti-Communist line of George Meany and Jay Lovestone which the CIA has so generously underwritten. The Histadrut is also involved in the Israeli pro-imperialist activities in Africa, as we have noted, through the investments of Hevrat Ovdim.

Ties With South Africa

Especially notorious are the relations of the government of Israel with the ultra-racist apartheid regime in South Africa. Political, economic and military links between the two have been maintained since 1948 and in recent years have been increased. And this has taken place in the face of nearly universal condemnation of the racist barbarism of South Africa's white rulers, and despite numerous UN resolutions calling for severance of relations with the South African Republic until it ends the policy of apartheid.*

South Africa was among the first countries to recognize the State of Israel. In 1953 its prime minister Dr. D. F. Malan visited Israel and was cordially received, despite his record of blatant anti-Semitism and wholehearted support of Hitler during World War II. And on Malan's retirement in 1954, his name was inscribed in the Golden Book as a proven true friend of Israel. The South African ruling circles had only unstinting praise for Israel.

This state of affairs lasted until mid-1961 when Israeli policy in relation to other African countries made it expedient to join in the UN condemnation of apartheid. In the ensuing years relations cooled considerably. But with the 1967 war all was forgotten and relationships became closer and more cordial than ever before. The South African government permitted volunteers to go to Israel to work in civilian and paramilitary capacities, and more than $28 million raised by Zionist organizations was released for transmission to Israel.

The South African Foundation, a propaganda organization representing big business interests, took steps to re-establish its Israeli-South Africa Committee as an instrument for seeking closer economic and political ties between the two countries. The Committee, among other things, arranged a meeting between South African Defense Minister P. W. Botha and Shimon Peres, currently a minister in the Meir government, for the purpose of discussing military affairs. In September 1967 General Mordecai Hod, commander of the Israeli Air Force, addressed a selected group of officers at the Air Force College in South Africa. And in December of that year a group of Israeli officials, businessmen and aviation experts made a tour of South Africa.

In May 1969 David Ben-Gurion and Brigadier General Chaim Herzog visited South Africa to launch a United Israel Appeal Campaign. And within Israel an Israel-South Africa League was formed to

---

*For example, the operative paragraph of General Assembly Resolution 2547 B (XXIV) on "Measures for Effectively Combating the Policies of *Apartheid* and Segregation in South Africa," adopted in 1962, "*Calls upon* all those Governments which still maintain diplomatic, commercial, military, and other relations with the racist Government of South Africa and with the racist and illegal minority regime in South Rhodesia to terminate such relations immediately in accordance with the relevant resolutions of the General Assembly and the Security Council. . . ." It should be noted that Israel voted for this resolution.

press for closer ties with South Africa. Its base is chiefly among the Right-wing elements.

In the economic sphere, Israeli exports to South Africa have risen rapidly, from $1.4 million in 1961 to $4 million in 1967 and $15 million in 1970. South African capitalists were prominent in the "millionaires' conferences" held in Israel since 1967 to seek foreign investment (see below). Recently the mining tycoon Henry Oppenheimer paid a visit to Israel. In this connection it should be noted that the diamond-cutting industry, supplied mainly by the South African firm of de Beers, is an important factor in the Israeli economy and a prime earner of foreign currency. In 1968, diamonds made up 34.4 per cent of the value of Israeli exports.

The roots of Israeli-South African relationships go deeper, however, than immediate economic, political or military interests. They lie in the racist, reactionary character which these two states have in common today. It is not accidental that Prime Minister Jan Christian Smuts was a lifelong supporter of Zionism and a close personal friend of Dr. Chaim Weizmann, or that others after him have likewise been strongly pro-Zionist. The attraction which Israel holds for the racist rulers of South Africa is based on their feeling that Zionism has much in common with apartheid.

Thus, former Prime Minister Hendrik F. Verwoerd stated that the Jews "took Israel from the Arabs after the Arabs had lived there for a thousand years. In that I agree with them. Israel, like South Africa, is an apartheid state." (*Rand Daily Mail,* November 21, 1961.) South African government spokesmen have repeatedly hailed Israel as constituting, together with the Republic of South Africa, the only barrier to the taking over of Africa by "world communism."

On their side the Zionist rulers of Israel are also cognizant of such a community of interests. Today U.S. imperialism, basing itself on countries like South Africa, Rhodesia and the Portuguese colonies, seeks to draw certain other African countries which are under neo-colonialist domination more closely into their orbit and so to establish a base for counter-revolution throughout Africa. Toward this end it attempts to promote "dialogue" between such countries and South Africa, as well as "dialogue" between Black Americans and South Africa.

It is precisely in these countries—Lesotho, Swaziland, Botswana and Malawi—in which South African influence is strong, that Israel has stepped up its development programs. Early in 1971 an Israeli mission visited Zaire, Gabon, Ivory Coast, Ghana and Kenya, all of whose governments (with the possible exception of Kenya) are gravitating toward South Africa. Thus do the Israeli Zionist leaders contribute, together with South Africa, in building a base for U.S. imperialism in Africa.

Brian Bunting, a leader in the South African freedom struggles, appropriately summarizes the situation in these words:

> The Israeli-South African alliance is an alliance of the most reactionary forces in the Afro-Asian world, backed by the forces of imperialism, and designed to hold back the tide of progress, preserve the stronghold of profit and privilege and perpetuate the exploitation of the oppressed masses in the interests of the tiny handful of racists and monopolists who are holding the world to ransom today. *Israel and South Africa are today the two main bastions of imperialism and reaction in the Afro-Asian world. The smashing of the alliance between them must be one of the foremost priorities of progressive mankind today.* ("The Israeli-South Africa Axis— A Threat to Africa," *Sechaba,* April 1970.)

Zionists in South Africa

A particularly shameful aspect of this unsavory picture is the role played by the Zionist-dominated Jewish organizations in South Africa.* The Jewish community in that country, numbering some 120,000, is one of the largest and wealthiest in the world. Overwhelmingly Zionist in its leanings, its financial contributions to Israel are second in size only to those from the United States. To be sure, not all South African Jews are Zionists. Many have been prominent in the liberation struggles and have suffered persecution for their activities as Communists or members of the African National Congress. But these are decidedly in the minority.

The dominant Nationalist Party, strongly pro-Hitler and anti-Semitic during World War II, drastically changed its attitude toward the Jewish community in the immediately ensuing years. This was moti-

---

*For a detailed and well-documented account, see Richard P. Stevens, "Zionism, South Africa and the Apartheid: The Paradoxical Triangle," *The Arab World,* February 1970. The author is Professor of Political Science at Lincoln University in Pennsylvania.

vated partly by the search for white solidarity in maintaining apartheid, partly by a fear of the withdrawal of Jewish capital, and partly by sympathy with Zionist policies in Palestine. Accordingly, the government waived restrictions on the export of goods and currency in the case of Zionist contributions to Israel, making them an exception to a usually very strictly enforced law. In return it exacted one vital concession: support of apartheid.

In the face of the unspeakable oppression inflicted on Black Africans and the scarcely less brutal oppression of Coloreds and Indians, the Jewish Board of Deputies and other spokesmen of the Jewish community have maintained total silence. Not even the horrible massacre at Sharpeville in 1960 evoked so much as one word of protest. The official position of the Board of Deputies in such matters was stated to be one of "non-intervention." Dan Jacobson, a prominent South African Jewish writer, defended this position, saying that other religions condemn apartheid because they have Black adherents, but there are no Black Jews. Hence the Jewish community "raises its voice when its own immediate interests are threatened . . . and for the rest keeps mum." (Dan Jacobson and Ronald Segal, "Apartheid and South African Jewry: An Exchange," *Commentary*, November 1957.)

But it has been more than a matter of "keeping mum," which is bad enough in itself. Not only was Malan honored by Israel; when Verwoerd became prime minister in 1958 a delegation from the Board of Deputies conveyed formal congratulations. Later, at the time of Verwoerd's death, the Chief Rabbi said of him that "a moral conscience underlay his policies: he was the first man to give *apartheid* a moral ground." (*Rand Daily Mail*, September 12, 1966.) In short, the official spokesmen for the Jewish community have become outright apologists for apartheid.

In this shameful stand they have been upheld by their colleagues abroad. World Zionist organizations, and particularly those associated with the Jewish advisory body to the UN, have carefully refrained from comment on the question of apartheid and from any criticism of the South African Jewish organizations for their support to it. Typical of the justification offered for this is the following statement by Rabbi Morris Pearlzweig, speaking for the World Jewish Congress:

The non-government Jewish organizations refrain from responding on the problems of South Africa because they do not want to make the situation of South African Jewry difficult . . . and they know that this policy is very much appreciated by the Jewish community there. More-over, the constitution of the World Jewish Congress does not permit any involvement in Jewish affairs of Jewish communities that have the freedom of self-expression, unless by explicit demand or permission of the Jewish community concerned. (Quoted by Baruch Shepi in "Israel, Zionism and South Africa," *Zo Haderekh,* May 19, 1971.)

As we shall see, no such delicate scruples are shown in the case of the Soviet Jews.

Such is the disgraceful record of Zionism in relation to this most hideous form of racism. And such is the role of the Israel-South Africa axis in fostering the aims of imperialism in Africa.

III ZIONISM IN THE UNITED STATES

3. THE ROLE OF MONOPOLY CAPITAL

Jewish Capital and Israel

Spearheading the Zionist movement in the United States today is a major section of the big Jewish capitalists. This group has provided the lion's share of the contributions which have helped the Israeli government to finance its enormous military expenditures. It is the main purchaser of Israel bonds. It has made substantial investments in Israel and has been a leading participant in the three "millionaires' conferences" held in Israel since 1967 for the purpose of securing increased foreign investment. And it has exercised preponderant ideological influence within the movement. Indeed, it is its class interests which are served by Zionism with its preaching of class peace.

It would be wrong, however, to regard Zionism as a movement initiated by the Jewish bourgeoisie. On the contrary, the main sections of Jewish big business were originally strongly anti-Zionist and assimilationist in their views. Part of them, including such Jewish families of finance capital as the Lehmans, Morgenthaus, Rosenwalds and Warburgs, became involved in Palestine from philanthropic and business standpoints. Only later, after the establishment of the State of Israel, did any considerable number of them become pro-Zionist. At the same time another grouping, associated with the American Council for Judaism, has remained completely anti-Zionist and assimilationist.

From the very outset the Zionists looked to the Jewish capitalists to finance their colonialization schemes, beginning with the settlements in Palestine supported by Baron Edmond de Rothschild in the 1880s and 1890s. In 1902 the Jewish National Fund and the Jewish Colonial Trust were established under the aegis of the World Zionist Organization as the Zionist movement's chief financial instruments. The purpose of the former was to raise funds for the purchase of land; the latter was set up as a bank with its headquarters in London. Among its stated purposes were "to promote, develop, work and carry on industries, undertakings and colonization schemes" and "to seek for and obtain openings for the employment of capital in Palestine, Syria, and any other part of the world." *(Survey of Activities and Financial Report, 1899–1922.)* Both appealed to Jewish capitalists as the chief source of funds. Aaron Cohen notes:

> As for the Jewish Colonial Trust, in 1908 it had a paid-up capital of £225,000, of which £36,000 was invested in the Anglo-Palestine Bank in Jaffa and another £15,000 in the Anglo-Levantine Banking Company. The Trust's board of directors opposed risking this money in direct investments in Palestine, and gave all too few money grants-in-aid to settlement projects." *(Israel and the Arab World, p. 41.)*

The Trust's career was not a distinguished one. After the Mandate, investments were made in a number of ventures in Palestine, among them the General Mortgage Bank, Bank Hapoalim and Palestine Electric Corporation. In 1933 it was reorganized, handing over its banking and investment operations to the Anglo-Palestine Bank (now Bank Leumi Le-Israel) and has existed since only as a holding company for that bank.

Subsequently other vehicles for Jewish capital investment in Palestine and later in Israel were established in the form of investment corporations, particularly in the United States. Prominent among these has been the Palestine Economic Corporation, which now designates itself as PEC Israel Economic Corporation. It was founded in 1926 under the sponsorship of the top Jewish financial groups, Kuhn-Loeb and Lehman Brothers. Felix Warburg, then senior partner in Kuhn-Loeb, became its largest stockholder. PEC was an offshoot of the American Jewish Committee, founded in 1906 by a group of Jewish bankers and industrialists, chiefly of German origin, and representing some of the most reactionary and most assimilationist sections of Jewish big capital. They were, however, evidently not averse to profitable investments in Palestine. The American Jewish Committee also became dominant in the United Jewish Appeal, thus combining philanthropy and profitable investment. *

Lehman Brothers and Kuhn-Loeb have retained an interest in PEC Israel Economic Corporation. As late as 1961 Herbert H. Lehman was honorary chairman and Edward M. Warburg was a vice president of the board of directors. In 1969 the honorary chairman was Robert

---

*For a more detailed account of these interrelationships in their initial stages, see A. B. Magil, *Israel in Crisis*, pp. 101–07.

Szold, a leading founder of PEC, whose family has been associated with Lehman Brothers.

The present chairman of the board is Joseph Meyerhoff of Baltimore, a big real estate operator and a director of the Beneficial National Life Insurance Company and of several Israeli banks. Among the board members is Eli M. Black, chairman of the board and president of the two-billion-dollar conglomerate AMK Corporation, which owns United Fruit Company. Another, Ludwig Jesselson, is president of the Phillip Brothers Division of Engelhard Minerals and Chemicals Corporation, prominent in South African gold mining. A third, M. L. Mendell, is a director of Interstate Department Stores, Inc., retired vice president of Bankers Trust Company and treasurer of Rogosin Industries, Ltd., leading manufacturer of synthetic fibers in Israel.

At the close of 1969 PEC held $24.3 million in investments and loans in some 45 Israeli enterprises, including some of the largest. It recorded a net profit of $1,104,000 for the year, an increase of nearly 27 per cent over the year before.

In July 1969 the IDB Bankholding Corporation, Ltd. was formed in Israel, a conglomerate-type company listing as its two subsidiaries the Israel Discount Bank and the PEC Israel Economic Corporation, and as affiliates four other Israeli banks. With a combined capitalization of more than $45 million and combined resources of some $950 million, the IDB Bankholding Corporation is the largest private enterprise in Israel.

There is considerable interlocking between PEC and the Israeli Discount Bank. Raphael Recanati, a managing director of the latter, is also a vice chairman of the PEC's board of directors. Another member of this financially prominent Israeli family, Daniel Recanati, is chairman and a managing director of the Israel Discount Bank and a member of PEC's national advisory board. Two other PEC directors are also directors of the bank. Several are directors or officers of IDB Bankholding Corporation.

"The Holding Corporation," the 1969 PEC Financial Report states, "will be dedicated and equipped to pursue the original objective of PEC—the development of the Israeli economy on a sound business basis." Which, of course, means a profitable one. At the same time, says the Report, "PEC will continue as an American company."

There are a number of other corporations serving as vehicles for investment by U.S. Jewish capitalists in Israel. Among them is the

Israel Investors Corporation with $22 million invested in Israeli enter-
prises, including a 50 per cent interest in the *Jerusalem Post* and $4.4
million of holdings in IDB. Other U.S.-based investment companies
include AMPAL American Israel Corporation* and Israel Research
and Development Corporation. To facilitate these and other operations there are several Israeli and Israeli-American banks with offices
in New York, among them Bank Leumi Le-Israel, Israel American
Industrial Development Bank, Ltd., Israel Discount Bank, Ltd., First
Israel Bank and Trust Company of New York and Republic National
Bank of New York (controlled by the Israeli-owned Safra bank of
Switzerland).

All this, it is clear, adds up to a very sizeable interest of U.S. Jewish
capitalists in Israel's economy.

The Stake of U.S. Imperialism

Financial support to Israel, however, is not limited to Jewish capital
and other Jewish contributors. Since its birth, Israel has received well
over $1 billion in grants and credits from the U.S. government, in
contrast to less than $60 million received by a country like Syria. Nor
are investments in Israel restricted to Jewish capital. Of the more than
$1 billion of investments to date by U.S. capitalists, the major part is
in the hands of non-Jewish capital. More than 200 U.S. firms have
invested in Israel, including 30 of the top 500 U.S. industrial corporations. Among these U.S. investors are such familiar names as Ford,
Chrysler, Monsanto Chemicals, Motorola, International Business Systems, Holiday Inns, American Can, Control Data, General Telephone and Electronics, Xerox Data Systems, National Cash Register
and others.

U.S. monopoly capital is a dominant factor in the Israeli economy
today. More than half of all foreign capital invested in Israel is
American. A great part of Israel's financial, industrial and commercial
institutions are in American hands. Of Israel's enormous foreign debt,
80 per cent is owed to the U.S. government and to U.S. organizations
and institutions. Of its large annual trade deficit, some 40 percent is
incurred in unequal trade with the United States. This includes the

---

*AMPAL provides credits to and has direct investments in Histadrut enterprises,
notably COOR, Solel Boneh and Bank Hapoalim.

huge purchases of arms of which the United States is now over-whelmingly Israel's chief supplier.

In 1971 alone the Israeli government received a $500 million loan from the United States for the purchase of Phantom jets and other arms. And President Nixon has made it clear that his administration is prepared to supply Israel with all the arms required to "maintain the balance of power" in the Middle East—that is, Israel's military superiority. But the $500 million and all other debts incurred for military goods must be repaid—and in U.S. dollars, not in Israeli pounds. Israel, it is clear, pays both an economic and political price for its government's reliance on U.S. support.

It is U.S. imperialism *as such* which has bolstered (and dominated) the Israeli economy and has supplied Israel with arms. It has followed such a policy because it accords with the interests of the dominant sections of U.S. finance capital in the Middle East, with their desire to use Israel as a weapon against the Arab liberation movement and its threat to U.S. oil investments. In this picture the top Jewish financiers play an important role, together with their counterparts in other capitalist countries. But it is at the same time a subordinate role. Powerful as they are, the big Jewish capitalists are a minor factor in the totality of U.S. finance and capital. Moreover, they are relegated to a peripheral status, thanks in part to the anti-Semitism which prevails in Wall Street as it does elsewhere in U.S. society. Of this, Victor Perlo writes: "The anti-Semitism of Wall Street . . . has had the . . . objective of keeping the Jewish bankers 'in their place' as intermediaries with the world of trade and light industry, a role from which the top oligarchy also derives substantial profits." (*The Empire of High Finance,* p. 186.)

Thus, the Lehman-Goldman, Sachs finance capital group has its main center of interest in retail commercial enterprises and the food and other light industries. Of total assets of $5.8 billion controlled by this group, $2.8 billion are accounted for by the following firms: Federal Department Stores, General Foods, National Dairy, Gimbel Brothers, May Department Stores, Sears, Roebuck and Company, McKesson and Robbins, McCrory Corporation, Allied Stores and General Baking. At the same time its orbit includes also such firms as American Metal Climax, Continental Can, General Dynamics and Owens-Illinois Glass, as well as Lazard Frères which acts as bankers for International Telephone and Telegraph and other corporate giants. Similarly Kuhn, Loeb has banking ties with the Rockefeller interests.

(S. Menshikov, *Millionaires and Managers*, pp. 266, 298–99). Here we see both their subordinate status and their ties with the top finance capital groups.

This in no way lessens the leading role of the big Jewish capitalists in the Zionist picture. Rather it indicates the centrality of Zionist dependence on U.S. imperialism and the fact that the role of Jewish capital is exercised in relation to this.

Dependence on Foreign Capital

Instead of seeking economic independence, Israel's ruling class has from the beginning tied the country's economy to foreign capital, chiefly U.S. and British. Since the 1967 war economic dependence on U.S. imperialism has grown considerably. In 1968–1970, U.S. government subsidies and loans, together with private investments and contributions, totalled almost half of the total import of capital.

Today, with the burden of military expenditures threatening Israel with economic bankruptcy, and with an increasingly desperate demand for foreign currencies, a way out is being sought through greatly increased foreign investment. Toward this end, three "millionaires' conferences" were held in Israel between 1967 and 1969, attended by representatives of foreign capital. These gave birth in 1968 to the Israel Corporation, an investment company whose purpose was to attract foreign capital. Its goal was $100 million, but by the end of 1970 it had succeeded in scraping together only $21 million.

The fact is that the inflow of private capital has fallen off markedly in recent years, while the outflow of profits has risen. In 1965, net foreign investment was $113 million while repatriated profits totalled $94 million. In 1970, net investment had fallen to $55 million while repatriated profits had jumped to $165 million. Moreover, capital investment has been increasingly devoted not to establishing new enterprises but to buying into already existing government-owned firms such as the ZIM Steamship Line. Israel Oil Refineries, Timna Copper Mines and Palestine Potash.

To secure these investments the Israeli government has willingly disposed of its holdings to a point where it has little left to sell. Thus, the Israel Corporation now owns 50 per cent of ZIM and 26 per cent of Israel Oil Refineries. Israel's first jet engine plant, Beit Shemesh Engines, Ltd., is owned 49 per cent by the Israeli government and 51 per cent by the French Turbomeca Company. And General Telephone and Electronics has a 35 per cent interest in Tadiran Electronics, with the remaining 65 per cent held by the Ministry of Defense and Histadrut.

To encourage foreign investment the government has also offered fantastic concessions, among them grants and long-term credits up to twice the amount invested, generous tax concessions, exemption from payment of duties on required imports, payment of export premiums, payment of half of research and development outlays, full rights of repatriation of principal and interest, and others. Thanks to these lavish grants and loans the actual value of foreign holdings is often as much as three times the amount invested.

The largest new venture is the Eilat-Ashkelon oil pipeline, built at a cost of $120 million. Its present capacity is 20 million metric tons a year (a metric ton is 1.1 U.S. tons), and is expected to reach 60–70 million tons a year by 1975. By way of comparison the Suez Canal in 1966, its last full year of operation, carried 176 million tons. Such a pipeline is clearly not required by the Israeli economy; its purpose is rather to provide the foreign oil monopolies with an alternative route to the Suez Canal (in this connection there is also talk of building an Eilat-Ashdod canal). And though the pipeline was built mainly with government funds it is operated as a concession by a subsidiary of Canadian A.P.C. Holdings, Ltd.

Thus does the Israeli ruling class barter away the country's economy to foreign monopolies and subject Israel to increasing imperialist domination. For U.S. monopoly capital, including Jewish capital, Israel exists primarily as another arena of exploitation, of the extraction of superprofits at the expense of the Israeli working people, to be milked for all it is worth. As a source of comparatively low-priced skilled and technical labor, it provides a profitable base of production of certain types of goods for export to Asian and African countries. Through these channels much of the money raised by the United Jewish Appeal in this country finds its way into the coffers of U.S. monopoly capital, Jewish and non-Jewish. This is the reality cloaked by high-sounding, hypocritical declarations of undying dedication to Israel's welfare.

IV A BULWARK OF REACTION

1. THE STRUGGLE AGAINST ANTI-SEMITISM

How Zionism Downgrades the Struggle

In the opening chapter we presented the Zionist conception of the Jewish question. It is, of course, quite at odds with the Marxist conception.

The Communist Party of Israel defines the Jewish question in these words:

> When we talk of the Jewish question, we mean the question of the discrimination, persecution and even annihilation (especially under Nazi rule) of Jews for being Jews. The problem of the solution of the Jewish question is, therefore, the problem of liberation of the Jewish masses from the virus of anti-Semitism, which appears in various forms in the society of class exploitation. The problem is, therefore, how to uproot the virus of anti-Semitism completely, how to ensure the Jewish popular masses freedom and equality of rights. ("The Jewish Question and Zionism in Our Days," *Information Bulletin, Communist Party of Israel*, Nos. 3–4, 1969, p. 187.)

National and racial oppression are instruments of capitalist exploitation, and national chauvinism and racism are forms of capitalist ideology designed to perpetuate that exploitation. They are means of dividing workers, of pitting workers of differing race and nationality against one another, not only to maintain the superexploitation of the working people of oppressed nationalities but to intensify the exploitation of the workers of the oppressing nation itself.

Like other forms of chauvinism and racism, anti-Semitism is an instrument of reaction, of the capitalist exploiters for sowing dissension among the people and dividing the working class. The struggle against anti-Semitism is part of the struggle for working-class unity, for democracy, against the class forces of reaction in our society.

It is part of the struggle against all forms of racial and national oppression. Historically the Jewish people have long been victims of persecution and the horrors of the Nazi holocaust are all too real. But they are by no means the only victims. Countless millions of Africans suffered death at the hands of slave traders and colonialists. The genocidal extermination of Indian peoples in the Western Hemisphere by colonialists and the advancing forces of capitalism is a matter of record. The Hitlerites are responsible for the death of twenty million Soviet citizens, of more than three million Poles and of many others in addition to the Jews. And today U.S. imperialism is engaged in the brutal mass slaughter of Vietnamese. Such mass murder and genocide are basic features of imperialism. To defend the rights and well-being of the Jewish people, therefore, it is necessary to defend the rights and well-being of all peoples.

Such is the Marxist view. It is based on recognition of the class roots of anti-Semitism and of the class struggle and working-class unity as the primary vehicles for its eradication. Zionism, on the contrary, views the Jewish question entirely apart from its class roots. Therefore it looks upon anti-Semitism as eternal and as a unique form of oppression.

In the Soviet Union and other socialist countries the Jewish question has been resolved with the elimination of the monopoly capitalist roots of chauvinism and racism. Of this we shall have more to say later.

In the United States, on the other hand, anti-Semitism is a problem of considerable proportions, both in its "respectable" forms and in the highly virulent forms propagated by the fascist ultra-Right. Professor Charles Y. Glock, who headed an extensive study of the subject by the University of California Research Center from 1960–1965, summarized its conclusions in these words:

> One third of Americans are not anti-Semitic at all. Another third have anti-Semitic beliefs but are not vocal or active about it. The last third are outspoken anti-Semites. Included in the last group is the one in ten Americans who advocate doing something to take "power" away from the Jews. (*Time*, December 17, 1965.)*

A survey by the American Jewish Committee in 1969 showed that in history and social studies textbooks used in junior and senior high

*For a detailed account of these studies see Charles Y. Glock and Rodney Stark, *Christian Beliefs and Anti-Semitism*, Harper and Row, New York, 1966.

schools, expressions of prejudice against Jews are common. Other surveys disclose widespread exclusion of Jews from top executive and administrative positions in colleges and universities, public utilities, industrial corporations, banks and other business institutions. There is also extensive discrimination in other employment, in college enrollments, in housing and in other aspects of Jewish life.

With the sharp swing toward reaction on the part of the Nixon Administration, and with the growing aggressiveness of the ultra-Right, fascist elements, has come a rise in open, virulent expressions of anti-Semitism. The circulation of vicious anti-Semitic filth has increased. Desecration of synagogues and similar actions have become more and more common. Financed by the dollars of "respectable" billionaire corporations, and finding fertile ground in the "respectable" anti-Semitism so widely prevalent in this country, the ultra-Right purveyors of racism and anti-Semitism hold forth the ever-present threat of a flareup of violent anti-Semitism.

Clearly, anti-Semitism in the United States is not a minor matter. Zionism, however, habitually downgrades the struggle against this real anti-Semitism. One finds no mass campaigns against its manifestations such as are organized for the "deliverance" of Soviet Jews. On the contrary, such actions are frowned upon, on the specious argument that they would only stir up the anti-Semites and make matters worse.

Actually, Zionism gives encouragement to anti-Semitism. First, it accepts the premise of the anti-Semites that Jews can never become full citizens of the lands in which they live. Illustrative is the following statement by Dr. Farrel Broslawsky, chairman of the Los Angeles chapter of Americans for Progressive Israel-Hashomer Hatzair:

> . . . in America, as in every Diaspora situation, Jewishness is a socially defined set of attributes forced upon individuals according to the dictates of society. It is not possible for the individual to assert himself subjectively as a Jew, nor is it possible for the individual to escape being objectively defined as a Jew. The social system removes the element of choice and forces a functional definition upon the individual. Since one cannot help being defined as a Jew, his only choice is to struggle against the social definition as a form of existential self-assertion. In the United States, most Jews have refused the option of struggle and have acquiesced in the system's objective definition for the sake of material benefits and the illusion of assimilation. . . .
>
> But no matter how much the Jew attempts to become thoroughly assimilated into American society, the tension between the subjective

and objective definitions prevents his acceptance by the rest of society. He may seek to deny his heritage, but the social system persists in identifying him as the Jew. As the social system objectively needs the Jew, so the Jew must continue to exist. He has no choice. ("Those of Us in Babylon," *Israel Horizons*, November 1971.)

This is simply an elaborate way of saying that the Jew must continue to be singled out as an alien element in American society, no matter what is his desire to be accepted.

It is, in effect, a sort of anti-Semitism in reverse, attributing to non-Jews as such the very same incompatibility that anti-Semites attribute to Jews as such. That is, Zionism and anti-Semitism both are rooted in racist concepts.

At the same time, Zionism relies on anti-Semitism as the cement which will hold Jews together as a distinct entity and bring them eventually to Israel. Any lessening of anti-Semitism is looked upon as opening the doors to assimilation and loss of Jewish identity. Indeed, assimilation is viewed as the chief threat to the Jewish people today. Speaking at the 26th Congress of the World Zionist Organization in 1964, Nahum Goldmann, then its president, stated:

. . . We are now living in a period when a very large part of our people, especially the younger generation, is threatened by an anonymous process of erosion, of disintegration . . . by lack of challenges which would arouse Jewish consciousness and make it evident why they should remain Jewish. . . .

This process, if not halted and if not reversed, threatens Jewish survival more than persecution, inquisition, pogroms, and mass murder of Jews had done in the past.

And, of course, nowhere does this terrible fate threaten Jews more than in the Soviet Union. Such a view, to put it mildly, is hardly conducive to fighting anti-Semitism. For Zionists the rise in anti-Semitic propaganda in the United States is not half as serious as the rise in intermarriage.

Suppression of the struggle against anti-Semitism has characterized Zionism throughout its existence. It became especially glaring with the rise of Hitlerism in the thirties. The mounting horrors of Hitlerite anti-Semitism evoked growing outrage and resistance among the Jewish people generally. The Zionist organizations, too, were impelled to oppose and combat it. But this came into conflict with the basic attitude of Zionism toward anti-Semitism, and it was the latter which predominated. Hence it was that leading Jewish organizations and spokesmen opposed any forthright expressions or demonstrative actions against the mounting horror of Hitlerite anti-Semitism in Germany on the grounds that this would only arouse the Hitlerite elements in the United States. Instead, millions of dollars were sent to Hitler for the relief of German Jews.

Nahum Goldmann writes:

> We complain today that the non-Jewish world did not take an effective moral and political stand against the Nazi regime but embarked instead upon years of appeasement and had to pay the price with the Second World War. Historically these charges are completely justified, but no less justified is the self-accusation of our people, which irresolutely and myopically watched the coming of the greatest catastrophe in its history and prepared no adequate defense. We cannot offer the excuse that we were attacked unexpectedly. Everything Hitler and his regime did to us had been announced with cynical candor beforehand. Our naiveté and complacent optimism led us to ignore these threats. In this mortifying chapter of Jewish history there is no excuse for our generation as a whole or for most of its leaders. We must stand as a generation not only condemned to witness the destruction of a third of our number but guilty of having accepted it without any resistance worthy of the name. (*The Autobiography of Nahum Goldmann*, pp. 147–48.)

This attitude continued even when Hitler's plans for the extermination of Jews became known. Weizmann encountered it on a visit to the United States in 1940, now projected in the name of maintaining "neutrality" and avoiding "war propaganda." He writes:

> . . . Now for the first time rumors began to reach us of plans so hideous as to be quite incredible—plans for the literal mass extermination of the Jews. . . . It was like a nightmare which was all the more oppressive because one had to maintain silence: to speak of such things in public was "propaganda"! (*Trial and Error*, p. 420.)

But it went much farther than this. Speaking at a symposium in 1966, Knesset Member Chaim Landau stated: "It is a fact that in 1942 the Jewish Agency knew about the extermination . . . and the truth is that they not only kept silent about it but silenced those who knew." (*Ma'ariv*, April 24, 1966.)

He could have said much more. As the trial involving Dr. Rudolf

Kastner held in Jerusalem in 1952 revealed, there was actual collaboration with the Nazis. Kastner had to admit that he and others, knowing that Hungarian Jews were being sent to the gas chambers, agreed not only to keep this silent but also to help "pacify" the victims in exchange for the promise of the Nazi hangman Adolf Eichmann that a small number of selected Jews would be permitted to migrate to Palestine.

Eichmann himself describes Kastner's role in these words:

> . . . This Dr. Kastner was a young man about my age, an ice-cold lawyer and a fanatical Zionist. He agreed to help keep the Jews from resisting deportation—and even keep order in the deportation camps—if I would close my eyes and let a few hundred or a few thousand young Jews to emigrate illegally to Palestine. It was a good bargain. For keeping order in the camps, the price of 15,000 to 20,000 Jews—in the end there may have been more—was not too high for me. . . . And because Kastner rendered us a great service by helping keep the deportation camps peaceful, I would let his groups escape. After all, I was not concerned with small groups of a thousand or so Jews. ("Eichmann's Own Story: Part II," *Life*, December 5, 1960.)

At the same time, Kastner was involved in efforts to save a small number of Jews, mainly Zionist leaders and wealthy pro-Zionists, in exchange for foreign currencies, trucks and military goods. But he was by no means alone in these Zionist operations. Thus, Jon and David Kimche relate the case of two Palestinian Jews, Pino and Bar-Gilad, who got the agreement of the Gestapo in Berlin and Vienna to set up pioneer training camps for young Jews to migrate illegally to Palestine. The Kimches state: "These two Jewish emissaries had not come to Nazi Germany to save German Jews. Their eyes were fixed entirely on Palestine and the British Mandatory." (*The Secret Roads*, p. 27.) They report also that Eichmann established an office, run by him, for illegal migration to Palestine.

Such is the sorry record of Zionism in relation to the Hitlerite slaughter of Jews.

A "New Ant-Semitism"

Since the 1967 war the Zionists have discovered a "new anti-Semitism"—an "anti-Semitism of the Left." Lothar Kahn, writing in the *Congress Bi-Weekly,* organ of the American Jewish Congress, spells it out in these words:

> For the first time in modern history, the Jew is imperiled from both the Left and the Right. . . . For the Left, the anti-Jewish course is hidden under the political label of anti-Zionism. It has been used by much of the Marxist camp, the so-called neutrals, and by Black Power groups and their sympathizers. It has served as a respectable political cover by Arabs inflaming their people to a new frenzy; by Communist states frustrated by their inability to assimilate Jews fully and exterminate every vestige of religious-cultural identity; by African nations eager to prove their solidarity with the anti-imperialist, socialist Soviet-Nasser bloc; by American Black extremists merging their pro-Moslem bias with the charge of Jewish capitalism and exploitation. Young Jewish radicals, in the forefront of the various movements, have through their silence backed the anti-Zionist campaign as part of the anti-Establishment, anti-imperialist package they have bought, possiby with some misgivings. ("The American Jew in the Seventies," March 6, 1970.)

The New York Times (November 29, 1969) cites Nahum Goldmann as speaking in a similar vein. It reports: "In place of the 'classic anti-Semitism of the old-line reactionary forces,' extremist elements of the New Left have engaged in such forms of anti-Semitism as attacking Zionism and equating Israel with 'colonial imperialism,' Dr. Goldmann said."

The device is obvious: to be anti-Zionist is to be anti-Semitic. On these spurious grounds the Soviet government, since it opposes Zionism, is declared to be anti-Semitic. And the anti-Zionism and pro-Arab sympathies that are widespread among Black Americans are declared to be evidences of a menacing "Black anti-Semitism."

Thus, notes Michael Selzer, statements by Black organizations condemning Israeli aggression are denounced as anti-Semitic. He states:

> The race relations coordinator of the American Jewish Committee told this writer bluntly: "We will cease to cooperate with any Negro organization which comes out with an anti-Israel stand; we regard such a stand as anti-Semitic." (*Israel as a Factor in Jewish-Gentile Relations,* p. 3.)

On the basis of such a criterion, "anti-Semitism" is found to be widespread indeed among Black people. The preface to the book *Negro and Jew: An Encounter in America,* containing a collection of articles from the magazine *Midstream,* opens with the following:

It is now accepted as an incontrovertible fact that, 1) there exists a pronounced anti-Jewish sentiment among the Negro masses in this country, despite the active participation of many idealistic young Jews in the Negro struggle for Negro rights, and the moral support given to the Civil Rights Movement by organized Jewish groups, and 2) that Jews are reacting to this with an emotional backlash.

This fiction of "Black anti-Semitism" has been magnified into a monstrous threat to U.S. Jews. Now, indeed, it is none other than the Black Americans who are alleged to be the persecutors of the Jews. Thus, Milton Himmelfarb writes in the publication of the American Jewish Committee, *Commentary* (March 1969):

> Is the president of the teachers' union a Jew? Then call him a Zionist and warn him that he will not be allowed to perpetrate in Harlem the genocide that the Israelis are supposed to be perpetrating in the Middle East. . . .
> If that is not bad enough, the quota system is being introduced. Or reintroduced—only this time not, as in the universities and professional schools of the 1920s, to keep those pushy Jews (greasy grinds) from dispossessing the gentlemen, but to do justice to Negroes.

Here the quota systems imposed on Jews by the dominant Anglo-Saxon ruling-class elements are flatly equated with the efforts of the oppressed Black people to secure some degree of equality in education through compensatory measures. The fact that they have suffered discrimination infinitely worse than has ever been imposed on Jews in the United States is totally ignored. The mere demand for a higher percentage of Black administrators, teachers and college students becomes the imposition of a quota system on Jews.

Such distorted views have emerged with particular sharpness in relation to the educational system in New York City, where the teaching and administrative personnel is chiefly Jewish. They were expressed in the shameful, racist strike of the United Federation of Teachers in 1969, led by President Albert Shanker and his cohorts—a strike directed against the Black and Puerto Rican peoples seeking to obtain some semblance of decent education in the ghettos through community control of the schools. The Shanker attack was marked by the wholesale distribution of propaganda charging "Black anti-Semitism."

These views came to the fore again in 1971 with the decision of the

Lindsay Administration to conduct an ethnic census of New York City's employees. The census was welcomed by Black and Puerto Rican spokesmen as a means of determining the extent to which these groups are excluded from city employment, especially in the higher-paying jobs. But it was energetically opposed by a number of leading Jewish organizations. Indicative of the character of this opposition is the following, appearing in a column in *Israel Horizons* (March–April 1972) whose author signs himself "Y'rachmiel." Responding to a column in the leading Black newspaper *Amsterdam News* by its executive editor Bryant Rollins, in which Jewish opposition to the census is challenged, he states that

> if Mr. Rollins thinks the Jews are fighting the questionnaire because they are afraid for their jobs and their livelihood, he is exactly right. I don't find it written in any law, religious or secular, that it must be the Jews, and the Jews alone, who are to make way for the upward mobility of the Blacks. If Mr. Rollins is looking for whipping boys, I would ask him to look elsewhere. We Jews have played that role much too long—longer by millenia than have the Blacks.

Here, instead of seeking to unite Jews and Blacks in common struggle against the ruling-class instigators of discrimination against both, Y'rachmiel pits one against the other and looks upon the employment status of Jewish teachers and administrators as something to be defended against the encroachment of Blacks and Puerto Ricans. Such a contest serves only the interests of the real racists and anti-Semites and undermines the struggle against them. In these circles, representing the interests of the giant monopolies, lie the sources of the growing retrenchments in an already grossly inadequate educational system while military expenditures continue to soar. But the Y'rachmiels, in the fashion typical of narrow nationalism and Zionism, see *only* the interests of the Jews and view all other peoples as their enemies.

Such views are carried to their ultimate extreme by the so-called "Jewish Defense League." "Anti-Semitic black racists," it asserts, "are battling for control of the cities. . . ." And this grave menace must be fought, arms in hand. Of this fascist gang and its actions we shall have more to say later.

Not surprisingly, the major Jewish organizations and their leaders have with few exceptions steered clear of the struggles in recent years against the brutal persecution of the Black Panthers and other Black militants. And they totally boycotted the fight for the freedom of Angela Davis. Judd Teller, writing in *Congress Bi-Weekly* (November 20, 1970), declares:

> Even if it were true that the Black Panthers are the victims of a judicial conspiracy—and this is yet to be proven, even as their guilt is yet to be proven—there are a number of questions that a Jew should consider before striking an instant liberal posture. Is there not good reason to fear that the monies for the Black Panthers' defense will be deflected to their political purposes, even as were the monies raised by the Communists in the 1930s for the defense of both real and fictitious victims of that time?

Apart from his slanderous allegations, Mr. Teller is among those who find fictitious stories of political repression in the Soviet Union real, and real cases of repression in the United States fictitious or questionable. He goes on to say:

> The abstention of Jews from contributing to the Black Panthers' defense or from conducting their defense will not jeopardize the outcome of their case. Jews are a very small percentage of the population. . . . Moreover, the Black Panthers are anti-Israel and anti-Jewish. Beneath all the euphemisms the two positions remain identical.

That they are victims of racist persecution and frameups (which the actions of juries in freeing them have by now made clear to everyone), and therefore deserve to be defended by all who are seriously anti-racist and who cherish democratic liberties, is apparently of no matter. They are anti-Zionist (which Teller equates with being anti-Israel) and therefore anti-Semitic, and this is what really counts. And anyhow, the weight of the Jewish community is inconsequential—a specious argument which, interestingly, is never raised when it comes to "freeing" Soviet Jews.

All the more was this attitude displayed in the Angela Davis case. She is a Communist, it was asserted, hence an anti-Zionist and hence an anti-Semite. And so it is that virtually no major Jewish organization, no Jewish religious congregation, no important Jewish leader spoke out in her defense. And not a few took a negative view of her acquittal. The only exception was the Jewish Left, and even here there was much accommodation to the Zionist-inspired chauvinism prevalent in the wider Jewish community. This stands in sharp contrast to the reaction in non-Jewish circles and particularly of churches, with white congregations as well as Black, to the especially blatant frameup character of the case and to the exceptionally brutal persecution inflicted upon her.

True, the anger and resentment among Black people against their oppression and degradation have at times found expression in anti-Semitic utterances. But studies have shown that anti-Semitism is distinctly less pronounced among Black people than among whites. Furthermore, as a statement issued by the New York State Communist Party points out:

> Is is not the Black people who are the source of anti-Semitism. It is not they who are responsible for the flood of anti-Semitic filth which befouls the country. It is not they who are guilty of the economic and social discrimination against Jews which exists in our country.
>
> In a word, it is not the Black people who are the oppressors of the Jews. On the contrary, it is the white power structure, including a small sector of Jewish capitalists, which maintains and benefits from the oppression of Black people.
>
> To fail to see these things is to divert the very fight against anti-Semitism into a racist blind alley. It is to fall victim to those who would use the fraud of "Black anti-Semitism" as one more club against Black Americans. (*Daily World*, February 19, 1969.)

In a word, the fraud of "Black anti-Semitism" serves to align the Jewish people with the forces of reaction and to divert them from the struggle against their real enemies. And it has its roots in the false identification of Zionism with the interests of the Jewish people and the consequent equation of anti-Zionism with anti-Semitism.

It is Zionism, therefore, which is the central obstacle to any real struggle against anti-Semitism.

2. THE "JEWISH DEFENSE LEAGUE"

Shift to the Right

We have dealt above with the reactionary role of Zionism within the Jewish community. We have called attention specifically to the retreat of Jewish organizations and leaders from the fight against U.S. aggression in Indochina, to the general downgrading of the struggle against anti-Semitism, and to the rise of racism and the creation of the fictitious monster of "Black anti-Semitism" which has served to drive a wedge between the Jewish and Black peoples. And in the next chapter we shall deal at length with Zionism as the spearhead of anti-Sovietism in the United States.

In these respects and others, Zionism has behaved as an instrument of the ruling-class forces of reaction and racism in this country. And this role is but an expression of the reactionary, racist character of Zionism itself, which, as we have seen, leads it into ever greater subservience to U.S. imperialism. In particular, since the 1967 war there has taken place a pronounced shift to the Right among the Zionist forces.

In addition to the forms noted above, this finds expression in the development of ever closer ties of Zionist groups with Right-wing politicians, on the grounds that, whatever their stand on other questions, they are "friends of Israel." Among these "friends" is California's Governor Ronald Reagan, who not long ago was awarded a Medal of Valor by the Los Angeles Bonds for Israel Committee with the presentation made by no less a person than Israeli Foreign Minister Abba Eban. In Philadelphia, B'nai B'rith presented a citizenship award to the ultra-racist Mayor Frank Rizzo. The Zionist Organization of America joined the procession by giving its Brandeis Award to Mayor Sam Yorty of Los Angeles. The chief speaker at the 62nd Annual Banquet of the Religious Zionists of America in June 1972 was Vice President Spiro Agnew. And so on.

At the celebration of the birth of Israel in New York's Carnegie Hall in April 1971, two of the main speakers were Senators Henry M. Jackson and James L. Buckley. Both are notorious Right-wingers and Buckley in the 1970 elections conducted one of the worst anti-Semitic campaigns by a major candidate in the history of the country. And the 1972 elections witnessed a major drive by Jewish leaders to swing Jewish voters into the Nixon camp.

Of course, this is not to say that all individuals or groups associated with Zionism follow an unrelieved course of support to reactionary views and policies. On the contrary, there are Jewish organizations and public figures that oppose the Indochina war. There are others who are disturbed by the rise in racism and the growing alliances with political reaction. Indeed, there is a rising opposition within Zionist circles which the Zionist Establishment, as we have seen, is doing its best to squelch. But this does not negate the fact that the basic thrust of Zionism within the Jewish community and the country as a whole is reactionary, and since 1967 increasingly so.

A Fascist Gang

The natural spawn of this reactionary trend is the so-called Jewish Defense League, embodying the extreme Right wing of Zionism. Originating in the mid-sixties as a vigilante group in Brooklyn, New York, ostensibly for the protection of Jewish residents from Black muggers, since 1968 it has blossomed forth under the leadership of the notorious Rabbi Meir Kahane in its present form—that of a gang of fascist hoodlums, of Jewish Brown Shirts.

As of late 1971, the JDL claimed a membership of some 14,000. In an interview with J. Anthony Lukas of *The New York Times Magazine* (November 21, 1971), Kahane stated:

In the [New York City] metropolitan area, we have 51 chapters, a little over 10,000 members, a little over 14,000 nationally. We have groups in Boston, Philadelphia, Miami, Chicago, Detroit, Cleveland, St. Louis, Houston, Albuquerque, Los Angeles and San Francisco. In Canada, we have them in Montreal and Toronto. In Europe we have them in London and Antwerp.

However, according to David A. Andelman (*The New York Times*, January 17, 1971), they concede "that they put on the membership list virtually anyone who sends them a sympathetic letter, much less the annual dues of $18 for an adult or $5 for a student. The hard core of trained cadres, however, numbers only a few hundred." But they involve substantial numbers of others in their activities, particularly groups of teen-age youth.

The Jewish people, according to the JDL, are in imminent danger of extinction, both in the Soviet Union and in the United States.

In the Soviet Union, Kahane maintains in his book *Never Again!*, the Jews are in danger of physical extermination no less than in Nazi Germany. He cries out: "There is no time! Another holocaust could well approach!" The "saving" of Soviet Jews, therefore, becomes the most urgent task before the JDL, and toward this end any action is justified. Its program calls for the cutting off of all relations with the

USSR, for relentless harassment of Soviet personnel in the United States, for unceasing demonstrations at Soviet offices, for sit-downs, chain-ins and other such acts. In Kahane's words, the aim is nothing less than "to provoke a crisis in U.S.-Soviet relations." That such a crisis brings with it a greatly heightened danger of nuclear war seems to disturb Kahane and his followers not in the least. Apparently, if nuclear war is required to "liberate" the Soviet Jews, so be it.

U.S. Jews are also in grave danger. A JDL leaflet declares:

We are talking of JEWISH SURVIVAL!
Anti-Semitism is exploding in the United States.
Revolutionary Leftist groups—hostile to Israel and to Jewishness—are capturing young people's minds and destroying law and order.
Right-wing extremism is growing at an alarming rate.
Anti-Semitic Black racists are battling for control of the cities.

This is a central theme in Kahane's book. And in an article in *The New York Times* (May 26, 1972) he states: "The first chapters are beginning to emerge in what will be the most critical Jewish issue of the next decade—the physical survival of the largest community of Jews in the world, the Jews of the United States." The prosperity of recent decades is fading, he says, and those who face the loss of the good life they had enjoyed will "turn to demagogues and racists who will promise them the good life in return for their liberties and at the price of the scapegoat—the Jew. . . . What has happened before can happen again and indeed, is beginning to happen already."

"The answer," he concludes, "is immediate mass emigration to Israel. But failing this, Jews must organize to defend themselves, arms in hand if need be, from those who would destroy them."

It is not, however, Right-wing extremism which concerns the JDL. In their activities they pay precious little attention to the fascist ultra-Right. The chief threat to Jewish existence, they maintain, comes rather from another source. Says Kahane: "The most flagrant and dangerous incidents of Jew-hatred in our times have occurred and are occurring at the hands of the minority racial, mostly black, militants." (*Never Again!*, p. 99.)

Thus, according to the JDL, the threat to Jewish existence today comes from two main sources: the Black militants—those whom they designate as "anti-Semitic Black racists"—and the Soviet Union. And it has gone forth in typical gangster fashion to do battle against both. Its chief stock-in-trade has been anti-Sovietism, and its attacks have been centered on Soviet institutions, personnel and cultural events in this country, as well as on the Left here, particularly the Communist Party. But at the same time it has carried on a racist offensive against Black Americans.

Politically, the JDL has followed a generally Right-wing line. This is manifested particularly in its all-out support for the Indochina war. Kahane himself, in 1965, had joined with one Joseph Churba in authoring a book entitled *The Jewish Stake in Vietnam*. The JDL has also sought ties with reactionary or disreputable elements, such as its alliance with the reputed underworld figure Joseph A. Colombo, Sr., founder of the so-called Italian-American Civil Rights League. One of this organization's chief functions is to supply a respectable image for underworld leaders. It has also attracted the support of the notorious New Jersey racist Anthony Imperiale, among others. Further, on at least one occasion the JDL has conducted joint actions with the Young Americans for Freedom, the youth arm of the Birchites.

In pursuit of its aims the JDL has been guilty of a shocking series of outrages and crimes. Space forbids a cataloguing of these here, but by an admittedly incomplete count, the list as of February 1972 includes 14 bombings, 34 cases of assault and injury, 1 attempted hijacking, 11 instances of vandalism, 19 instances of rioting, 10 invasions of offices or meetings, 7 disruptions of cultural events, 15 cases of arms violations and about 1,200 arrests for disorderly conduct. (Rick Nagin, "A Force for Fascism," *World Magazine*, February 19, 1972.)

Most shocking are the bombings and attempted bombings, whose targets include the offices of the Palestine Liberation Organization, the New York Aeroflot office, the Soviet Embassy, the Iraqi UN Mission, the national headquarters of the Communist Party, the offices of the Soviet trade agency Amtorg, the Soviet UN Mission residence in Glen Cove, Long Island and the Washington headquarters of the Soviet news agency TASS. Each case was accompanied by anonymous telephone callers crying "Never Again"—the JDL slogan. Especially outrageous were the following incidents:

On October 20, 1971, four shots were fired from an adjacent roof into an eleventh-floor room of the Soviet UN Mission in New York in which four children were sleeping. Fortunately, none were hit.

On January 26, 1972 the offices of Sol Hurok Enterprises and Columbia Artists Management, Inc. in New York were firebombed. Both are agencies booking concerts for Soviet artists. In the Hurok offices a young Jewish woman was killed and 13 other individuals were injured.

As might be expected, the JDL has publicly denied responsibility for these crimes, though often applauding them. In the case of the Hurok and Columbia bombings, Kahane declared that these were the acts of "insane" people, while JDL vice president Bertram Zweibon attributed them to "provocateurs of the radical Left seeking to discredit the League." There is no doubt, however, that it is the JDL which is guilty of these criminal actions.

First of all, in May 1971 Kahane and six other JDL members were indicted in Federal Court in Brooklyn, New York, on charges of conspiring to transport a large arsenal of weapons across state lines and "to make, receive and possess explosive and incendiary devices." Subsequently Kahane and two other defendents pleaded guilty to the charge of conspiring to manufacture explosives, and considerable quantities of such explosives were afterward found. Kahane told newsmen that he and his followers would not be deterred from using explosives against Soviet facilities if they felt it necessary.

Secondly, in every case in which the culprits have been discovered, they have proven to be members of the JDL. In September 1971, seven JDL members were indicted on charges of conspiring to bomb the Amtorg offices and to plant a bomb at the Soviet Mission's Glen Cove estate. And in May 1972, four more JDL members were charged with plotting to bomb the Glen Cove estate during Nixon's visit to Moscow. In February 1972 a 17-year old youth described as a "former JDL activist" was arrested on charges of making a false statement in the purchase of the rifle used in the Soviet UN Mission shooting. And to cap it off, in June 1972, four JDL members were arrested on charges of bombing the Hurok and Columbia offices.

In November 1972, two of these indicted in the Glen Cove plot, who had pleaded guilty, were sentenced to prison terms of three years and a year and a day respectively. Other cases were still pending.

In addition to its anti-Soviet activities the JDL plays the role of a spearhead of extreme racism and chauvinism. Among its earliest claims to notoriety were its attacks on Black militants.

In May 1969, when James Forman, author of the *Black Manifesto*, announced that he would appear at Temple Emanu-El in New York to ask for reparations for Black people, a JDL gang lined up in front of the temple, armed with chains, sticks, pipes and baseball bats to prevent him from speaking. As it happened, Forman did not appear. Shortly afterward, when Muhammad Kenyatta spoke—by invitation—at the Main Line Temple in Philadelphia, a similar gang was on hand which, as he left, threatened him with violence should he ever return. Other exploits included an attempted attack on Black Panther headquarters in Harlem, and subsequently a physical assault by Kahane and a hundred of his goons on a group of Black students in the cafeteria of Brooklyn College. The alleged reason for this Nazi-like attack was that Black students had broken a Hebrew recording in the cafeteria juke box. At all times the JDL has done its utmost to sow dissension between Black and white and to create a lynch spirit against Black people.

The JDL's chauvinism is not confined to Black people, however; it extends equally to Arabs. Aside from the bombings of the Palestine Liberation Organization and the Iraqi UN Mission, in May 1970 three leaders of Arab organizations were severely beaten by groups armed with weighted clubs. Asked if the JDL took credit for the beatings, Kahane replied: "If we did we'd be open to all sorts of problems. You can quote me in exactly that manner." (*The New York Times*, May 23, 1970.)

Not even Jewish organizations are exempt from the JDL's gangsterism. In April 1971 a JDL mob forced its way into the offices of the New York Board of Rabbis and committed considerable damage. The reason, they said, was that the board had refused to provide bail for one Avraham Hershkovitz, a JDL official who was arrested with his wife at Kennedy Airport when they sought to board a London-bound United Arab Airlines plane with a grenade and four guns hidden in their clothing. According to authorities, they had planned to hijack an Arab airliner from London to Tel Aviv. Hershkovitz was sentenced to five years in prison for making false statements in his passport application. His wife jumped $15,000 bail and fled to Israel.

Hershkovitz was also one of the seven indicted for conspiring to bomb Amtorg. In January 1972 he pleaded guilty and was ordered deported to Israel upon completion of his prison term (evidently much abbreviated) in May. Apart from the comparative mildness of Hershkovitz's punishment, what is noteworthy is the way in which this case, in glaring contrast to that of the Soviet hijackers, has been hushed up by U.S. authorities, the communications media and the Jewish organizations. To this point we shall return later.

Such is the despicable crew which parades itself as "defenders" of the Jewish people. It has all the earmarks of a fascist gang—irresponsible warmongering, pathological anti-Communism and anti-Sovietism, extreme racism and chauvinism, and hoodlumism as a way of life. And its mentor, Kahane, is a fitting fuehrer for such a gang. *

Spawn of Zionism

The JDL is not some sort of fortuitous aberration. It is not an accidental development. On the contrary, it is the logical outgrowth of present-day Zionism and its increasingly reactionary trend. Its views are basically those of the "respectable" Zionist organizations, carried to their extreme limits. Does the JDL advocate the removal of as many Soviet Jews as possible to Israel? So do the others; indeed, it is they who are leading the drive. Does the JDL inveigh against "Black anti-Semitism"? So do the others. Does the JDL fully support the expansionism of Israel's rulers? So do the others. And so on. The JDL's complaint is that the others do not conduct a real fight on these questions, and especially that they are derelict in the struggle to "save" Soviet Jews. It defends its own methods as being both necessary and effective.

The JDL, to be sure, has been strongly condemned by all major Jewish organizations and by many Jewish leaders. The Anti-Defamation League of B'nai B'rith has labeled it "a group of self-appointed vigilantes whose protection the Jewish community does not need or want." Rabbi Maurice N. Eisendrath referred to it as a collection of "goon squads" and compared it to the Ku Klux Klan. The New York Division of the American Jewish Congress called on U.S. Jews "to repudiate the lawlessness and self-defeating conduct of the Jewish Defense League." Many more statements of a similar character could be cited. What must be noted about all these statements, however, is that they condemn not the *aims* but only the *methods* of the JDL. * *

---

*For further details on the activities of the JDL and on the background of Kahane, see Hyman Lumer, *The "Jewish Defense League"—A New Face for Reaction.*
* *On one point disagreement does exist. Kahane's call for mass aliya on the grounds of a threat to Jewish existence here has, as one might expect, been widely rejected in leading Jewish circles, which strongly deny that any serious danger of anti-Semitism exists. Thus, in an article replying to Kahane (*The New York Times*, June 2, 1972) Morris B. Abram, honorary president of the American Jewish Committee, says: "No country, to my knowledge, has sustained individual liberty and group security at so

They reflect the JDL's violence as morally wrong, and they maintain that its methods "will not bring one additional Jew out of the Soviet Union."

One would expect that an organization so clearly fascist in character and guilty of such heinous crimes as the JDL would not merely be condemned, but that the "respectable" Jewish elements would join in bringing these criminals to justice and putting this gang out of business. But no such thing has happened. Despite the verbal condemnations, there has been widespread toleration of the JDL. More, it enjoys a not inconsiderable body of sympathy in both Jewish and non-Jewish circles. On April 24 and 26, 1971 the Yiddish daily *Day-Jewish Journal* carried a by no means unfriendly interview with Kahane. At about the same time, *Look* published an article by its senior editor, Gerald Astor ("The Agonized American Jews," April 20, 1971), which treats Kahane and the JDL as a legitimate current in the Jewish community, on a par with the American Jewish Congress and the New Left.

Particularly significant are the events which took place at the international conference for the "liberation" of Soviet Jews held in Brussels in February 1971. Kahane appeared on the scene and asked to address the conference. He was refused admittance and was shortly afterward expelled from the country. But this, according to *The New York Times* of February 25, 1971, "threw the conference into an uproar, embarrassed its organizers and sharpened a split between a majority favoring peaceful pressure on the Soviet government and those who think that violence is necessary."

While Kahane has been refused permission to speak at their gatherings by most Jewish organizations, it is noteworthy that he was given the platform at the 1971 convention of the Zionist Organization of America. More recently, on March 20, 1971, he was guest speaker at the annual luncheon, held in New York, of the Jewish Teachers Association, an organization with some 30,000 members. The audience of 1,200 according to newspaper accounts, gave him a rising ovation and frequent bursts of applause.

The JDL has succeeded in establishing a base on a number of college campuses. At Brooklyn College it currently has a majority in

---

high a level as has America during a period so beset with pressures. . . ." He adds: "The latest opinion polls show that since the end of World War II, there has been a dramatic decrease in anti-Semitism in the United States."

the Student Council and is the dominant force on the campus, which it has virtually turned into its own private preserve.

Other examples could be given. But the foregoing are sufficient to make it clear that the JDL cannot be written off as an isolated handful of crackpots shunned by all decent people. On the contrary, it is a far greater menace than is indicated by the size of its membership. It has become an increasingly dangerous instrument of the forces of reaction, and there is reason to suspect that it operates as a direct tool of the CIA in its anti-Soviet intrigues. But it derives its main base from the fact that it is part of the Zionist movement, that it expresses in its own extreme fashion the views of Zionism. On all counts, it cannot be ignored.

Historical Roots

If the ideas of the JDL are not a mere isolated aberration, neither are they something new. The JDL has its historical roots in the Revisionist Party headed by Vladimir Jabotinsky, the original embodiment of the extreme Right wing of Zionism. This heritage is acknowledged by Kahane in his book. Jewish youth, he writes, should be taught about the great heroes of the Jewish people. And who are these heroes? None other than Jabotinsky and his most fanatical followers.

It was Jabotinsky's followers who in the days of the British Mandate organized the terrorist groups Irgun Zvai Leumi and the Stern gang, the former of which was responsible for the ghastly massacre of hundreds of Arab residents of the village of Deir Yassin in 1948. It is their tactics which serve as the model for the terrorist gangster methods of the JDL today.

The fascist character of Revisionism was evident long before these events. A. B. Magil writes:

It must also be admitted that long before the Irgun began bombing British police stations, the Revisionist gangs used bullets and bombs against the Jewish and Arab peoples of Palestine. Their youth group, Brit Trumpeldor (Betar for short), and specially organized goon squads broke strikes, bombed workers' clubs, and attacked meetings. Revisionist leaders developed a cult of violence whose resemblance to the tactics of Hitler and Mussolini could hardly have been accidental. In fact the Revisionists were at one time quite brazen about their ideological affinities. "Mussolini is the man who saved humanity from Communism," wrote one of them, who was tried in 1934 for membership in a secret terrorist band organized by his party. "We are the pioneers in the struggle against socialism, Marxism and Communism. For ten years we have been seeking a Jewish Mussolini. Help us find him." (*Israel in Crisis*, p. 120.)

Jabotinsky's own record of support to reaction goes back much further, to the days of his open collaboration with the Ukrainian White Guard pogromist Simon Petlura in the civil war following the October Revolution in Russia.

Today's heirs of Jabotinsky and the Revisionists are Menachem Begin and his ultra-Right Herut Party. Its youth organization, still called Betar, plays the same fascist hoodlum role in Israel that the JDL plays in this country. Betar, it may be noted, has a branch in the United States; in fact, it was as a member of this group that Kahane got his start.

The Revisionists and their successors have never been ostracized by the rest of the Zionist movement but have generally been an accepted part of it. Thus, Begin and his Right-wing Gahal group were represented in the Golda Meir government as part of the national coalition until mid-1970 when its representatives resigned in protest against the government's verbal assent to the U.S. initiative, which included an expression of readiness to implement UN Resolution 242. Jabotinsky himself, it is worth noting, is today viewed as a hero by all sections of the Zionists.

With these elements the JDL has close ties. Kahane himself commutes between the United States and Israel, where he is also engaged in organizing the JDL with at least the tacit approval of the Israeli authorities. Uzi Burstein writes in *Zo Haderekh*, organ of the Communist Party of Israel:

"The new world"—the rabbi Meir Kahane—has come to Israel, where during the last year a number of evident fascist organizations have sprung up, like mushrooms after rain. The arrival of the rabbi Kahane from the USA had been prepared by the establishment of organizations of the so-called "Jewish Defense League" in Israel and also by the establishment of additional fascist organizations, such as DB (Dikui-Bogdim, Hebrew for "suppression of traitors"). These organizations are mainly composed of members of Betar and of Herut. Their heroes are Menachem Begin and Ezer Weizman.

These organizations have set themselves the aim of creating a regime of terror and fear in Israel; to attack public meetings, demonstrations, clubs of any party or organization which opposes occupation and struggles for peace. The members of the fascist organizations are busy training in Judo, karate and methods of violence, wrapping their activities in a veil of mysticism of underground work, though the authorities and police do not impede their activities; on the contrary, they draw encouragement from the permissive attitude of police and the judicial bodies in this country, as happened at the trial against members of Betar who attacked the offices of the Communist Party of Israel, and as happens whenever they attack meetings and demonstrations of fighters for peace. (October 20, 1971.)

Thus the JDL has not only close ties with similar groups in Israel but also a base of toleration and support within Israeli ruling circles.

A Slap on the Wrist

The JDL has been repeatedly condemned by leading public officials, and on the occasion of each fresh outrage pledges have been made to put a stop to its criminal activities. Nevertheless, it has been able to carry on with relatively little hindrance. True, there have been numerous arrests and indictments. But the courts and other authorities have on the whole been remarkably lenient in these cases.

Kahane himself was twice convicted of comparatively minor offenses, suffering a fine of $500 in one instance and $250 in the other. In the more serious case, referred to above, of his indictment with others for conspiracy to transport arms across state lines and to manufacture explosives, a top-level deal said to involve the U.S. Attorney General's office permitted them to go free. Kahane and two other defendants pleaded guilty to the explosives charge. In return all charges against the others were dropped. The judge then proceeded to give the three individuals suspended sentences, place them on probation and fine them. Kahane received a five-year suspended sentence and probation period and was fined $5,000. The others received three-year suspended sentences and probation periods and lesser fines. The conditions of probation, as specified in the judge's written decision, included among others that "they may have nothing to do directly or indirectly with guns, bombs, dynamite, gunpowder, fuses, Molotov cocktails, clubs or any other weapons." But despite these conditions, Kahane has continued to be freely involved in the subsequent exploits of the JDL. And the other two were soon afterward indicted again, this time in connection with the attempted bombing of the Soviet Glen Cove residence.

Then there is the Hershkovitz case previously referred to. Guilty of two serious crimes, he spent less than a year and a half in prison (apparently the longest period any JDL member has been imprisoned) and was then "deported" to Israel, to which his wife had already fled.

Courts have also been easy on JDL defendants in the matter of bail. The defendants in the Amtorg bombing, for example, were released on $10,000 personal bond (which meant that each had to put up 10 percent or $1,000 in cash), with one exception who was released on his own recognizance. Even in the bombing of the Hurok offices, which involved actual murder, the bail was no more than $35,000.

The authorities, moreover, have done little to halt the anti-Soviet outrages of the JDL, despite repeated Soviet protests. In December 1970 the USSR found it necessary to cancel a projected visit to the United States of the Bolshoi opera and ballet companies because of "provocations perpetrated by Zionist extremists against Soviet institutions in the United States, as well as against Soviet artistic groups." In the following month a Soviet note was delivered to the U.S. ambassador in Moscow, calling attention to the persistent failure of U.S. authorities to protect Soviet facilities and personnel. In addition, the note charged that though the U.S. government had promised protection it was in fact "conniving at criminal actions" with the perpetrators of these provocations. And as late as May 1972 the Soviet Embassy in this country delivered a note to the State Department listing the numerous anti-Soviet acts of the JDL and requesting information on the steps taken to discover those guilty of them. As of a month later, no reply had been received.

To be sure, President Nixon has at times been impelled to express "regrets" and to make promises, and so has New York City's Mayor Lindsay. But in actual fact, government authorities have failed to take anything remotely approaching the measures required to curb Kahane and his fascist cohorts.

This failure, be it noted, stands in glaring contrast to the vindictive, murderous assaults on the Black Panthers and other Black militants, and to the trumped-up charges against them—charges of which juries later found them innocent. Furthermore, while Kahane and his friends have been permitted their freedom on low bail or personal recognizance, these Black victims of racial persecution have been held in prison for months and even years either without bail or—what amounts to the same thing—under astronomically high bail. Especially shocking is the contrast with the inhuman persecution of the heroic Black Communist woman Angela Davis, imprisoned without bail for some eighteen months, nearly all of it in solitary confinement, on a crude frame-up which literally fell apart in court.

Though glaring, the contrast is not surprising. From the extreme leniency toward the JDL one can only conclude that the Soviet government was fully justified in charging "connivance at criminal actions" with these elements. And indeed, the monopolist rulers of our country and their political spokesmen—notably the Nixons, Agnews, Reagans and their ilk—are not basically hostile to the JDL. On the contrary, they fully share its anti-Sovietism and racism. And they find such fascist gangs useful in the pursuit of their policies of aggression abroad and repression at home, just as the German monopolists once found Hitler's Brown Shirts useful. Hence the spectacle of the all-powerful U.S. government "unable" to protect the property or personnel of foreign governments in this country, or to curb the criminal conduct of a group of petty hoodlums.

To conclude, it is important to emphasize once more that the JDL is not an isolated aberration but is an integral part of the Zionist movement. Its own reactionary role derives from that of Zionism *as a whole*, not excluding its so-called "Left" or "socialist" sector. The JDL is but Zionism in its ugliest garb.

While others in the Zionist camp may sincerely repudiate it, therefore, they cannot do so on fundamental grounds but can only deplore its methods as reprehensible and harmful to a common cause. Above all, they are incapable of comprehending its essentially fascist character and of combatting it on these grounds. Hence, to conduct a serious struggle to put the JDL out of business it is necessary to fight against the reactionary trends within the Jewish community generally, which means that it is necessary to do battle against Zionism itself.

V A SPEARHEAD OF ANTI-SOVIETISM

1. THE FRAUD OF "SOVIET ANTI-SEMITISM"

Zionism's Enmity toward Socialism

If Zionism displays a lack of concern about anti-Semitism in the capitalist countries, it is utterly tireless in its crusading against alleged anti-Semitism in the Soviet Union and other socialist countries. The Zionists are driven to prove that anti-Semitism is indeed ineradicable and that it exists in socialist society no less—in fact, even more—than in capitalist society. They are imbued with a bitter enmity toward the socialist world for having removed the Jews living within its bounds from the Zionist orbit. It is an enmity which goes back to the October Revolution in 1917 and is directed first and foremost against the Soviet Union.

The Russian Zionists were bitterly hostile to the Bolsheviks. They opposed the October Revolution. In May 1918 a clandestine conference of Zeire Zion took place, which adopted a program to fight Communism. In the period of the civil war, Zionists took part in the counter-revolutionary governments of Denikin, Skoropadsky and Petlura, and established Zionist military units to fight with the White Guard forces. This enmity has never disappeared.

Zionists are totally blinded to the spectacular achievement of Soviet socialism in ending the degraded, poverty-stricken, pogrom-ridden ghetto existence of the Jewish people under tsarist oppression and elevating them to the status of Soviet citizens enjoying full equality with all others. They reject the fact that socialism, which eliminates the social basis of anti-Semitism, has effectively solved the Jewish question and has thereby removed all grounds for the existence of reactionary separatist movements.

Weizmann, in his memoirs, performs the remarkable feat of dealing with the entire period from 1917 to 1948 with virtually no mention of the Soviet Union other than some sorrowful references to the absence of Soviet Jews from Zionist world congresses. He makes no mention whatever of the role of the Soviet Union in saving untold Jewish lives from the Nazi butchers, in the establishment of the State of Israel or in supplying military aid to the newly born state to defend its independence. And he is totally silent on the liberation of the Soviet Jews from tsarist oppression.

To Ben-Gurion the wiping out of pogroms and ghettos and the integration of Soviet Jews into the life of their country seems little less than a calamity. In his address to the 25th World Zionist Congress in 1960 he speaks only of "the isolation and paralysis of Russian Jewry for the last forty years." He asserts that

> . . . this Jewry has for forty years been condemned to silence and bereavement; its creative powers have been crushed by a foreign hand, its schools closed, its literature stifled and its authors led to execution, and an Iron Curtain has been erected between it and world Jewry, between it and the renascent homeland.

With the merits of these assertions we shall deal shortly. But the essence of Ben-Gurion's position is clear: oppression of Jews is no less under socialism than it was under tsarism.

Meir Kahane, feuhrer of the so-called Jewish Defense League goes even farther. To him the cramped, ghettoized poverty-ridden life of the *shtetl*, with its religious medievalism, was a golden age of Jewry which the October Revolution destroyed.

Of the saving of Jews from the Hitlerites, Ben-Gurion has only this to say:

> Only one Jewish community in Nazi-occupied Europe was saved from Hitler's hangmen—that of Bulgaria, when the Bulgarian king told the Nazi conqueror that the Jewish people would be destroyed only over his dead body.* This exception casts a heavy and terrible load of guilt on Hitler's other allies, who could have saved the Jews if they had wanted.

The implications of this statement are frightening. Ben-Gurion's complaint is not that these others were allies of Hitler; it is only that they did nothing to save Jews. One is reminded of those German Jews who were fully prepared to support Hitler if only he would abandon his

---

*Ben-Gurion is entirely wrong on this point. It was not the intervention of the pro-fascist king which saved the Bulgarian Jews but the struggles of workers and other sections of the people—and of the Jews themselves—largely led by the Bulgarian Communists. The documents of this heroic struggle are published in the 1971 *Annual* of the Social, Cultural and Educational Association of the Jews in the People's Republic of Bulgaria.

anti-Semitism. But twenty million Soviet citizens, among them Soviet Jews, gave up their lives to defeat fascism and to save the lives of Jews everywhere in the world, including Palestine. In the view of Ben-Gurion, this never happened.

According to Amos Elon, in his book *The Israelis: Founders and Sons*, this falsification of history is general. "When Israeli historians reflect upon events prior to and during World War II," he writes, "they invariably conclude that, during this greatest calamity that has befallen the Jewish people in their long history, few non-Jews and no single sovereign state had actually come to their rescue with a specific intention to save them" (p. 277).

Such is the overpowering hatred of the Soviet Union and socialist in these Zionist circles. True, there were at one time other, Leftward-leaning sectors of the Zionist movement which took a more positive attitude toward the Soviet Union. But these, never more than a small minority, have long ago joined the anti-Soviet pack. And not surprisingly, for this is the logic of Zionism.

The Anti-Soviet Crusade

Zionist hostility toward the Soviet Union reached new extremes with the 1967 war. Since then there has developed an anti-Soviet drive unprecedented in its ferocity.

On the one hand the Soviet Union is charged with supporting those forces which seek the destruction of the State of Israel, and with arming the Arab states for that purpose. In his speech to the Biennial Convention of the American Jewish Congress in 1970, its president Rabbi Arthur J. Lelyveld spoke of "the increasing boldness of Soviet intervention to give direct support to the Arab threat to Israel's existence." Avraham Avidar, Minister of Information of the Israeli Embassy, declared in his address to the Convention: "Soviet imperialism is today the single most important factor blocking the road to peace in the Middle East." He added: "The world must know, Russia must know that Israel will not be another Czechoslovakia." (*Congress Bi-Weekly*, June 19, 1970.)

Ira Hirschmann, in his book *Red Star over Bethlehem*, states:

The Soviet leaders know that the United States, regardless of the extent of American economic and sympathetic ties with the Arab states, cannot in good conscience or in good politics support a policy aimed at eradication of the State of Israel or any other independent state. Genocide can never become an instrument of American political policy, but it is a fair assumption that it is a tactic from which the Kremlin would not flinch if it suited their purpose (p. 44).

Mr. Hirschmann is apparently unaware of what has been happening in Indochina. But we shall return to his "fair assumption" below.

On the other hand the Soviet Union is accused of the most inhuman persecution of its Jewish citizens, of forcibly depriving them of their religious and cultural rights, of grossly discriminating against them in employment and education, of preventing them from migrating to Israel where they can "live as Jews," and of a host of other abuses. Soviet Jews are said to be living in fear and terror. The "liberal" American Jewish Congress speaks of nothing less than the "Soviet inquisition of Jews." (*Congress Bi-Weekly*, January 22, 1971.) Indeed, not a few of the accusers go as far as to liken the lot of Soviet Jews to that of the Jews under Hitler, and to speak of genocide.

So hysterical and divorced from reality have these charges become that even spokesmen who are by no means pro-Soviet have been impelled to caution against going to such extremes. C. L. Sulzberger, in a *New York Times* column datelined Moscow (July 1, 1970), states that "the regime itself is not committed to internal anti-Semitism" and that "real anti-Semitism is concentrated among relatively few bigots." *The New York Times* Moscow correspondent Bernard Gwertzman writes (December 27, 1970): "There is certainly no wave of officially-inspired anti-Semitism sweeping the Soviet Union" (though there are, he says, individual instances of anti-Semitism). Nahum Goldmann has repeatedly noted that Soviet Jews enjoy equal civil rights with all other Soviet citizens and has warned against distortions on this point.

2. SOVIET JEWS AND ISRAEL

The Disillusioned

What of those Jews who have gone to live in Israel? It is by now clear that there is much dissatisfaction among them and that many have come to regret their action and have returned or seek to return to the Soviet Union. No precise statistics are available but it is evident that the number who want to go back is far greater than a mere handful, as the Israeli authorities have claimed. According to some estimates, about 20 per cent have applied to return within a year of their arrival.

Among the religious Georgian Jews, much of the dissatisfaction is over their treatment with regard to religious matters. So serious has the situation become that in May 1972 one of their leaders, Rabbi Yehuda Butrashvili, came to the United States to alert the U.S. Jewish community to their problems. At a press conference he stated that "Georgian Jews who came to Israel to live a more religious life are finding it increasingly difficult to do so." (*New York Post*, May 18, 1972.)

Their chief complaint is the disruption of their communal life. They have a different religious tradition than the Ashkenazi or Sephardic Jews and they live in close-knit communities centered around their religious life. They have demanded, therefore, that they be settled in Israel in communities of 200 families or more and that special synagogues and schools be provided for them. They have complained that they are instead being dispersed, that their children are compelled to go to secular schools and that they have been compelled to work on the Sabbath. In fact, according to a story in the *Jerusalem Post Weekly* (February 15, 1972), some 200 Georgian Jews staged a demonstration at Lod Airport in protest against the dismissal of a number of Georgian Jews employed there for refusing to work on the Sabbath.

Not a few of them have concluded that they enjoyed more religious freedom in Georgia than in Israel and have decided to return. Thus, the *International Herald-Tribune* reported on November 27–28, 1971 that about 200 (it was not clear whether this meant individuals or families) had cabled Soviet President Nikolai Podgorny, asking for permission to return to the Soviet Union. And undoubtedly there have been others.

The main source of dissatisfaction, however, is the conditions of life encountered in Israel. Soviet Jews, accustomed to living in a socialist society, discover with a rude shock what it means to live under capitalism. In a speech to the Knesset, Communist member Emile Habibi states:

> The Jews who come from the Soviet Union to Israel come very quickly to know matters, and they are perplexed. I have read what Georgian Jews now living in Affuleh have said, published in *Davar* of January 10, 1972:

Shabbetai Mikhalshvili, aged 31, reports that his material state in Tbilisi in the Soviet Union was very good. He had a flat of four rooms, central heating, all conveniences, gas and electric appurtenances. No, he did not suffer from any anti-Semitism. He paid 2 rubles a month for rent of the house, all services included. His monthly wage was 220 rubles, which is more than 1,000 Israeli liras, and in addition he had all sorts of benefits. He was not only able in the Soviet Union to ensure the holiness of the Sabbath but also, and this is the main thing, to ensure the future of his children, their education and health, and all this at the expense of the socialist society. Here he is perplexed. He is still unemployed. There is no heating in his house. His wife works in a textile factory and receives 12 liras a day. (*Zo Haderekh*, February 16, 1972.)

Soviet Jews are indeed perplexed when they learn that they must now pay a high proportion of their income for rent and utilities, often for very inferior quarters, that they must pay considerable sums for health insurance, that they must pay for child care, for both high school and college education. And they are even more disturbed when they find they must work long hours at miserly wage rates for an employer who can fire them at will—that is, if they are fortunate enough to find work at all, let alone in their own trades or professions. And they express their dismay in the letters they write.

For instance, a letter sent by A. L. Cherches from Israel to the Soviet UN Mission in New York in March 1970, asking for help in returning to the USSR, says the following:

. . . I had been given an apartment, but I paid 150 pounds a month for it, besides 20 for electricity, 10 for gas, and 19 for water. Then, 30 pounds were deducted every month for the right to use the polyclinic. From 70 to 85 pounds a month went for bus fare. How much did all that add up to? More than 300 pounds. And for ten hours of work, after which I could hardly stand on my feet from fatigue, I was paid only 500 pounds a month.

Roughly, what remained: less than 200 pounds. That was barely enough to make ends meet, not to die of hunger, to preserve enough strength and energy to get through another shift the next day. And besides, I had to fawn on the boss, be grateful to him for giving me a job he could deprive me of any minute. In the Soviet Union, on the other hand, I enjoyed all the rights every other citizen did and slept tranquilly, knowing that my life did not depend on the whim of the boss, that the right to work was guaranteed me by the Constitution. (Quoted in B. Prahye, *Deceived by Zionism*, p. 43.)

Another letter, sent by Fishel Bender to relatives in Odessa, states:

An education is more than a poor person can afford in Israel. There is a
tuition fee for all schooling beyond the eighth grade, and it's quite high
at that. To attend a secondary school, for instance, it costs 70 Israeli
pounds a month. Tuition fees are especially high when it comes to
higher education.

But why talk about a university education. Even first aid is beyond the
reach of the rank-and-file inhabitant of Israel. There are polyclinics in
the country which cater only to those who contribute a definite sum
every month to the hospital fund. Should you default on the next
payment, you will be refused medical aid even if you have contributed
regularly over a number of years and all the money you have paid in until
then will be lost (*ibid.*, p. 55).

But this is not all. On arrival the Soviet immigrant, after initial
processing, is assigned an apartment. However, the apartment most
often turns out to be located not in an urban center like Tel Aviv or
Jerusalem but in some development town in the Negev, miles from
anywhere and devoid of cultural life. In many cases it is also far from
the relatives whom the immigrant wants to rejoin. To Soviet Jews,
accustomed to the availability of extensive cultural facilities, this is an
added blow. It is worth noting that the Israelis themselves generally
shun these towns; hence the availability of apartments in them.

In addition, the financial assistance given to the newly-arrived
immigrant is mainly in the form of loans. These may cover his travel
expenses in coming to Israel, expenses connected with obtaining and
furnishing an apartment and other outlays. These are substantial sums
which the immigrant is required to repay over a period of time. Should
he change his mind and decide to return, as we have noted, he must
repay the loans in full before he is permitted to go.

Finally, those Soviet Jews who migrate to Israel because they seek
Jewish culture (which to them means Yiddish), quickly learn that
nowhere is the use of Yiddish discouraged as it is in Israel. Some report
that when they address questions to Israelis in Yiddish they are not
infrequently told to speak Hebrew, not Yiddish. And they find that the
Yiddish theater, literature and music are at a low ebb. Yet the Zionist
ruling circles conduct an all-out campaign to get Soviet Jews to go to
Israel on the grounds that Yiddish culture is being stifled in the Soviet
Union! What irony!

It is small wonder, then, that a growing flood of letters has been received by the Soviet Ministry of Internal Affairs and other agencies from Soviet Jews in Israel, pleading for permission to return. To be sure, the majority of the migrants can he expected to remain in Israel, but the desire of so many to go back testifies to the unquestionable superiority of the conditions of life for Jews in the USSR ovei those that prevail in Israel.

The important fact is that those who have sought to leave and on whom the anti-Soviet crusaders have based their clamorous propaganda are only a tiny minority. The overwhelming majority of Soviet Jews consider the Soviet Union their motherland and have no desire whatever to leave it. They are proud to be Soviet citizens, and in reply to the anti-Soviet slanders many of them have most emphatically said so. And with good reason. The transformation from the ghettoized and pogrom-ridden Jews of tsarist days to the Soviet Jews of today is little short of miraculous.

In tsarist Russia nearly 55 per cent of the Jewish working population consisted of traders, small shopkeepers, dealers and persons with no definite occupation. About 18 per cent were handicraftsmen, 11 percent worked in cottage industries and 10 per cent were office workers. Only 4 per cent were factory workers and about 2 percent were peasants. (*Soviet Jews: Fact and Fiction*, pp. 22–23.) Today, however, Jews work in all occupations. The so-called "Jewish occupations" are a thing of the past. The discrimination in employment and housing that one finds in the United States are absent. Jews live everywhere. There are no "Jewish neighborhoods," nor even the "gilded ghettos" of U.S. suburbia. The flood of anti-Semitic filth and acts of desecration which so disfigure our country are unknown there; indeed, anti-Semitic acts and utterances are forbidden by law.

In a word, Soviet Jews enjoy a status of equality with other Soviet citizens which is unmatched in any capitalist country. More, they are citizens of a *socialist* country, working devotedly, side by side with others, to build the communist future for themselves, their children and their grandchildren.

This is the reality which the slanderers and detractors of the Soviet Union seek to distort or conceal. What is most shocking about their anti-Soviet campaign is not so much the endless succession of individual lies which they propagate; it is rather the all-encompassing Big Lie which presents a totally false picture of the status of Soviet Jews, of who are the friends and who are the enemies of the Jewish people, of where their real interests lie. Its dissemination and the campaigns of slander built on it do incalculable damage to the Jewish people themselves as well as to the cause of progress for all mankind.

3. THE SOVIET UNION AND THE MIDDLE EAST

The Issue is Oil

We have noted above the Zionist charges that the policy of the USSR in the Middle East is to support those forces which seek the destruction of Israel and to arm the Arab states for that purpose. Underlying these is the proposition generally accepted in bourgeois circles that Soviet foreign policy, like that of the imperialist states, is based on the pursuit of power politics—of domination over other countries.

Soviet policy in the Middle East is treated as merely a continuation of tsarist policy. Its aims, it is asserted, are to secure warmwater ports, to protect the USSR's southern flank and to gain a foothold in Middle East oil. To achieve these aims the Soviet Union seeks to gain the favor of the Arab states, and toward this end it is prepared to countenance the annihilation of the State of Israel, which has been the steadfast purpose of these states. Such is the Zionist version. It is no less false than the allegations of "Soviet anti-Semitism."

In the Zionist view, the central conflict in the Middle East is that between Israel and the Arab states; hence, if the Soviet Union supports the latter it is *ipso facto* against the existence of Israel. But this is completely erroneous. The central conflict in this region, as it is in Asia, Africa and Latin America generally, is that between the forces of imperialism and those of national liberation. Here, as elsewhere, it is U.S. imperialism which is the chief protagonist of the imperialist forces, while the Soviet Union comes forward in support of the anti-imperialist forces.

The issue is oil. The Middle East has the most fabulous oil resources in the world. It contains two-thirds of the capitalist world's oil reserves and accounts for one-third of its production. The bulk of Western Europe's oil supply, and nearly all of Japan's, come from the Middle East.

Nearly the whole of this immense bonanza is in the hands of eight giant oil companies: Standard Oil (New Jersey), Standard Oil (California), Texaco, Gulf, Mobile Oil, Royal Dutch Shell, British Petroleum, and Compagnie Français des Pétroles. Five of the eight are U.S. firms; in fact, U.S. oil companies control more than 55 per cent of Middle East oil and British firms almost another 30 percent.

Profits on these investments are the most phenomenal in the entire world. In 1965, reported profits of the U.S. oil companies on their Middle East operations averaged no less than 76 per cent of their stated investment as of the first of the year. The *Wall Street Journal* (March 14, 1966) reported that the 1965 pre-tax profits of Aramco, which controls the entire oil output of Saudi Arabia, amounted to 85 per cent on sales, as against an average of less than 10 per cent for all U.S. manufacturing corporations. Although investments of U.S. oil companies in the Middle East come to scarcely three per cent of total foreign investments, they account for 22 per cent of all repatriated profits on foreign operations. (*Survey of Current Business,* October 1968.) These fantastic profits are made possible by the extremely low production costs in the area, arising in part from the fact that the oil-bearing strata lie near the surface, but also in part from the fact that wage scales are among the lowest in the world.

It is the pursuit of these profits, as well as the strategic importance of the Middle East as a crossroads of the world, that has shaped U.S. policy there and has given rise to unceasing machinations designed to secure and expand the empire of the U.S. oil monopolies at the expense of their rivals and of the Arab peoples.

The history of the Middle East since World War II has been one of constant struggle and a succession of revolts against imperialist domination: in Egypt, Yemen, Syria, Iraq, Algeria, and more recently in Libya and Sudan. These states have freed themselves from their former colonial or semi-colonial status and some of them, notably Egypt and Syria, have taken the path of non-capitalist development and are moving in the direction of socialism.

The role of imperialism, and especially of U.S. imperialism, has been one of striving to stem and reverse the tide of revolt. In 1953 the Mossadegh government in Iran, which had nationalized the country's oil industry, was overthrown with the active involvement of the CIA. As a result the Anglo-Iranian Oil Company, which had held complete control of Iranian oil, was replaced by a consortium in which U.S. companies held a 40 per cent interest.

In 1955 the Baghdad Pact was engineered, with five official participants—Britain, Pakistan, Turkey, Iraq and Iran—and one unofficial participant: the United States. In 1959, after the withdrawal of Iraq, it was renamed the Central Treaty organization (CENTO). Its chief purpose was to deal with "subersive" activities in the region.

In 1956 there took place the ill-starred invasion of Egypt by Britain, France and Israel. In 1958, after the revolution in Iraq, U.S. troops were sent into Lebanon on the pretext of protecting that country from the threat of Iraqi attack. And in more recent years, U.S. imperialism has connived at the overthrow of the governments of Egypt and Syria.

Against Imperialism

Such is the basic contest of forces in the Middle East, in the context of which all other conflicts must be judged. The question is: for or against imperialist rule? The Israeli ruling circles, as we have shown in Chapter 3 above, have been consistently on the side of imperialism. And this has necessarily brought them into conflict with the Soviet Union and other socialist countries, which have been just as consistently on the side of the anti-imperialist forces.

When Czechoslovakia sold arms to Egypt in 1955, the purpose was not invasion of Israel (the cold facts are that Egypt has never invaded or even contemplated invading Israel), but defense of Egypt against attack. And Egypt *was* attacked, in 1956 and in 1967, and both times by Israel in collusion with imperialist powers.

The Soviet Union has not indiscriminately supplied arms to Arab states; it has done so only in the case of those countries which needed them for defense against threatened imperialist aggression, principally Egypt, Syria and Iraq. By the same token, U.S. imperialism has supplied arms to those Arab countries with the most reactionary, pro-imperialist regimes, such as Saudi Arabia and Jordan.

The Soviet Union has also given considerable economic aid to Arab countries, in the form of long-term loans at extremely low rates of interest and of generous technical assistance. The most prominent example is the aid given in construction of the giant Aswan Dam in Egypt. Syria is similarly receiving assistance in the construction of a series of dams on the Euphrates River. In short, Soviet policy is to give all possible help to Arab countries seeking to ensure their independence, political and economic, and to develop modern industrial economies.

With regard to the Middle East oil resources, the Soviet Union is charged with pursuing its own policy of "Soviet imperialism." But there is no such thing. In Soviet society there are no private corporations, no private investments, no private profits. The Soviet government's only interest is to help the oil-producing countries to free themselves of foreign exploitation and to develop their resources for their own benefit. In addition it purchases a limited amount of oil. (Actually the Soviet Union is an exporter of oil, mainly to other socialist countries.)

That this is indeed the role of the Soviet Union is recognized by even so conservative a publication as *U.S. News and World Report.* An article in its issue of June 26, 1972 notes that in Libya it has an agreement to provide technical assistance and is buying some oil from the nationalized oil fields; in Egypt and Syria it has long-term agreements to assist in explorations for oil and gas; in Iraq it has aided in developing the nationalized oil fields in North Rumaila and purchases some oil (and will undoubtedly aid in developing the more recently nationalized oil fields in Kirkuk); in Iran it also gives assistance in developing gas and oil fields and imports natural gas.

Again, the Soviet Union is on the side of the forces of political and economic independence in the Middle East, and it is precisely for this reason that its policies are anathema to the forces of oil imperialism and their supporters.

The attitude of tne Soviet Union toward Israel is equally clear. Not only was it instrumental in bringing about the establishment of the State of Israel; it also supplied the new-born state with arms in defense of its independence. And since 1948 the Soviet Union has firmly upheld the rights of *all* states in the Middle East. It has opposed not Israel's right to exist but the aggressive policies of its leaders. This was made plain by Soviet Premier Kosygin in his speech before the UN General Assembly on June 19, 1967. He said:

> . . .The Soviet Union is not against Israel—it is against the aggressive policy pursued by the ruling circles of that state.
>
> In the course of its 50-year history, the Soviet Union has regarded all peoples, large or small, with respect. Every people enjoys the right to establish an independent national State of its own. This constitutes one of the fundamental principles of the policy of the Soviet Union.
>
> It is on this basis that we formulated our attitude to Israel as a State, when we voted in 1947 for the UN decision to create two independent states, a Jewish and an Arab one, in the territory of the former British

colony of Palestine. Guided by this fundamental policy the Soviet Union was later to establish diplomatic relations with Israel.

While upholding the rights of peoples to self-determination, the Soviet Union just as resolutely condemns the attempts by any State to conduct an aggressive policy towards other countries, a policy of seizure of foreign lands and subjugation of the people living there.

Soviet condemnation of Israeli aggression has been sharp indeed but, we maintain, it has been fully warranted, and in its stand the Soviet Union has performed a service in the cause of peace. Nor have its efforts for peace been one-sided; it has worked also to restrain threats to peace from the Arab side, as even Zionist spokesmen have felt obliged to admit.

Thus, at the annual Policy Conference of the American-Israel Public Affairs Committee in early 1967, a panel of experts discussed the Soviet role in the Middle East. *Israel Horizons* (February 1967) reports their conclusions as follows: "These men were in full accord that Russia did not want a war and would do everything possible to prevent one, and would step in very quickly to stop it if one developed. Moscow is evidently making this clear to the Arabs themselves, and especially to Syria. . . ."

These words are almost prophetic. The Soviet Union did in fact do everything possible to avert war in the Middle East in the only way it could be averted—by exposing and combatting the aggressive policies of the Israeli ruling circles, as well as by seeking to prevail on certain forces within the Arab countries to exercise restraint. In the explosive situation on the eve of the 1967 war the Soviet ambassadors in Cairo and Tel Aviv called Nasser and Eshkol, respectively, in the small hours of the morning to obtain assurances from each that his side would not be the one to fire the first shot. And when war broke out nevertheless, a war which served the interests of neither the Arab nor the Israeli peoples but only those of imperialism, the Soviet Union made every effort to bring it to the quickest possible end, pressing for an immediate cease-fire.

The danger of war in the Middle East persists, thanks to the annexationist policies of Israel's rulers in league with U.S. imperialism. The chief roadblock to peace is the adamant refusal of the Israeli government to commit itself to withdrawal from the conquered territories, in keeping with the UN Security Council Resolution of November 1967. Insistence on retaining these territories leads not to peace, not to security for the Israeli people, but to mounting hostility and the ever-present threat of the flareup of full-scale warfare with all its deadly implications. The road to peace lies only in abandonment of this policy, in accepting the UN resolution in its totality as Egypt, Jordan and Syria have already done.

The Soviet Union stands in the forefront of those who press for Israel's acceptance of the resolution and abandonment of its expansionist policy. In doing so, it continues to work for peace in the Middle East and for the best interests of all its peoples, Jews and Arabs alike.

VI. THE STRUGGLE AGAINST ZIONISM

Zionism vs. The Jewish People

To sum up, Zionism must be regarded as a deadly enemy of the best interests of the Jewish people and of working people in general. It is an enemy of peace, freedom and progress everywhere. It must be thoroughly exposed and its poisonous influence on the Jewish masses abolished. Moreover, an end must be put to the pro-Zionist mythology which has been so diligently cultivated among the people of the United States as a whole.

But one should not make the mistake of equating Zionism with the Jewish people. The masses of Jewish people, mainly working people, who join the various Jewish organizations and take part in their fundraising and other activities, are not consciously Zionist in their thinking. Rather, they are motivated by such feelings as a sense of national pride and an emotional attachment to Israel, as well as apprehension for the future of the Jewish people growing out of the frightful experiences of the Hitler period. In themselves, these are natural and healthy sentiments; however, they have been perverted by the Zionist Establishment and harnessed to the support of reactionary policies both in Israel and in this country, policies which are falsely identified with the interests of Israel and the Jewish people.

Opposition to Zionism in the U.S.

Among non-Jews, support for the Zionist position has been declining. The Zionists' demand for unreasoning support to the policies of the Israeli government and their labelling of all opposition as anti-Semitic have helped to alienate growing sections among gentiles. Particularly noteworthy has been the challenge to the Zionist stand among Christian religious groups.

An outstanding example is the study *Search for Peace in the Middle East*, published by the American Friends Service Committee in 1970 and revised later that year. Prepared by a Quaker-sponsored committee of various religious denominations and released at the United Nations, the study is sharply critical of Israeli policies, though it is at the same time not uncritical of Arab policies. However, it stresses the need of a change in the Israeli position if peace in the Middle East is to be achieved, saying:

It is the judgment of the authors of this paper that without certain first moves by Israel, which only the militarily dominant power can make, progress toward a settlement of the Middle East situation cannot be made. Those first moves should involve firm public commitments to withdraw from Arab territories as part of a comprehensive peace settlement and to aid in the search for positive solutions to the Palestinian refugee problem (pp. 114–15).

With regard to the situation in leading Jewish circles in this country it states:

> Our impression, confirmed by many comments from Israelis inside Israel, is that there is a tendency for some of the leaders of the American Jewish establishment to identify themselves with the more hard-line elements inside the Israeli cabinet, and to ignore or discount the dissident elements, in and out of the Israeli government, that are searching for more creative ways to solve the Middle East problem.

It calls upon U.S. Jewish leaders to reassess the nature of their support to the Israeli government (pp. 116–17).

Needless to say, the Quaker study has greatly aroused the ire of the Zionist Establishment, which has gone out of its way to attack it. However, it offers the basis for a serious challenge to the Zionist position.

These and other expressions of opposition which are developing are, of course, not directed against Zionism as such; in fact, they arise mainly within the framework of acceptance of the premises of Zionism and take issue only with certain specific policies of the Israeli government. But such policies, as we have sought to show in these pages, stem directly from the precepts of Zionism. A basic change in policy and direction for Israel, therefore, requires the abandonment of these precepts and the conclusions flowing from them. If the movement against the present policy of aggression is to grow and to acquire effective organized form, it is essential to lay bare the reactionary bourgeois-nationalist character of Zionism and its domination by big Jewish capital in league with U.S. monopoly capital as a whole.

A fight must be waged against the idea of Israel as the state of all the Jewish people and of Jews exclusively, and for an Israel conceived of as the land of the Israeli people—a land of full equality of all Israeli citizens, whether Jew or Arab, Western or Oriental. It is necessary to fight for an Israel which will become part of the Middle East and will seek its ties not with the forces of imperialism which oppress the Arab peoples but with the anti-imperialist forces among the Arabs. It is necessary to strive for Israeli independence of foreign monopoly capital, for economic relations with the socialist countries, and for the achievement of economic independence as the only foundation for a viable economy and a secure future. It is necessary to press for recognition of the right of self-determination of the Palestinian Arabs, including a just solution of the refugee question. It is necessary, in a word, to fight for the de-Zionization of Israel. The unfolding of such struggles is the task of the Israeli people in the first place—but not of the Israeli people alone.

In the United States—the heartland of world imperialism and the home of the world's largest Jewish community—the fight against Zionism takes on exceptional importance. It is here, above all, that the dangerous machinations of U.S. imperialism in the Middle East must be combatted. It is here, next to Israel itself, that the pressures to compel a basic change in Israeli foreign policy must be generated. And it is here that the struggle against the slanderous attacks on the Soviet Union and other socialist countries must be focused.

The great hoax perpetrated by Zionism on the Jewish people—indeed, on all the people of our country—can and will be exposed. The eradication of Zionist influences will mark a big step forward for the Jewish people. It will permit them, in Israel and in other countries, to turn their creative energies in more fruitful directions. It will go far toward freeing them of racist and chauvinist influences. It will open up the way toward Jewish-Arab brotherhood and peace in the Middle East. And it will contribute greatly to securing world peace.

5

MIDDLE EAST PEACE:
A NEW STAGE IN THE STRUGGLE*

HYMAN LUMER

The war which broke out on October 6 between the Israeli military forces and those of Egypt and Syria, and which culminated in the cease-fire voted by the UN Security Council in its resolutions of October 22 and 23, has profoundly altered the balance of forces in the Middle East and has created new and more favorable conditions in the struggle for a just and durable peace.

To understand the meaning of these changes and the consequences which flow from them it is necessary first of all to understand clearly the nature of the war itself, about which the forces of reaction have done their utmost to spread confusion and misunderstanding. The Zionst rulers of Israel would have us believe that this was a war of aggression by Egypt and Syria. In this they are faithfully parroted by the degenerate Mikunis-Sneh group (MAKI) in Israel, which says in a statement issued on October 7: "The Political Bureau . . . strongly condemns the aggressive war acts of the Egyptian and Syrian governments against the State of Israel. We, together with the whole nation, are sure that Zahal (the Army) will succeed in repelling the aggressors and defends the security and peace of the nation." This notion was widely propagated in the United States, among others by the *Morning Freiheit*, MAKI's faithful ally in this country, which wrote: "Egypt and Syria have begun a new war, following a series of attacks by the terrorists whose professed aim is to destroy the State of Israel as quickly as possible." (October 14, 1973.)

This notion that Egypt and Syria attacked Israel with the aim of annihilating it gained considerable credence among the U.S. people;

From *Political Affairs*, December 1973. Excerpts only.

it is, however, totally false. And it is based on completely erroneous criteria for judging the character of a war. This cannot be determined on the basis of who fired the first shot, of the flow of events immediately preceding the fighting or of the self-serving statements of this or that government spokesman. On the contrary, the basis of judgment, as V. I. Lenin repeatedly stressed, is that contained in the famous maxim of Clausewitz that "war is the continuation of politics by other means" (that is, by violent means). To understand correctly the character of a war waged by a particular state, therefore, it is necessary to examine the political line pursued by its ruling circles over an extended period of time preceding the outbreak of war. The war itself does not change this line; it changes only the methods used to achieve it.

A Long-Range Policy of Aggression

In this light, let us survey briefly the politics of the Israel ruling circles. To begin with it is essential to recognize that the central conflict in the Middle East is that between the forces of imperialism and those of national liberation, and that in this conflict Israel's rulers have been found almost at all times on the side of imperialism. Motivated by the Zionist goal of a Jewish state embracing all of Palestine—a goal attainable only at the expense of the Palestinian Arabs—they have pursued from the very birth of Israel a policy of aggression and annexation, in league with the forces of imperialism and especially U.S. imperialism.

When the UN partitioned Palestine into Jewish and Arab states in 1947 the Zionist leaders accepted the partition, but they were opposed from the outset to the establishment of a Palestinian Arab state, and in the 1948 war they seized more than half the territory allotted to that state and incorporated it into Israel. A large part of the Arab refugees came from these areas, whose population was almost totally Arab before the war and is now almost wholly Jewish.

In the early fifties there developed an alliance with French imperialism which supplied the Israeli government with arms in return for the latter's support in the UN to the imperialist moves against Algerian liberation. By 1956 this grew into a full-blown collusion with both British and French imperialism to invade Egypt with the aim of overthrowing the Nasser government (which had committed the unpardonable crime of nationalizing the Suez Canal) and, in the case of

Israel, of annexing the Sinai Peninsula. But the aggression failed and they were forced to disgorge their booty.

They thereupon entered into alliance with U.S. imperialism, which had by now become the most potent imperialist force in the Middle East and which likewise sought the overthrow of the anti-imperialist Arab regimes and the defeat of the national liberation movements. This new collusion culminated eventually in the June 1967 war—a war of aggression aimed at toppling the governments of Egypt and Syria on the one hand and at territorial conquest on the other. The transparent fiction that this, too, was a war of national defense has now been completely exploded by the admissions of leading Israeli army officers themselves that in 1967 Israel was in no danger whatever of attack by the Arab states.

The effort to bring about the overthrow of the Egyptian and Syrian governments failed, but Israel emerged from the war with a considerable body of conquered territory—the Sinai Peninsula, the Gaza Strip, the West Bank of Jordan and the Golan Heights. The policy pursued by the Israeli ruling circles since June 1967 has had as its aim *the incorporation of these territories in their entirety into the State of Israel.*

But the policy of aggression and expansion goes even beyond these acts. Under the pretext of retaliation for terrorist acts by Arab guerrillas, Israeli armed forces have conducted repeated large-scale raids into Arab territories, making use of napalm and taking a considerable toll of civilian lives and property. For these raids the Israeli government has been again and again condemned by the UN Security Council.

Such were the politics of Israel's ruling class from 1948 up to the eve of October 6. Clearly the war launched on that date was on the Israeli side a war of "continuation of [these] politics by other means." It was a war whose purpose was *to maintain and expand Israel's military conquests,* a war to retain by force territories to which Israel has no legal or moral right. It was a war whose roots lay in Israeli aggression, in the persistent refusal of the Israeli government to return the occupied territories to the countries to which they rightfully belong.

The Victims of Aggression

The Israeli ruling clique has from the outset sought to justify its policy of military force and expansionism on the spurious grounds that this was necessary to safeguard Israel's security. Indeed, it has been endlessly reiterated, there is no other choice since the Arabs flatly refuse to recognize the right of Israel to exist and are motivated only by an irrational urge to bring about its annihilation. As Golda Meir expressed it in a recent interview concerning the recent war, Israel must win "because to lose is to be annihilated." (*Jerusalem Post Weekly,* October 16, 1973.)

This, it can readily be shown, has never been true. To be sure, Arab spokesmen have all too often engaged in bloodthirsty calls to "drive the Jews into the sea" and the Israeli leaders have used such utterances to their advantage. But the fact is that since 1948 no Arab state has attacked Israel or sought to seize any part of its territory. On the contrary, it is Israel which has more than once invaded the territory of its neighbors and now holds sections of their lands by force. Moreover, it is Israel which now holds most of the land inhabited by the Palestinian Arabs and which denies to more than a million Palestinian Arab refugees the right to return to their homes.

The purpose of the war which Egypt and Syria have been waging is to regain the territories taken from them. To call this a war of aggression is as absurd as it would be to call the struggles of the people of Mozambique to drive out the Portuguese colonial oppressors a war of aggression. In short, the war of Egypt and Syria is a *just* war, a war *against* aggression, a part of the struggle for liberation, against the forces of imperialism whose interests Israel's rulers serve. Such as the "continuation of politics" on the Arab side.

The story that their purpose is the destruction of Israel can only be characterized as an outright lie. First of all, Arab spokesmen have made their aims crystal clear. On October 9, Ashraf Ghorbal, adviser to President Sadat, stated on Cairo television that all that Egypt wanted was recovery of the Sinai Peninsula and recognition of the rights of the Palestinian Arabs. And shortly afterward, speaking to the National Assembly and the Central Committee of the Arab Socialist League, Sadat himself stated: "We wish to tell the Israelis that we do not call for their annihilation, as has been claimed." And in return for Israeli withdrawal to the borders preceding the 1967 war, he offered a lasting peace with internationally guaranteed borders.

Moreover, this position is not something new. It was expressed already some years ago when Egypt, Jordan and Lebanon declared their acceptance *in toto* of UN Security Council Resolution 242 soon after its adoption in November 1967. And they were later joined in this action by Syria. Under the terms of the resolution, Nasser repeatedly stated, and after him Sadat, that in return for the withdrawal of Israeli forces from the occupied territories Egypt was prepared to agree to "termination of all claims or states of belligerency and respect for and acknowledgment of the sovereignty, territorial integrity and political independence of every State in the area and their right to live in peace within secure and recognized boundaries free from threats or acts of force." More than that, in response to a memorandum of Gunnar Jarring in February 1971, the Egyptian government explicitly stated that in return for withdrawal it was prepared to sign a peace treaty with Israel—an act which the Israeli leaders had for more than two decades declared to be their fondest desire.

All this has been common knowledge for some years; yet the Israeli ruling clique has persistently behaved as though none of these things had ever occurred. In fact Golda Meir, in a lengthy article entitled "Israel in Search of Lasting Peace" (*Foreign Affairs*, April 1973) performs the remarkable feat of never once mentioning the stand of the Arab states, even to reject it, and confines herself to the lament that peace is impossible until the Arabs give up their mad desire to exterminate Israel. And this absurd fiction is maintained to this very moment even though, as President Habib Bourguiba of Tunisia notes, all Arab countries now accept the existence of Israel. (*New York Times*, October 14, 1973.)

The truth of the situation was expressed in no uncertain terms at the World Congress of Peace Forces in Moscow, whose 3,200 delegates in their overwhelming majority expressed their wholehearted support to the Arab peoples in their just struggles. The Report of the Commission on the Middle East states: "The Commission displayed near unanimity in its appraisal of the basic causes of the renewal of hostilities: the continuing Israeli occupation of Arab territories in defiance of repeated UN resolutions and the denial of the national rights of the Palestinian Arab people."

The Palestinian Arab Question

At the very heart of the Israeli-Arab hostilities over the past 25 years lies the grave injustice done to the Palestinian Arab people, who have been deprived of their land and reduced in great part to the status of refugees who, since 1948, have been denied the right to return to their homes. Throughout these years they have waged an ongoing struggle for their national rights—a struggle which, since 1967, has assumed major proportions and has emphasized increasingly the right to self-determination. This is today a pivotal issue, without whose resolution there can be no stable peace in the Middle East.

Especially glaring, however, has been the refusal of Israel's Zionist leaders to face reality on this specific question. In 1948 the UN General Assembly adopted a resolution affirming the right of the refugees either to be repatriated or to receive compensation for their property. This resolution has been reaffirmed every year since then. On every occasion the Israeli delegation has voted against it and the Israeli government has at all times flatly refused to honor it. Had it been willing to do so, the conflict could long ago have been peacefully resolved. Thus the Bandung Conference in 1956 adopted a resolution, signed by all the key Arab states, calling for the peaceful solution of the Palestine problem on the basis of the UN resolution. But the Zionist leaders of Israel, motivated by their racist concept of an exclusively Jewish state, wanted as few Arabs within the borders of Israel as possible.

In 1967 Israeli armed forces occupied the West Bank and the Gaza Strip, territories inhabited entirely by Palestinian Arabs. In the process an added mass of refugees was created and in the years since 1967 the population of these territories has suffered severe repression at the hands of the occupying forces.

Israel's rulers deny not only the national rights of the Palestinian Arab people but even its existence. There is, says Golda Meir, no such thing as a Palestinian Arab people and the proposal of a Palestinian Arab state is nothing more than a plot for the destruction of Israel. Besides, the Arabs already have fourteen states; why do they need a fifteenth? As for the refugees, why should they want to live in Israel? Would they not be happier among their own people? As reported in the *British Morning Star* (October 29, 1973), she rejects any idea of negotiations with the Palestinian Arabs, saying: "There is room for the refugees in Jordan, it is the natural place for Palestinians."

Thus does Mrs. Meir graciously perform the act of self-determination on behalf of the Palestinian Arabs. Her cohort Moshe Dayan carries it even a step further. "After the Jews established Israel in their part of Palestine," he says, "the Arabs preferred to join the Jordanian Hashemite Kingdom and give up their distinctive Palestinian status— thus putting an end to political Palestine." (*The Israel Digest*, July 6, 1973.)

Such is the warped chauvinist mentality of the Meirs, Dayans and their ilk, who are utterly insensitive to national distinctions and sensibilities among Arabs and to whom all are simply "Arabs." But unfortunately for their schemes the Palestinian Arabs think otherwise. A militant movement for liberation and self-determination has developed, whose chief organized expression is the Palestine Liberation Organization headed by Yassir Arafat. The Israeli spokesmen have sought to brand this organization as a gang of irresponsible terrorists and to hold it responsible for certain senseless acts of terror committed by isolated groupings. But such a characterization is today utterly groundless. The PLO has not only disassociated itself from such acts but has come to be widely recognized as a responsible and accepted spokesman for the Palestinian Arab people.

The World Peace Congress was warmly endorsed by Arafat, and though he himself could not attend, the PLO was well represented and took an active part in the deliberations, both in the plenary sessions and in the Commission on the Middle East. They fully associated themselves, as did the other Arab delegates, with the Commission's Report, which states: "Nearly all of those participating called for implementing Resolution 242 and all who did so linked it with the just achievement of their national rights by the Palestinian Arab people." They associated themselves also with the Congress's call for implementation of the UN Security Council ceasefire resolutions. These are hardly the actions of a gang of "terrorists" seeking the extermination of Israel.

This is not to say that the PLO has abandoned its idea of a single secular Palestinian state within which the State of Israel would be absorbed and cease to exist as an independent political entity. However, this was now raised not as an inflexible demand but as a proposal for discussion in negotiations along with alternative proposals for Palestinian Arab self-determination. What *is* demanded—and with justice—is the inclusion of this question in any negotiations growing out of the cease-fire resolutions.

The Israeli government will be compelled to come to terms with the just demands of the Palestinian Arabs no less than with the growing world-wide insistence that it relinquish the occupied territories. Indeed, these demands are closely interlinked with the implementation of Resolution 242, for the exercise of the right of self-determination is inconceivable without ending the occupation and without assuring the right of the refugees to return to their homeland. "In any endeavor to decide their future," says the Report, "The Palestinian Arab people must take part; and it was pointed out that the Palestine Liberation

Organization has been recognized as its spokesman in the present circumstances by international bodies such as the Non-Aligned Conference and the Arab League, as well as numerous countries."

The U.S. Role in the Middle East

U.S. policy in the Middle East is designed basically to defend the interests of the oil monopolies and other sectors of finance capital. But within this framework the policy has assumed an ambivalent character.

Its predominant feature has been all-out support to Israel as an instrument against the anti-imperialist Arab forces. It is this support, as is well known, which has made possible the whole aggressive policy of the Israeli government. The U.S. policy has been enunciated by Nixon as one of "maintaining the balance of power" in the Middle East, by which is meant maintaining Israeli military superiority at all costs. This policy has never been modified or repudiated and remains in force to this day.

At the same time, however, the U.S. ruling circles have sought, under pressure of the leading oil companies, to maintain amicable ties with the oil-producing Arab states, particularly with such a state as Saudia Arabia, which leads in oil output and capacity and is governed by a reactionary feudal regime. This aspect of U.S. policy has received increased emphasis during the past few years, thanks largely to the struggles waged by the Organization of Petroleum Exporting Countries (a group of eight Middle Eastern countries plus Nigeria and Venezuela) for better prices and terms of production, also to the growing nationalization and threats of nationalization of oil properties. The problem of oil shortages has added to these pressures. An indication of this shifting emphasis in Middle Eastern policy was given by Nixon in September when he said: "Both sides are at fault. Both sides need to start negotiations. That is our position. We are not pro-Israel and we are not pro-Arab. . . . We are pro-peace." (Quoted in *New Republic*, October 20, 1973.)

The war came as a shock to the Nixon Administration. As one observer put it: "The war is a great big firecracker that has exploded in Nixon's face." The response was two-sided. On the one hand there were calls for a cease-fire based on return to the 1967 cease-fire lines. On the other hand, as soon as Israel's military plight became clear, a military airlift was instituted. In Congress, demands for large-scale supply of arms to replace Israeli losses were made, spearheaded by such "friends of Israel" as Senators Henry Jackson and James L. Buckley. And Nixon himself leaped to the rescue with a proposal for a $2.2 billion grant for military aid to Israel.

All this was done in the name of countering alleged large-scale Soviet aid to the Arab states. Secretary of State Kissinger spoke of a threat to the détente which, he declared, "cannot survive irresponsibility." But Mr. Kissinger placed the shoe on the wrong foot. The burden of "irresponsibility" lay not in Moscow but in Washington, which was providing arms to an aggressor in defiance of international law and UN decisions. It was this policy which threatened the détente, not the assistance given by the Soviet Union to the victims of aggression—assistance such as it has freely given to the people of Vietnam and to all others fighting for their freedom.

As in the case of Israel, the U.S. policy has led also to its growing isolation. In the UN Security Council the U.S. spokesmen found few takers for their plea for a cease-fire based on the 1967 lines. Ten of the Council's fifteen member states made it clear that they would support no cease-fire proposal not based on Israeli withdrawal from the occupied territories. Moreover, the U.S. found itself increasingly at odds with its NATO allies. Britain placed an embargo on arms shipments. The position of the French government was epitomized in the question asked by Foreign Minister Michel Jobert: "Is it necessarily unforeseen aggression to go home?" The West German government sharply protested the shipment of U.S. military materiel to Israel from its ports. Only fascist Portugal allowed the U.S. airlift to operate from its bases.

In the end the U.S. government was impelled to accede to the Soviet initiative and to join in introducing the cease-fire resolution adopted by the Security Council on October 22 (Resolution 338), which provides for a) a cease-fire on the lines as of that date, b) full implementation of Resolution 242, and c) opening of negotiations leading toward a just and stable peace. The resolution was immediately accepted by Egypt and Israel and soon after by Syria. The terms of this resolution represent a major political victory for the forces of peace and anti-imperialism, since they embody the one truly valid basis for a peaceful settlement of the conflict.

However, the cease-fire has only opened the door to placing the struggle for peace on a new plane. The struggle itself is far from won and it is by no means precluded that fresh outbursts of war may occur.

6

AGAINST APOLOGISTS FOR IMPERIALISM, ZIONISM, RACISM*

HENRY WINSTON

To our chairman, to our honored guests and to all our comrades and friends present—warmest greetings! Even though the introduction of our chairman was overstated, I was moved by the spirit of his remarks and by your inspiring response to them. Esther Carroll, with her usual warmth and humanism even makes me a "doctor." It is known that this is not my status, yet I applaud the beautiful sentiments and hopes expressed in the remarks of Esther Carroll, for they are truly reflective of the democratic, anti-monopoly and anti-imperialist unity that is growing between Jew and gentile, Black and white, and all oppressed minorities whose interests are as one in a common struggle against monopoly, against imperialism.

The strengthening of unity and its further development is largely dependent upon the quality and quantity of the struggle against the main weapons of a decadent, dying system which is consciously fanning racism in general and anti-Semitism in particular.

It is indeed a pleasure to find here a conscious understanding that anti-Communism, racism and anti-Semitism are needed by the reactionary, militarist, ultra-Right and fascist forces not only to undermine the struggle for detente and peaceful coexistence, not only to place obstacles in the way of the fight of labor and the people to defend their living standards against the monopolies, but also to establish a safe rear for the monopolists by crushing the liberties of the people, and making possible a more aggressive military policy in the international arena.

Implicit in all the speeches from this platform is the simple truth

From *Jewish Affairs*, Jan/Feb 1974. Address to the Second Annual *Jewish Affairs* Dinner, December, 1973.

that the realization of the cause of democracy and peace makes man
datory a vigorous struggle against anti-Communism, racism and anti
Semitism.

Jewish Affairs has played and is playing a very fine role in helping to
bring that kind of clarity to our class and our people, and is at the
same time actively giving leadership to larger and larger numbers of
Jewish masses seeking answers, at a time when the ideologists of
imperialism in general and Zionism in particular have pulled out all
stops in their barrage within the Jewish community.

What is the aim of this barrage? It is a conscious effort to spread that
kind of confusion which would make it appear as if the Zionist-
directed policies of the Israeli government are identical with the
healthy national aspirations of the Jewish masses. The Zionists receive
the unstinting support of finance capital as a whole in the U.S.
Without such support the barbaric racist and militarist occupation of
Arab lands could never take place.

The defense of the vital interests of the Jewish masses is identical
with the needs and aspirations of all lovers of democracy, equality and
peace. The realization of these goals by forward-looking humanity
necessitates an understanding of the conscious efforts of imperialism to
muddy the waters. With that it is necessary to rapidly make a break
with the misleading ideologies of imperialism and to take the path of
practical organization to advance programs of struggle corresponding
to the needs of the working class and all democratic strata against
monopoly. *Jewish Affairs* is playing an important role in helping to
bring about this kind of understanding. Hyman Lumer, the editor of
Jewish Affairs, is playing a splendid role in this respect.

I am very proud to have been given the honor of representing the
Political Committee of the Communist Party of the United States and
to convey its warmest greetings to *Jewish Affairs* and to its editor,
Hyman Lumer, for its contributions in bringing the science of Marxism-Leninism to ever greater numbers of people who are playing a
growing role in the sharpening struggles within the country. The
Communist Party fully supports *Jewish Affairs* because it is an active
fighter for the unity of Jewish masses with all democratic forces,
especially labor, with a conscious outlook of an anti-monopoly
character. Such an outlook necessarily means vigorous struggle against
anti-Semitism in all its forms. Anti-Semitism is a conscious weapon of
the forces of reaction in this country. The struggle against anti-
Semitism is part of the struggle for democracy, for peace, for the

strengthening of solidarity within the ranks of the working class, for unity between Black and white, for unity of all forces seeking social progress. Anti-Semitism is a crime against all that is decent, a crime against everything the people of the U.S. hold dear. Anti-Semitism must be outlawed. This is the position of the Communist Party of the United States.

I recently spoke at an All-People's Rally in Chicago at the National Anti-Imperialist Conference in Support of African Liberation Movements. Among other things, I said the following:

"My dear friends—if we wish to achieve this objective we must learn what Africans have already learned: that if you're going to defeat the man, you cannot play the man's game. And the man's game is anti-Communism—and he who practices anti-Communism is playing the man's game. The road to victory is to take away from him his two main weapons. What are these weapons? They are anti-Communism and racism. Wherever you find an anti-Communism you will find a racist. And wherever you find a racist you will find an anti-Communist.

"That is why, together with South Africa you will find U.S. imperialism supporting Israeli aggression. What is their weapon? It is anti-Communism, it is Zionism. And Zionism is imperialism; it is racism.

"That is why you can have a barbarous assault upon the Arab lands. The struggle of the Arab peoples for the mastery of their land and for driving out the aggressors is a just fight and Communists in the U.S. fully support that fight. Therefore to the Zionist occupiers we say—get out and stay out of Arab lands. The struggle of the Arab people is a struggle which is serving the interests of all humanity. That is why today, within Israel itself, among the Jewish masses there is a growing groundswell against the Zionist leadership of Golda Meir, Moshe Dayan and Abba Eban. The struggle of the Jewish people, if supported by us, will grow and the true national spirit among the Jewish masses in Israel will assert itself."

The Anti-Defamation League is disturbed by this. I pick up the *New York Times* and find it taking exception to the thought that "Zionism is imperialism" or "Zionism is racism." I cannot say that I am surprised. The rebuff given by the Arab peoples, more united than ever and supported by all peace-loving people throughout the world, among them the Soviet Union and other socialist countries, helped smash the myth of Israeli military invincibility and also revealed to the bulk of the world's peoples the imperialist essence of Israeli aggression.

I am not surprised at the conscious effort of the Anti-Defamation League to conceal the simple truth that Israel is a capitalist country and that Zionism is a political movement which directs the affairs of the entire state. I am not surprised that the Anti-Defamation League deliberately covers up the false concept of a "chosen people." In point of fact, failure to distinguish between Zionism and Judaism is not accidental at all. Perhaps the Anti-Defamation League, performing the role of all apologists of imperialism, would assert that the racist practices against the Arab peoples in general and the Palestinian Arab people in particular accompanied by the discrimination against the Sephardic Jews, should be regarded as a "civilizing" mission. Is this not a justification of Israeli aggression and a defense of racism?

In point of fact an axis exists between Pretoria and Tel-Aviv in which there is full cooperation on the political, economic and military level. This unity of the white fascist apartheid regime in South Africa with Zionism is explained by Prime Minister Vorster, who said in a speech in Ketmaskhan, Namibia: . . . "We are in solidarity with Israel in its war. . . ." The South African newspaper *Die Burger* was even more precise. It said outright that "from the point of view of South Africa, Israel was guarding the northern gates to Africa, while from the point of view of Israel, South Africa was guarding the continent's southern gates, and so it is in the interests of both that the other side survives."

I do not think that any sincere person should dismiss the meaning of such relationships. Some people have the mission in life of helping to make things palatable to the imperialists, and cannot be bothered by such facts. Naturally they do not agree with me. But in their haste they are tripped by the cleverly peddled falsehoods. Mr. Max Lerner is such a person. For example, in the *New York Post* of December 21, 1973, he writes: "The old Lenin-Hobson theory of imperialism died with the twilight of the imperialism of the 'haves' after world war I" and "In the 1930's and 1940's it was the 'have-not' nations—Italy, Germany, Japan—who turned the tables and had their own imperialist adventure."

It is very easy to see through this deliberate confusion. Present-day events are daily and hourly revealing the profundity and truth of Lenin's teachings on imperialism. Lessons from these teachings are the basis of study and action guiding hundreds of millions of oppressed people on to the highway of struggle which will achieve political and economic independence. These developments are irreversible.

For example, Mr. Lerner does not tell us the simple truth revealed by Lenin that imperialism is capitalism in its highest phase of development. To Mr. Lerner imperialism becomes simply the difference between "have" nations and "have-not" nations, and regards the Rome-Berlin-Tokyo axis as being only "an imperialist adventure."

Let us take Germany alone. Germany was a major imperialist power with colonies, and, locked in battle with other imperialist states during world war I, was stripped of its colonies. The German state never ceased to be an imperialist state even though its struggles with rival imperialist powers resulted in the loss of its colonies. But Mr. Lerner sees Germany only as a "have-not" nation between the first and second world wars.

Why does not Mr. Lerner tell us that behind anti-Communism in general and anti-Sovietism in particular, and more specifically anti-Semitism, was the drive of the German monopolies for *"lebensraum"?* Why does he not tell us that it was the imperialist policies of the Krupps and Thysens which brought us Hitler fascism that outlawed democracy and destroyed all political opposition and the trade union movement, that developed the idea of Nordic superiority to the extreme, that gave us concentration camps and crematoria which took the lives of many millions, including six million Jewish people, and that engulfed the entire world in the second world war. This was a titanic struggle against Hitler's efforts to establish German imperialist dominance and a "thousand-year regime" of Aryan terror.

Mr. Lerner fails to tell us that the most significant event in human history occurred when, in October, 1917, the working class and peasantry of Russia, led by the Bolshevik Party under Lenin achieved power and detached from the system of imperialism 160 million people. Nor does he tell us that in 1922 this victory of the Russian working class and its allies was followed by the founding of the Union of Soviet Socialist Republics—an expression in life of the equality of formerly oppressed nations and peoples.

Thus, when the Nazis launched war against the Soviet Union there emerged a courage, heroism and fighting spirit unequaled in all human history. This role played by the Soviet people was an integral part of the struggle of democratic and peace loving peoples in all lands and of bourgeois-democratic governments opposed to fascism.

The lives of some 20 million Soviet people were lost in this struggle. If democracy is still alive in many lands, if the struggles for national independence in Africa, Asia and Latin America are advancing, this is primarily due to the decisive role played by the Soviet Union in this epic struggle against imperialism. This is a lesson which should never be forgotten. I say that not only because I feel that world humanity owes a debt to the Soviet Union which can never be fully repaid, but also because of the urgent requirements of the moment in helping to build a movement for detente and peaceful coexistence, and for support to all movements of national liberation. Such a cause is not helped when it is declared that the teaching of Lenin on imperialism is "dead."

Mr. Lerner's notion about imperialism being a matter of "have" and "have-not" nations makes it possible for him to write this nonsense: "With the ending of World War II it was the Russians who spread their wings and became the imperialist power in the whole of Eastern Europe, and then with Vietnam it was the U.S. which tried the role." Mr. Lerner is developing notions exactly like those of the CIA, the ultra-Right and all forces of imperialism, especially U.S. imperialism, which is the top dog in the system of world imperialism. He erases with a stroke of the pen the tremendous contributions of the Soviet Union, an achievement made possible by the Soviet people under the leadership of the CPSU and based on the teachings of the great Lenin.

Mr. Lerner is a learned man, and the fact that he writes about "Russia" is not accidental. Thereby he does two things at once. On the one hand he conceals the splendid achievement in the sphere of equality among peoples magnificently growing and developing in a period of Communist construction. On the other hand he conceals the contribution of this great union of peoples to the liberating underground democratic, anti-fascist struggles in such countries as Estonia, Latvia, Lithuania, Poland, Hungary, Czechoslovakia, the German Democratic Republic, Yugoslavia and Albania. These struggles successfully put an end to fascist dictatorship in these countries, making it possible for them, for the first time in their history, to have stable borders and a full national development of their economic, social and cultural life.

Everyone is acquainted with Mr. Lerner's anti-Communism. But new millions will quickly become acquainted with his falsification of the role of the Soviet Union, and will understand that he needs such falsification to justify his apologies for imperialism.

He would have us believe, for example, that the defeat delivered to U.S. imperialism in Vietnam, first of all by the courageous and heroic people of Vietnam, together with the Soviet Union and other socialist countries, as well as the peace-loving people throughout the world, including the people of the U.S., has put an end to what he calls "the adventure" of these imperialists who, in Vietnam, "tried the role."

Mr. Lerner needs this manipulation of logic in order to make it difficult to notice an unpardonable racist sin. His "have" and "have-not" concepts are used to sustain the specious thesis which states: "It is the Arabs who are the "haves," when it comes to their rich crucial oil supply, and it is the Western states which are the "have-nots." Mr. Lerner goes on to say that "the true imperialism today is no longer Western capitalist imperialism, but Arab oil imperialism."

To Mr. Lerner, U.S. imperialism is no longer imperialism. It is simply a democracy. The class nature of this democracy, the existence of state monopoly capitalism, the existence of brutal class, national and racial oppression, the economic controls of U.S. imperialism in Arab lands and their unity with reactionary capitalists and land-owners—all this is not even mentioned. Nor is the just struggle of the Arab peoples for control of their own resources and the use of oil to advance the fight for their national rights—the rights to determine their own lives and the nature of their relations with other states, and to stop the flow of their riches to foreign banks. It is a struggle in which victory can come about only on the basis of the ousting of foreign imperialism. The Arab states will become "have" states only when they become the masters of their lands in all aspects of life. This is the nature of the struggle now. Mr. Lerner, turning logic upside down, calls this "Arab oil imperialism."

Mr. Lerner is angered at such a just struggle. After all this kind of struggle is injurious to his imperialist masters.

That is why it is difficult for Mr. Lerner to restrain himself. He issues a warning to these people fighting imperialism. He writes: "But let them too beware. For they are compelling the disunited West to close ranks in order to meet the threat. The Kissinger idea of a joint crash program of America and Europe, to develop new oil and energy resources, is a handwriting the Arabs should heed. If pre-industrial nations start playing with technology as a political weapon, it is not they but the technological countries who will end the game."

This voice reflects the iron-fist policy of U.S. imperialism and Zionism in support of Israeli aggression. This policy has the aim if strengthening and extending U.S. imperialist influence in the Middle East, establishing military bases there to dominate this area, including the whole of the Mediterranean. This policy also has as its aim slowing down and undermining, with the hope of ultimately destroying the movement for national independence and ouster of imperialism. At the same time, the aim is to create bases of operation directed against the Soviet Union.

Mr. Lerner's "have" and "have-not" concepts are related to these imperialist objectives. It must be made plain that great dangers are involved in the continued occupation of Arab lands. The implementation of UN Resolution 242 must be speeded.

The millions of Jewish masses must come to understand that such concepts as those of Mr. Lerner are knocking at the door of war, not peace. Let us not forget Charles A. Lindberg's propaganda about the so-called "Asiatic hordes" during the second world war. This does not differ in essence from Max Lerner's propaganda about so-called "Arab blackmail" and "Arab oil imperialism," in relation to the dangers of a third world war.

The magazine *Jewish Affairs* is making a very fine contribution to an understanding of this question. It must be built—it must constantly grow—and it must help to bring light to Jewish masses in these troubled times.

So I wish to greet this magazine once more, and to wish it new and greater successes.

7

ZIONISM: IS IT RACIST?*

HYMAN LUMER

On October 17 the Social, Humanitarian and Cultural Commission of the UN General Assembly adopted a resolution declaring that "Zionism is a form of racism and racial discrimination." Needless to say, this action evoked a flood of angry protests from the Zionists and their supporters.

Typical of these reactions are the following:

An ad in *The New York Times* (November 2), by the Zionist Organization of America, says, in part:

> Who is it that presumes to sit in judgment on Zionism? International conspirators, oppressors, dictators, terrorists and murderers . . .
> Free mankind esteems Zionism as one of the noblest liberation movements of modern history.
> Zionism is synonymous with Judaism. An attack on Zionism is an attack on the Jewish people.
> Zionism built and sustains the state of Israel, the only democracy in the Middle East. . . .
> Zionism inspired subjected peoples in Africa and Asia to free themselves from colonialism.

Abba Eban, in an article in *The New York Times* (November 3), charged that the UN "is on the way to becoming the world center of anti-Semitism" and stated that "Hitler himself would have felt at home in a forum which gave applause to a gun-toting Yasir Arafat and an obsequious ovation to the murderous Idi Amin." He charged a

"Moslem-Communist coalition" with seeking to defame Zionism—"an ideology, a historic doctrine and a spiritual faith endorsed by the United Nations itself 28 years ago."

Vernon E. Jordan, Jr., executive director of the National Urban League, wrote in a letter to *The Times* (November 5):

> I am appalled at the grotesque attempt to equate Zionism and racism in the draft resolution . . . Zionism is the national liberation movement of the Jewish people, seeking exactly what other national movements seek: statehood and self-determination. The attack upon Zionism amounts to the grossest form of anti-Semitism, since it is clear that the term Zionism is used by its opponents as a code word for Judaism and Jews."

The *AFL-CIO News* reacted on November 1 with an editorial statement saying that "the United Nations General Assembly faces one of the gravest challenges in its 30-year history . . . the question of whether it will officially endorse anti-Semitism."

Statements of condemnation were issued by a number of groups of academic figures, professionals, public officials and others. In addition, virtually the whole House of Representatives and the entire Senate endorsed a resolution declaring that the UN resolution "wrongfully equates Zionism with racism and racial discrimination.:" In short, a campaign of unprecedented proportions was already developing.

When, on November 10, the resolution submitted by the committee was adopted by the entire General Assembly (72 to 35, with 32 abstentions), the floodgates were opened wide. The anger and outrage of the pro-Zionist forces knew no bounds, and they could scarcely find language strong enough to express these sentiments.

The Israeli UN representative, Chaim Herzog, melodramatically tore up a copy of the resolution on the podium and charged that the UN was on the way to becoming a world center of anti-Semitism. Others spoke of it as an obscenity, a curse and an abomination. The question was raised in a number of areas whether the U.S. should continue its adherence to the UN. A resolution introduced in the U.S. Senate called for "hearings immediately to reassess the United States' further participation in the United Nations General Assembly." A mass demonstration in New York City's garment center on November 11 served further to whip up the anti-UN hysteria. The communications media and numerous organizations and public figures have added their voices to the outcry that the UN is being converted by a "Communist-Arab bloc" into an organ of anti-Semitism.

Much more could be said about the current wave of hysteria, but the foregoing will suffice to demonstrate the ability of the Zionists and their supporters to stand truth on its head and, with the help of the ruling class, to portray Zionism as a great liberating movement. But this picture is utterly false.

To begin with, Zionism is not in any sense "the national liberation movement of the Jewish people." The fountainhead of national and racial oppression is imperialism, and real national liberation movements are by their very nature anti-imperialist. How, then, are we to explain a "liberation movement" which has based itself from the outset on alliance with the forces of imperialism, and which is today a vassal of U.S. imperialism?

From whom are the Jewish people to be liberated? Is it from the Arab peoples, and particularly the Palestinian Arabs, themselves struggling for their own liberation? Are these the real oppressors of the Jewish people?

And not least, is it not a strange liberation movement which numbers among its chief supporters the forces of political reaction in this country and counts among the leading "friends of Israel" such right-wing racists and anti-Semites as the Buckleys, the Reagans, and now the disgusting racist Moynihan, who has been elevated to the status of a national hero?

To term such a movement, associated with the world forces of imperialist reaction, racism and fascism (note, among other things, the Meir regime's recognition of the former puppet Thieu government in Vietnam, also the present close ties of the Israeli government with the fascist Chilean junta and with the bestial apartheid regime in South Africa), a movement of national liberation is sheer mockery.

Equally false is the claim that branding Zionism as racist is *ipso facto* a form of anti-Semitism, since Zionism and Judaism are allegedly identical. This piece of sophistry is most clearly expressed in the above-cited *Times* article by Abba Eban. He says: "There is, of course, no difference whatever between anti-Semitism and the denial of Israel's statehood. Classical anti-Semitism denies the equal rights of Jews as citizens within society. Anti-Zionism denies the equal rights of the Jewish people to its lawful sovereignty within the community of nations. The common principle in the two cases is discrimination."

This is a fraudulent presentation of the issue. First of all the question is not the "denial of Israel's statehood." Virtually all of the countries which voted for the resolution do not deny this right. In particular, the Soviet Union has expressed itself very clearly on this point. In his address to the World Congress of Peace Forces in Moscow in October 1973, Leonid Brezhnev stated: "Our firm stand is that all the states and peoples of the Middle East—I repeat, all of them—must be assured of peace, security and inviolability of borders. The Soviet Union is prepared to take part in the relevant guarantees."

This position has been repeatedly stated. Yet the Soviet leadership is and always has been totally opposed to Zionism and the policies flowing from it.

Zionism cannot be made synonymous with Judaism and the welfare of the Jewish people. On the contrary, it is a reactionary nationalist ideology which is hostile to their interests.

It is inherently a racist ideology which gives rise to racist practices. The Communist Party of Israel, in its theses for its 17th Congress, states:

> Zionist ideology is reactionary because its point of departure is nationalist, racist. Zionism claims that the solution of the Jewish question, the liberation of the Jews from persecution and from anti-Semitism, lies in their leaving the countries in which they live and in their immigration to Israel. Thereby it ignores the capitalist class roots of anti-Semitism and denies the sole correct and realistic solution, which is the change of regime and the triumph of democracy and socialism. This theory is racist because it assumes a priori that under no regime can members of different peoples live in brotherhood and friendship and that this is valid in particular for the Jews. This is a sort of inverse anti-Semitic doctrine. The Zionist ideologues attribute to members of other peoples, to non-Jews, because of their not being Jews, the same characteristics which the anti-Semites attribute to Jews because of their being Jews. The two theories, Zionism as well as anti-Semitism, have one origin: racialism; and their aim is division between the workers of different peoples to the satisfaction of the class enemy. (Information Bulletin, CPI, Special Number, 1972)

Accordingly, the Zionists conceive of the State of Israel not as a state in which Jews and Arabs live together in equality and friendship but as one designed to serve exclusively the interests of the Jews, who hold a privileged position by law in all aspects of life. The Arabs are looked upon as an impediment, as a fifth column, at best to be tolerated and kept under strict control, and where possible to be gotten rid of. The result is a society permeated with racist practices and attitudes, whose source is the ideology of Zionism.

Space forbids a detailed account of this racism. We can present only a few examples. But these will suffice to show beyond question that Zionism is truly a racist ideology. First, it should be noted that whereas any Jew anywhere in the world is given the privilege of migrating to Israel and claiming all the privileges of Israeli citizenship, no such rights are granted to Arabs, including the more than a million refugees who were driven or fled from Israel and the occupied territories, even though they and their ancestors may have lived there for centuries.

Second, with the establishment of the State of Israel the British emergency regulations of 1945 were removed for Jews but not for Arabs. Among other things these permitted the closing off of areas of land on grounds of "security" and forbidding their former residents to re-enter. Many of these have become "internal refugees," living in shacks in nearby villages, while others have found their way into crowded slum ghettos in the cities.

Israeli law permits the expropriation of land also for cultivation, development and construction. This has been used as a device for dispersing the Arab population, concentrated in the Galilee, in which the Jews now constitute 45% of the total population. In the fifties and sixties, large areas of land were requisitioned adjacent to Nazareth, a totally Arab city, and a modern all-Jewish suburb, Upper Nazareth, was constructed. It is now larger than Nazareth itself. Other Jewish towns were similarly constructed in the area. Now a new wave of requisitioning is developing whose ultimate objective, according to Arab leaders, is the taking over of some 15–20,000 acres, with the aim of creating a Jewish majority.

Altogether, more than half the land belonging to Arabs has been expropriated. To be sure, compensation is frequently offered but the amounts are grossly inadequate. Moreover, all this has been done by compulsion, regardless of the wishes of the Arabs concerned.

Third, the Israeli Arabs suffer severe discrimination in all spheres of life. The annual incomes of Arab families are less than two-thirds of those of Jewish families, even though the number of earners per Arab family is larger. Only half of the Arab workers are members of the Histadrut (to which they were first admitted only in 1957) compared to three-fourths of the Jewish workers. And only one-third are members of the Health Insurance Fund as against 72% of the Jewish workers. Moreover, the Fund has few clinics in Arab villages, hence the service received by Arab members is far inferior to that received by the Jewish members.

Arab farmers are discriminated against by the government in the granting of credits, in providing irrigation and in assistance with mechanization. Many Arab villages are not yet provided with electricity.

There is gross discrimination in education. Arab schools receive far less in the way of funds, facilities and teacher training than do the Jewish schools. To cite but one illustration, Shulamit Aloni, Member of the Knesset, quotes a letter from the head of a Bedouin settlement in Galili, who describes "a school for four hundred pupils that lacks all services and water. (The lack of water still exists, even though inhabitants paid long ago for connections to waterlines that have not yet been made.) Is there any Jewish settlement, even the newest, without such school services and without water?" (*Yediot Aharonot,* October 10, 1975.)

While Arabs comprise 12% of the population, they constitute only 1.5% of the student body of institutions of higher learning. The small number who graduate find it almost impossible to obtain employment in their professions, and from some professions Arabs are completely barred as "security risks."

Nor is such discrimination confined to the Arab population. It is visited also upon the darker-skinned Oriental Jews who make up well over 60% of Israel's population. They are confined to the lowest-paying jobs; they are packed into crumbling "old city" ghettos; they suffer the same educational disabilities as Arabs; and they are subjected to all sorts of indignities and insults.

Especially outrageous is the treatment of the Arab people in the occupied territories, which has been repeatedly condemned in the UN as well as by the World Peace Council and other bodies. Here people are denied all democratic rights. Instead of abiding by the Geneva Conventions the Israeli Occupation authorities have applied the infamous British emergency regulation of 1945. They have outlawed all forms of political action and organization. They have instituted administrative arrests with no charges, no trial, and no definite period of imprisonment. They have resorted to collective punishments such as imposing endless curfews, blowing up houses of people suspected of aiding Arab guerrillas, and they have engaged in the widespread use of torture. They have driven additional scores of thousands of refugees from these territories and have summarily deported many leading public figures without charges or trial.

At the same time, a process of "creeping annexation" is taking place, with the establishment of growing numbers of Jewish settlements in the occupied territories, the aim being to annex these territories to Israel through a succession of "accomplished facts." And this is justified in the name of the historical right of the Jews to all of Palestine.

The foregoing is of necessity an abbreviated account of the racial and national oppression in Israel. . . . Nevertheless, it is enough to show beyond question the racist character of the present State of Israel and its oppression of other peoples, stemming from the principles of Zionism by which its policies are guided.

The racist character of Zionism is shown also by the conduct of Zionists elsewhere. Thus, in South Africa the Zionist organizations are staunch supporters of the apartheid regime. In the United States, the racist influence of Zionism is evident in the support of leading Jewish organizations to Shankerism, in their campaigns against preferential hiring and open admission, in their attacks on so-called "Black anti-Semitism," in their alliance with reactionary, racist political figures and in other ways.

The essence of Zionism is the thesis that the interests of the Jewish people are opposed to those of non-Jews, and from this arises the concept of an exclusively Jewish state in which Arabs are to be repressed or driven out. But the maxim that those who oppress others cannot themselves be free still holds good, and the inescapable fact is that the Jewish people cannot solve their problems at the expense of others. The insecurity of the State of Israel alone amply demonstrates this.

Zionism holds no future for the Jewish people. It is, on the contrary, their worst enemy. It can only serve to isolate them from their real allies—the working class and national liberation forces—and to place them at the mercy of the forces of imperialist reaction, the very source of racism and anti-Semitism. For the Israeli Jews it can lead only to ultimate catastrophe.

Zionism sees Israel as the state of all Jews everywhere who supposedly constitute a single nation. And when people like Abba Eban speak of the right of self-determination they refer not only to the people of Israel but to the totality of Jews on a world scale.

But by no means do all Jews accept these ideas. On the contrary, the great majority reject the concept that they are members of a world Jewish nation and that their homeland is Israel. They view themselves rather as citizens of the countries in which they live and the fight for liberation as a fight for full equality with all other citizens and against all anti-Semitic discrimination. This struggle, in alliance with the struggles of the working class and all oppressed peoples, is part of the anti-monopoly movement, and ultimately of the movement for socialism.

This is how, the slanders of its Zionist enemies notwithstanding, the Jewish question was resolved in the Soviet Union and other socialist countries and this is the path to its solution in the United States.

In Israel, support of Zionism is by no means unanimous. The Communist Party has always opposed it, together with other sectors of the left. Among these is Uri Avneri, editor of the widely read weekly *Haolam Hazeh*, and author of a book entitled *Israel Without Zionists*. A growing section of Israeli youth, despite intense indoctrination, is beginning to question the validity of Zionism.

Zionism cannot claim to speak for the Jewish people as a whole. It has few supporters in the Soviet Union, and in this country most Jewish people are not Zionists but are motivated by a sympathy and concern for Israel as a country of fellow Jews and a desire to assist and support it as such. It is these sentiments which the Zionists seek to pervert for their own ends.

To recognize Zionism as a form of fascism is not an expression of anti-Semitism. On the contrary, those countries which supported the UN resolution have performed a service to the struggle against racism in general and the Zionist poison in particular.

The right of the Israeli people to self-determination must be defended. But so must the rights of the Palestinian Arab people and all other peoples. Only by abandoning the reactionary, racist line of Zionism and by fighting side by side with all workers and oppressed peoples can the Jewish people truly serve their own best interests.

8

RETHINKING ON ISRAEL*

LEWIS M. MOROZE

The unprovoked invasion of Lebanon, referred to as "The Longest War," by Jacobo Timerman, breached both its time and geographic limits. Victory was to come in four days. Five months later the Israeli aggressors are preparing to winter in Lebanon alongside U.S. forces. The 25 kilometer limit was breached upon receiving the signal from the U.S. when it vetoed the U.N. Resolution calling for the withdrawal of the Israeli forces from Lebanon. The murderous march on to Beirut was protected by the U.S. fleet hugging the shore line.

The blood-letting continues as the war enters its sixth month. The enormous costs of the aggressive and annexationist policies of the Begin-Sharon-Eytan junta has deepened the economic crisis in Israel. Arrogantly the Israeli ruling circles are demanding larger grants from the U.S. for carrying out U.S. policy in the Middle East. El Al may be closed down rather than meet the demands of the workers and recently a half million public workers went out on strike.

As surrogate of the U.S. administration in the Middle East, the Begin-Likud government, is pursuing its plan to dismember Lebanon and is preparing for an attack upon the anti-imperialist government of Syria. U.S. economic and military aid continues to flow to the aggressors while poverty stalks our land as U.S. ruling circles strengthen their position for grabbing the natural resources of the Middle East.

The Israeli Commission of Inquiry is exposed for what it is, an in-house inquiry uninterested in and incapable of guaranteeing that the perpetrators of the Beirut massacres are brought to justice. Begin and Sharon are handled gingerly, being notified that they may face a

*From *Jewish Affairs*, Nov/Dec 1982

charge of "non-fulfillment of duty." Begin and Sharon have already defied the Commission of Inquiry by refusing to submit themselves to further interrogation. Raful Eytan and General Yaron were notified that they may face charges of "breach of duty." The ruling circles contempt for the Commission is underscored by brazenly arranging for the butcher of Beirut, Sharon, to go to Honduras to arrange for the sale of arms to massacre the Nicaraguan people and bring down the anti-imperialist government of Nicaragua for their U.S. imperialist masters. Foreign Minister Shamir went to Zaire to buttress the repressive Mobuto regime.

The Commission of Inquiry called no representatives of the Lebanese and Palestinian victims of the massacres while the Commission of Inquiry is fully aware of the fact that the Israeli Intelligence Agency, Mossad, was serving as liaison at the Phalangist headquarters during the massacre. It was an Israeli intelligence officer, General Drorin, who revealed this damning fact.

It is patently clear that only an international tribunal similar to the one that conducted the Nuremburg Trials can bring forth the truth and bring the guilty to the bar of justice.

The Palestinian people are more determined than ever to establish a Palestinian State and the prestige of the P.L.O. has grown throughout the world though the aim of the war was to destroy once and for all the P.L.O. and, thereby, put an end to the demand for an independent Palestinian State. Most recently the Arab League delegation, including a representative of the P.L.O. met with the permanent members of the Security Council. Only Britain and the U.S. refused to talk with the delegation in the presence of the P.L.O.

It was the historic opposition to the war by the 400,000 Israelis under the banner of Peace Now that electrified the world. The peace sentiment of the Israeli people had a profound impact on the Jewish community in the U.S. About three and a half years ago, "Breira," the organization championing an alternative program for the solution of the Middle East Crisis, was smashed by the Jewish establishment. But the search for an organizational base to differ from and oppose the Jewish establishment position and to break its hold on the Jewish community brought forth New Jewish Agenda, a vibrant organization of young Jewish men and women who are making significant contributions in their persistent struggle for a just and lasting peace in the Middle East, for world peace, against racism and for economic democracy at home.

202 Rethinking on Israel

Prior to the war, the eminent U.S. Jewish leader, Philip Klutznick, was attacked and maligned by the Jewish establishment for his determined efforts to bring about peace in the Middle East by calling for negotiations with the P.L.O. After the invasion and the massacres at Shatilla and Sabra Camps, Klutznick was invited to speak at a prestigious Chicago Synagogue on: "Dissent in the Jewish Community."

The aggressive war has caused much agonizing in the Jewish community in the U.S. and reappraisals of readily accepted Zionist positions. Rethinking is going on in top circles as well as amongst the masses of U.S. Jewry.

Rabbi Alexander Schindler, head of Reform Jewry's Union of American Hebrew Congregations called on U.S. Jewry "to affirm our own identity" apart from Israel. Rabbi Schindler is currently deeply troubled by the Jewish establishment's equation: "Judaism equals Zionism equals Israel." This equation is one of long standing. On November 2, 1975 the Zionist Organization of America, in an ad in the *N.Y. Times* made a vitriolic attack on the nations approving the U.N. Resolution declaring "Zionism is a form of racism and racial discrimination."

Inter alia, the ad says: "Who is it that presumes to sit in judgement on Zionism? International conspirators, oppressors, dictators, terrorists and murderers. . . . Zionism is synonymous with Judaism. An attack on Zionism is an attack on the Jewish people." It is a matter of fact that many anti-Semites equate Zionism and Judaism basing their positions on the writings of Zionist theoreticians and writers.

In 1973 in his work, "Imperialism Today," Gus Hall, General Secretary of the C.P.U.S.A. observed:

> Both from circles within the Jewish movement, and from non-Jewish ultra-right groups there is a drive to make Zionism, bourgeois nationalism, national pride and the Jewish religion one thing. For the ultra-right it is an instrument of anti-Semitism.

Rabbi Schindler, referring to the equation mentioned above called it "sloppy." This equation is not merely "sloppy," it is deadly, having played havoc in the Jewish community and in the peace movements. Elaboration on his call to U.S. Jewry "to affirm our own identity," Rabbi Schindler observed that: "The weak, the helpless cry for relief. Will we heed them or block our ears so long as we see President Reagan's benign smile when he speaks of Israel?"

Rabbi Schindler called for closer ties with the poor especially because of the Reagan Administration's decision "to multiply missiles rather than to mitigate human misery." Continuing, Rabbi Schindler made the observation that "We do ourselves irreparable harm when we permit our Jewishness to consist almost entirely of a vicarious participation in the life of the State (of Israel)." This type of rethinking will lead to even deeper probing by U.S. Jewry.

For all who consider Zionism a national liberation movement there is need for reflection on the characteristics of such a movement. In probing to make an accurate and scientific assessment of a trend or political movement that describes itself as national, as do the Zionists, one must assess the relation of this movement and its ideological underpinnings to the struggles of the peoples throughout the globe against imperialism and its allies. Further to be probed is the aid and assistance rendered to such movement by the democratic, liberating forces from around the world. This is the measuring rod to be applied in the assessment of Zionism and its ideology, piercing through the various and sundry demagogic mouthings of the Zionist hierarchy.

In 1974 Emile Touma, a leading member of the Communist Party of Israel, stated that: "The crisis of Zionism concerns strategy, not tactics. It is the basic Zionist ideological concepts that are involved, not this tactic or that; and because Zionism, like other capitalist reactionary ideologies, cannot change their nature or characteristics, the present crisis will deepen and envelope Zionism ultimately."

Many who have been misled by Zionist demagogy are, nevertheless to be found involved in many democratic movements involving domestic and foreign policy issues. In 1972 Wolf Ehrlich, a member of the Central Committee of the Communist Party of Israel stated in an article: "He who opposes imperialism, conquests, dependence upon foreign capital, fascism, reaction and capitalist, all together or any one of them, is already an inconsistent Zionist. He may still sincerely believe in certain theses of Zionism. He may believe that he is still a Zionist, but he is no longer a prisoner of all its tenets and no longer a supporter of all Zionist practices. A process of emancipation from Zionism has begun in people like that, even if they do not themselves understand it and even if they object with all their might to such a statement."

Since the war in Lebanon, the differentiation is proceeding at a more rapid pace than in the '70's. At a gathering of the American Jewish Congress to honor Felix G. Rohatyn, Chairman of the Municipal Assistance Corp of N.Y.C. and Victor H. Gotbaum, Executive

Director of District Council 37 of the A.F.S.C.M.E., both honorees addressed themselves to the role of Israel and the relationship between Israel and the U.S. Jewish community.

Rohatyn asserted that "Many Jews critical of the policy of the Israeli government . . . were pressed into that position by explicit suggestions of Israeli officials and Jewish leaders that such criticism played into the hands of Israel's enemies and ultimately fostered anti-Semitism . . . Such silence was a disservice to Israel." This lesson is yet to be learned by Howard Squadron, President of the American Jewish Congress.

Victor Gotbaum, in his remarks noted that "If we want the right to be Jews, we must recognize the Palestinians." Rohatyn disclosed that Gotbaum and himself "had been agonizing over our feelings on the issue." Hopefully Gotbaum will follow up his thinking with the mobilization of trade unionists into the campaign for a just and lasting peace in the Middle East.

On the TV program, "60 Minutes," Jacobo Timerman sharply condemned the brutal practices of the Israeli armed forces and the chauvinist and racist practices of the Israeli government. The depth of his feeling was expressed in his exclamation, "I am a Jew, not an Israeli!" It is during this period of rethinking and much agonizing that that 30th World Zionist Congress is taking place (Dec. 7–16, 1982). It is being held in Jerusalem and its opening was attended by great turbulence. The Congress was postponed more than once. There was serious question as to whether it would take place at all. Emergency steps had to be taken by the W.Z.O. Executive to make this possible.

The Zionist Organization of America, announcing that it was reluctant to spend the necessary funds to conduct an election for delegates, caused panic in the W.Z.O. leadership. We must recall that the 1976 Congress was delayed until 1978. This was a reflection of its waning influence said the Israeli journalist, Boas Evron of *Yediot Ahronot.*

It was no wonder then that Arye Dulzin, Executive Chairman of the W.Z.O., as late as November 22, 1982, observed that it was "unimaginable" that the Congress could take place without the U.S. delegation. To guarantee U.S. participation Dulzin invoked a "temporary provision" in the W.Z.O. by-laws permitting the W.Z.O. Executive to ask the High Court of the 30th World Zionist Congress to allocate U.S. delegates without elections. This provision has been employed only in those rare cases when countries were in distress making it impossible to conduct elections.

Well, there is great distress in the U.S.—widespread agonizing and rethinking with growing questioning of Zionist practices and Zionism itself. The Congress, including the U.S. delegation created in Jerusalem, will have to come to grips with the current scene.

As we go to press the WZO Congress voted to condemn the Israeli government for establishing settlements in the occupied territories. Chairman Dulzin overruled the body declaring Zionists must not criticize any Israeli government. The session broke up in pandemonium.

In Jewish establishment circles there is still a clinging to rigid positions but here too the truth will out. At a meeting of the General Assembly of the N.Y. Jewish Community Relations Council held on November 29 it was revealed that they had launched a campaign against the outstanding TV program, "Like It Is," conducted by Gil Noble, outstanding Black TV producer. The reason for the attack was a report by two leading Black leaders on their trip to the Middle East. Their highly objective report was not to the liking of the JCRC leadership. As a result of the pressure, Gil Noble interviewed two Black leaders who were sent to the Middle East by the Jewish establishment. The Zionist press has been levelling bitter attacks on the Black media for daring to be critical of Israeli policy. Instead of racist attacks on the Gil Noble program, there should be a mass call by all democratic forces for putting it on a nationwide hook-up precisely because it is such an outstanding program.

At this same meeting of the NYCRC an appeal was made for mass pressure on Reagan and the Congress to increase economic and military aid to Israel and that the aid should be in the form of grants since such aid "benefits the U.S." as much as it does Israel.

"The Zionist Dimension" was also discussed at this gathering. Professor Steven M. Cohen, commissioned to undertake an extensive study of the Jewish community in the U.S., reported that "American Jews are not Zionists. American Jews reject classic Zionist doctrines." The survey revealed that only 12% accepted, in theory, the concept of Aliyah (the migration to Israel of Jews from around the world) and that over 66% felt secure living in the U.S. where "there is a bright future for American Jews." Such findings are in agreement with a position taken by the Economic and Social Commission of the World Jewish Congress in January of 1981 and are in sharp contrast and contradiction to the Zionist tenet that there is no future for Jews anywhere outside of Israel, in the so-called "diaspora."

Arye Dulzin announced that among his objectives at the 30th World Zionist Congress is to call for the establishment of a mass Aliyah movement, placing at the top of "diaspora communities" priorities "ensuring a Zionist orientation" in light of his finding that "the Zionist organization has become increasingly weak, from year to year and losing its leading role in the diaspora." Dulzin's approach, if adopted, will make the W.Z.O. more of an appendage of the Israeli ruling class and divorce it further from the Jewish people around the world, presaging further decline and the onset of the twilight of Zionism.

The reassessment now going on in the Jewish community and in peace movements has resulted in National SANE issuing a position paper on the Middle East. Over the years SANE has made significant contributions in the struggle for disarmament and world peace. For years it has remained tongue-tied and impotent on the question of the Middle East due to Zionist generated pressures. In light of the invasion of Lebanon by Israel, SANE issued their position paper in September. This is a welcome development. It carefully notes that the Middle East crisis could trigger a world nuclear holocaust. SANE, over the years has informed its membership that it is the U.S. that has caused the proliferation of nuclear weaponry and heated up the arms race. The position paper is seriously weakened by the statement that "the governments of the U.S. and the Soviet Union fuel the confrontation and military escalation" in the Middle East, calling on both to stop the arms race. Surely SANE leadership is aware that the U.S.S.R. borders on the Middle East and not the U.S. but it is U.S. Rapid Deployment Forces that are now stationed in Egypt, Lebanon and in the Persian Gulf States and not troops of the U.S.S.R.

The U.S. and the U.S.S.R. are Co-Chair of the International Conference for a Lasting Peace in the Middle East. The U.S. has violated the agreements establishing the Conference. While the U.S.S.R. has persistently called upon the U.S. to convene the Conference, the U.S. has consistently turned a deaf ear to that call. The U.S. has, at the same time, rejected a call from the U.S.S.R. to make the Middle East a nuclear free zone.

Advocates of peace in the Middle East must face reality: yielding to anti-Sovietism in the guise of even-handedness is self-defeating. Temporizing will only encourage the aggressive forces in the U.S. and the Begin-Sharon-Eytan junta now ruling Israel.

The new situation means new and greater possibilities for success in calling for a just and lasting peace in the Middle East. Essential components of such a call include: (a) no U.S. economic or military aid to Israel, (b) withdrawal of Israeli troops from Lebanon; (c) removal of U.S. troops from Lebanon; (d) recognition of the P.L.O. and the reconvening of the International Conference with participation of all parties in the area including the P.L.O., the sole legitimate representative of the Palestinian people.

9

REAGAN, BEGIN AND THE REAL
INTERESTS
OF THE
JEWISH PEOPLE*

HERBERT APTHEKER

Major organizations of Jewish people in the United States are dominated by an extremely wealthy elite. This leadership is ultra-nationalist; it supports the expansionist, occupationist and brutal policies of Begin, and the imperialist, counter-revolutionary and war-threatening policies of Reagan. Since reaction and racism are twins, the Begin-Reagan vaudeville act is permeated with chauvinism. One may say with confidence that the Reagan Administration is the most racist in U.S. history since that of Buchanan.

Recently there has been published (by a subsidiary of the Hearst Corporation) an authoritative book-length statement of this leadership's policy. Its title is *The Real Anti-Semitism in America* (Arbor House, N.Y., 1982, $15.50). Its chief author* is Nathan Perlmutter, presently National Director of the Anti-Defamation League of B'nai B'rith, formerly Associate National Director of the American Jewish Committee and a Vice-President of Brandeis University.

Mr. Perlmutter and his class brothers insist that their pro-Begin, pro-Reagan stance is necessary to the well-being of Jews in the United States and to the security of Israel. Further, with unabashed ethno-centrism, our author emphasizes that that well-being and that security are his fundamental, if not sole, consideration. Indeed, this line explains the book's title; Mr. Perlmutter means—and in the foreword explicitly states—that old fashioned, "crude," anti-Semitism does not seriously threaten Jews, or Israel, today; rather, certain policies constitute that threat. They are: affirmative action, the present peace

*From *Jewish Affairs*, July/Aug 1983.
**Ruth Ann Perlmutter is given as junior author, but almost the entire book is written in the first person, that of Nathan Perlmutter.

movement and its anti-nuclear weapons emphasis, and its "depreciation of military preparedness."

Perlmutter feels that "the preference Jews have manifested for the political Left over the Right requires reconsideration" and that "nowadays war is getting a bad name and peace too favorable a press." Like General Haig, Perlmutter is sure that war may be preferable to peace; like President Reagan he would rather see the children of the world dead than living in a globe whose politics was distasteful to him. Perlmutter demagogically supports his position by reference to World War II. Here, characteristically, what he notes is its relationship to the fate of Jews and not to humanity as a whole; further there is a failure to observe its anti-fascist character.

It is relevant also to observe that Perlmutter, like his Reagan-Kirkpatrick mentors, blames the coming of World War II upon the peace movement which preceded it, and equates it with an appeasement policy which eventuated in Hitler's aggressions. He uses this analogy to support his theme of the alleged danger today flowing from Left policies. But the analysis of the past is as erroneous as his prescriptions for the present. In the first place, the present peace movement seeks to prevent World War III—that would be omnicide, not war. Secondly, Hitler was created, financed and maintained by the world bourgeoisie which saw in his platform the annihilation of socialism in Germany and the destruction of the Soviet Union. Fascism was allowed anything, including the rape of Ethiopia, the crucifixion of Spain, and the swallowing of Austria and Czechoslovakia (as Japanese imperialism was encouraged to swallow China with, again, the understanding that the ultimate target was the U.S.S.R.).

Only the policy of collective security of all anti-and non-fascist Powers—of the Soviet Union and the bourgeois-democracies—could have curbed Hitlerism. That policy was rejected, by the Right; *this* led to World War II, the annihilation of fifty million peoples, including six millions Jews. The democratic, the Left policy finally was implemented, in blood and with the colossal losses noted; but when that policy *was* implemented, fascism was smashed—with the contribution of the U.S.S.R. being decisive. Thus was the human race saved from fascist enslavement.

There is an accurate depiction of the respective roles of Left and Right in the epoch of World War II. The line of opposing the Left and embracing the Right almost did enslave humanity and complete the utter extinction of its Jewish component. Today, that Perlmutter line, if followed to its logical conclusion, namely, Right domination and its offspring, a Third World War, will assure the end of humanity.

* * *

The line of the Right in Israel—the line of Begin, the fascist (as Albert Einstein correctly called him in 1948)—has meant for Israel not security but insecurity, not honor but disgrace, not peace but war. That line has meant over 20,000 dead in Lebanon and 3,000 dead and wounded among Israelis. It has meant Jews in the roles of occupiers, jailers, tormentors of other peoples; it has meant the coming into being of an Israel which is a pariah state, like its ally, the Republic of South Africa. It has meant that tomorrow begins the second year of Begin's "short war" which in May 1983 cost Israel ninety new casualties.

Can you believe that in a book published in September 1982, which is permeated with phrases about the danger to Israel's security, there is absolutely no mention of the "longest war" to ensnare Israel?* Perhaps one can extract something hopeful from this extraordinary fact; possibly Perlmutter omitted this "detail" because he—even he—is ashamed of this particular Begin atrocity? Further, except for repeated denunciations of an alphabetized and dehumanized P.L.O. there is no mention in the book of the Palestinian *people*; apparently Mr. Perlmutter has not discovered them.

The Perlmutter leadership detests liberalism and embraces reaction; it wants the United Nations dissolved, and Reagan's armaments program implemented. Perlmutter reserves his venom for Eugene V. Debs and Che Guevera, for Karl Marx and V.I. Lenin. The forward looking National Council of Christian Churches and the theology of liberation are anathema to him; the fundamentalists from Jerry Falwell to Pat Robertson are embraced. This is the Pat Robertson who in October 1981 (in *Church and State*) insisted that the principle of separation of State and Church reflected "not the Constitution of the United States, but of the U.S.S.R." Robertson advocated a Constitutional amendment "over and above the First Amendment" that would affirm this Republic to be a Christian state. He wrote: "We're the majority

---

*On p. 261, Perlmutter mentions the Israeli bombing of Beirut which cost 800 lives (he omits that, of course). But here he is referring to the attack of July, 1981 and denounces the "hypocrisy of Western protestations" about this bombing of an alleged P.L.O. center "unconscionably situated in residential Beirut"!

. . . Why don't Christians do something? I'm ready to go out in the streets and revolt."

Such "revolutionaries" are all right for Perlmutter; it is the martyred Che Guevera who reminds him of a "Hitlerian hurricane."

To Perlmutter a Black militant and a Ku Kluxer are undifferentiated. He thinks it absurd to distinguish what he calls a Black "brute" from a white one because one is "deprived" and the other is "depraved." With this outlook there is precious little to choose between a bedraggled General Washington and a bespangled Lord Cornwallis, between a John Wilkes Booth and a Nat Turner, between a Jefferson Davis and a John Brown.

Perlmutter's sharpest attacks are reserved for affirmative action; he attacks this at greater length than he does the Soviet Union! His arguments are as stale as they are insipid; he merely repeats the arguments offered by Professor Glazer of Harvard back in 1976.

In a manner more crude and more chauvinist than that manifested by the Harvard scholar, Perlmutter labels affirmative action reverse discrimination when, in fact, it is a way to reverse discrimination. He makes affirmative action the foe of merit when in fact racism is exactly a device for the undercutting of merit. He equates the quota efforts of affirmative action with the anti-Semitic quotas that characterized Czarism (and Ivy League colleges until the end of World War II) when in fact the quotas associated with affirmative action are precisely the *opposite* of the anti-Semitic quotas. The quotas of affirmative action are designed to *permit* entry, not to bar entry, to *open*, not close the gates to a decent education and good employment to all peoples in some equitable proportion to the general population so that decent incomes and homes and educations are realities for all our inhabitants regardless of race or color or religion or gender. That is what really combatting racism requires.

Perlmutter makes racism a matter of the past; he actually insists that it no longer exists! The fact, of course, is that the social order of the United States has been and is absolutely immersed in a racist sewer. Not only does every social index confirm this—from employment to income, from health to education, from housing to police brutality— but the ominous fact is that all such indices of racism have been intensifying during the past decade and especially so with the blatantly racist Reagan Administration.

Perlmutter especially objects to affirmative action's application to *groups* of people rather than to individuals, but of course racism afflicts specific groups. Racism *is* slander directed against designated peoples; racism *is* the special oppression of designated peoples. To seriously tackle racism *requires*, therefore, grappling with and combatting this group reality, by illegalizing the racist practice and instituting a democratic one.

Above all, Perlmutter objects to affirmative action's insistence that the test of its implementation is not a promise and not even a law; the test of its implementation is in *results*—in actual bread and butter, in employment, in income, in education, housing, health, in the quality of life, not the promises of politicians or Harvard professors or *Commentary* editors or Directors of million-dollar organizations. That is the content of the present state of the Afro-American liberation movement. Its achievement and advance are fundamental to the health of U.S. society in general, and that certainly includes the well-being of the Jewish component in that society.

Reaction needs and breeds anti-Semitism. To support reaction is, for Jews in particular and for humanity in general, to court disaster.

Indeed one sees in the present United States, the relationship between a resurgent Right and resurgent anti-Semitism. Perlmutter minimizes what he calls "crude" anti-Semitism, but the data of his own Anti-Defamation League show the following:

Reported Cases, ANTI-JEWISH vandalism and assaults 1978: 49; 1979: 120; 1980: 377; 1981 (latest year for complete figures) 900. This is an increase of about 1800% in four years! Furthermore, the A.D.L. itself reports, as Perlmutter notes, "that only a fraction of such depredations are formally brought to the league's attention." One should add that surveys by the A.D.L. over the years show a decline in the number of convinced anti-Semites in the United States, but its latest announced finding was a total of *seventy millions* of such bigots!

These figures seem to suggest enough "real anti-Semitism in America" to keep so-called Jewish leaders fully occupied without seeking, in addition, to destroy the United Nations, to eliminate affirmative action and to participate in an anti-Soviet crusade!

I have another suggestion to keep such "leaders" fully occupied in vitally important and relevant work. Early this year the Council of Jewish Federations reported that its twenty-two affiliates were swamped with appeals for help from unemployed and impoverished Jews. The Philadelphia Federation of Jewish Agencies, the Chicago Jewish

Federation, the Detroit Jewish Welfare Federation and similar organizations in Cleveland, in Baltimore, and in New Jersey report Jews without roofs over their heads, needing a meal, requiring clothing. Tens of thousands of Jews are newly poor. These federation employees report increased break-ups of marriages, suicides, child abuse, wife beating, and they say these are traceable to unemployment. *

Indeed, such experts believe that there are today in the United States—in Golden America—about one million Jews who are at or near the poverty level—are "Jews Without Money" in the words of our immortal Mike Gold. Perhaps the billions for Reagan's weapons and Begin's bombs might better be used to see to it that Jewish men and women have decent employment and that Jewish children have substantial, healthy meals?

In fact, Mr. Perlmutter, with his obsession against affirmative action, may not know (and certainly if he did know would be loath to publicize) that there exists a Bureau on Jewish Employment which has become especially active lately, thanks to Reaganomics. It is visiting corporate headquarters with the objective of checking out available jobs. This Bureau states that it does not seek quotas, but it *is* seeking out the big corporations which have anti-Semitic employment policies and it *is* threatening them—quietly, so far—with public exposure if they do not add some Jews to their employment rolls!

This Bureau on Jewish Employment demands not promises, not expressions of good will; it demands, Mr. Perlmutter, precisely "results"! (See the column by Peter Waldstein, the *Chicago Jewish Sentinel,* May 12, 1983.)

Permit me to quote a paragraph from my own writings published in *Jewish Affairs* some years ago (May–June 1979):

> Evidence has multiplied during the past fifteen or twenty years of the critical need of a national organization of Jewish men and women who understand the deepest requirements of our society, who understand the relationship between reaction and anti-Semitism and particularly between racist attacks upon colored peoples and anti-Semitism. Such Jewish men and women—steeped in the finest democratic and revolutionary traditions of Jewish masses for centuries—should act now to retrieve the reality of this tradition from the hands of the like of B'nai B'rith and the editors of such disgraces as *Commentary.*

*Data from Jewish Telegraphic Agency report, New York City, in *Jewish Sentinel,* May 19, 1983, pp. 2 and 44.

Happily, we have lived to see action along these lines. Outstanding in this regard has been the creation and very rapid growth of New Jewish Agenda, with its young, fresh leadership, its anti-war emphasis, and its commitment to an anti-racist, progressive outlook. This development is part of a national upsurge of labor militancy, campus stirrings, farmer activism, the women's movement, the inspiring anti-war and anti-nuclear weapons movement. It is part of such stirring events as the election of Harold Washington as Chicago's mayor and the defeat of the racist Rizzo in Philadelphia. These victories, and others, represent the development of a new politics with significant Black-Puerto Rican-Chicano-trade union and progressive unity. It should be observed that in Mr. Washington's victory last April [1983] over 43% of the Jewish voters chose the Black, progressive candidate, though his Republican-Reaganite-racist opponent happened himself to be Jewish.

Mr. Perlmutter's concluding chapter bears a title quoting from one of our Jewish sages: "If I Am Not For Myself . . .". Perlmutter stops his quotation quite abruptly at that point, but the full admonition is: "If I am not for myself, who will be for me?" *And,* it concludes "If I am for myself alone, what am I?"

Yes, it is necessary to speak up for oneself and not to keep silent. But it also is necessary to understand that to speak up only for ourselves, to forget that we are part of all struggling humanity and that our strength lies in unity—to forget this is to forget the teachings of our prophet and to court catastrophe.

Jews in the United States need what all peoples in our nation need: A progressive policy of anti-racism, anti-imperialism, anti-monopoly, anti-war, or, in one phrase, anti-Reaganism.

For equality, for national liberation, for peace, for People before Profits—that is the path for security for Israel, for effectively fighting real anti-Semitism in the United States, for realizing the precious dreams of our Prophets.

10

SETTING THE RECORD STRAIGHT: THE BIG LIE AND THE JEWISH-AMERICAN COMMUNITY*

GUS HALL

Today we are in a sense celebrating three related anniversaries: The 36th anniversary of the State of Israel; the 50th anniversary of Birobidjan, the Jewish Autonomous Region of the Soviet Union; and the 14th anniversary of *Jewish Affairs* magazine.

Considering past history and experience, I will base my remarks on the premise that the masses of Jewish Americans are concerned about and involved in movements, struggles and problems faced by the majority of Americans. They are an integral part of all the movements to defeat Reaganism, to stop the nuclear insanity, to end racism and in the struggles for jobs, peace and equality.

I look back with a sense of pride on my presence at the first discussion about publishing the magazine, *Jewish Affairs*, especially because I was in the company of such leading comrades as Henry Winston, Hy Lumer, Alex Kolkin, Herbert Aptheker, Philip Honor, Jack Kling and Abe Wise. And I am therefore especially honored to be here on this proud day to join in the celebration and recognition of *Jewish Affairs'* consistent contributions to the Jewish-American community in helping to clarify and give direction on some very complex and sensitive questions affecting Jewish national pride and identity. Since the very first issue, *Jewish Affairs* has been a consistent tried and tested voice of truth, a voice of truth against a cascade of slander and lies.

The new magazine was made necessary because most of the institutions and publications dealing with Jewish affairs had become engulfed in the tidal wave of reactionary cold war anti-Sovietism, a wave that was whipped up by the policies of U.S. imperialism worldwide and the

*Address at the 12th Annual *Jewish Affairs* Dinner, June 10, 1984, New York City.

policies of expansion and annexation by the ruling circles of Israel in the Mideast.

Jewish Affairs has established itself as a true voice for peace, an unrelenting fighter against racism, against Reaganomics; a clear voice for human and civil rights, for democracy and against all forms of anti-Semitism. Because *Jewish Affairs* is an advocate and defender the true interests of Israel it has never opportunistically remained silent. Nor has it distorted the truth when criticism of Israel's policies was, in fact, truth.

The Big Lie Brainwashing Fog

The big lie—the so-called "Soviet threat," "evil empire," anti-Communism—is the most massive brainwashing scheme in all of history. There has never been a bigger lie, repeated more times, in all of history. It is a diabolical, ideological trap. It is the real opium of the people. It is a brainwashing drug that transposes reality into its very opposite. It is designed to create a danger where none exists and to cover up when the danger is real. Under its hypnotic influence, those who should be honored and supported are vilified and condemned. The heroes are turned into villains and the villains are painted as heroes. It turns people against their very best self-interests. For humanity, the big lie about a Soviet military nuclear threat has now become a matter of life or death, because the main ideological weapon in the Reagan Administration's arsenal in preparation for a nuclear war is the big lie of anti-Communism. It is the brainwashing fog to cover up the Reaganite drive toward nuclear confrontation and a final nuclear holocaust.

Many believed the big lie of anti-Communism when Hitler used it. The fifty million lost lives should be a horrible reminder to the whole world that, unless challenged and checked, the same big lie anti-Communism may well become the final funeral dirge for all of humanity—when there is no one left to raise a voice. All the slander about a Soviet military threat is an unmitigated big lie. But the vile, vicious anti-Soviet brainwashing campaign is not limited to lies about a Soviet military threat.

Soviet Anti-Semitism'— Truth On Its Head

The charge of anti-Semitism in the Soviet Union is just as big a lie. In fact it is an integral part of the big lie. It also turns historical facts on their head. According to this slander, the real fighters against anti-Semitism become the anti-Semites. And the anti-Semites become freedom fighters.

The truth is there is anti-Semitism. But it is in the capitalist world. And, like racism, it is on the rise right here in the United States.

It is one of those ironic brainwashing twists that the socialist countries are accused of anti-Semitism, when the fact is that they are the only countries that have political, ideological, legal and constitutional bars against all forms of racism, chauvinism and anti-Semitism. Their philosophical world outlook consciously rejects and leaves no room for racism and anti-Semitism.

The Soviet Union is accused of anti-Semitism while it is the only country in the history of the world that has, for over 65 years, pursued a policy of affirmative action, the Leninist policy of equality and justice for all peoples and nationalities. It is an ingenious policy that has literally wiped out the effects of generations of feudal and capitalist inequality, chauvinism and anti-Semitism. Soviet socialism completely wiped out the degrading oppression, the poverty-stricken, pogrom-ridden ghetto existence of the Jewish people under czarism. And with these material conditions, it also removed the social and economic roots of racism and chauvinism. Thus guaranteeing that never again will it happen on socialist soil.

The country that was known throughout the world as "the prison-house of nations" has been turned into a highly developed, technologically advanced, union of equal republics and peoples who live in peace and harmony.

The big lie brainwashers work to cover up or turn history upside down. We must not forget that during the Hitler-fascist onslaught, with its genocidal anti-Semitic thrust, there was only one country in the world that took special measures, including mass evacuation, to protect and save its Jewish population.

It was not an accident of history that this country was the Union of Soviet Socialist Republics, where the working class is the dominant force.

The Truth About World War II

While every capitalist country in the world, including the United States, turned a deaf ear to the appeals for help and anti-fascist unity, the Soviet Union responded with heroic actions that saved more Jewish lives than any other single act in history. Millions more, including millions of Jewish people, would have been saved had the United States, Great Britain and France responded to the Soviet appeal for a joint effort when Hitler continued his aggression with the invasion of Czechoslovakia.

In fact an early, anti-fascist, collective security, united front might have prevented World War II. And, after Hitler's invasion of Europe and the attack on the Soviet Union, even more millions could have been saved if the allies, the United States and Great Britain, had responded to the Soviet appeal to open up a Second Front against Hitler in Europe—earlier. They did not join in the anti-fascist struggle in time because they were still hoping, and in fact maneuvering, to join forces with Hitler against the Soviet Union.

The Truth About Normandy

These days much is being made of the 40th anniversary of the Normandy invasion. But this is another clear example of big lie distortions because it is an attempt to rewrite history. In the volumes of commentary, nothing is said about the absolute truth that the U.S.-British invasion took place long after the Soviet Union had already broken the back of the Nazi armed forces on blood-soaked battlefields at Leningrad, Stalingrad and Kursk. It is also absolute truth that during the Hitler holocaust, of all the political parties in the capitalist countries, only the working class Communist Parties pursued policies of concrete actions to block the mass murder.

The Truth About Israel

Setting another historic record straight, when the question of setting up and recognizing Israel as a sovereign state was on the United Nations agenda, the U.S. government spent months debating whether to support such a move. The U.S. oil monopolies were against it. They already dominated the rich oil fields in the Mideast/Persian Gulf.

While all this was going on, the Soviet representatives at the United Nations had already taken supporting public positions and a firm lead in the establishment of the state of Israel. The Soviet Union supported either of two concepts: two separate states, Arab and Jewish, or one united Jewish-Arab state. This Soviet policy was not accidental, arbitrary or subjective. It was a policy leading to actions based on a solid partisan class position. The Soviet Union well understood that anti-Semitism, like racism, is an instrument of the capitalist class exploitation. And that active opposition to racism and anti-Semitism is a working-class position.

Contradictions in History

Contradictions have often arisen in world history between the interests of nations and the interests of peoples. The U.S. itself is a product of such contradictions.

In its early years, the interests of the mass of immigrants coming to the U.S. from around the world and the interests of the Native American Indian peoples developed into a contradiction. This contradiction arose within the framework of developing capitalism. The U.S. government and the capitalist class position has always been based on maximum corporate profits. Because of this there have been no adjustments, reparations or even attempts at a just solution. The brutal, genocidal offensive against the American Indian peoples was, and remains, a capitalist approach to the question. It was, and remains, criminal, unjust and wrong. A just solution remains on the agenda of our nation.

Solutions for Today

However, a just correction of the wrongs cannot be a return to the very beginning. Corrections and solutions must be made within the framework of today's realities. A just solution must start with the elimination of all forms of racism and discrimination through affirmative action programs to wipe out all the inequalities suffered by the Native American Indian peoples.

Likewise, the Palestinian people and the Jewish people have historic ties to Palestine. But the mass influx of Jewish immigrants, especially after World War II, created a contradiction between the interests of these immigrants and the interests of the people of Palestine. The explosive, violent and—yes, genocidal—policy pursued after the United Nations decision to create two separate states was a capitalist, Zionist approach to the question. For the Palestinian people, the outcome was criminal, unjust and disastrous. It was, and remains, a crime against five million people. But here, also, it is difficult to think of a just solution in terms of going back to the conditions of the very beginnings—neither historical nor Biblical. A just solution remains on the agenda of Israel and the world.

Today the solution must start with Israel's withdrawal of its forces from Lebanon, from the West Bank, from the Gaza Strip and Golan Heights. Israel must withdraw and return to its 1967 borders. The solution must include creating conditions of total equality, with affirmative action programs to undo the wrongs of the past. The solution must include the right of the Palestinian people to establish an independent homeland. The solution must encompass basic recognition of the sovereignty, independence and rights of all existing states, including Israel.

There has been, and remains, a basic difference between the Mideast policies of the Soviet Union and the United States. The U.S. policy has always been based on oil and corporate profits. The Soviet policy has always been based on the original, basic United Nations resolution, on the existence of Israel and an independent, sovereign Palestinian state.

Understandably, Jewish people pay particular attention to developments in Israel. Progressive people worldwide supported the achievement of Israel's independence. But progressives supported an independent state, with equal rights for Jewish and Arab inhabitants of the former Palestine.

Position of Israeli Communists

In celebration of Israel's 36th anniversary, the heroic, multinational Communist Party of Israel said:

On the 36th anniversary of the establishment of the state of Israel, we note with concern that Israel is today much further from true independence than ever before in her history.

The realization of the hope of the masses for peace, the strengthening of independence and progress have evaded us further as a result of the dirty war in Lebanon, which was unleashed by the Likud ruling clique and the U.S. Reagan Administration.

As a result of adventurist policies, three-quarters of the country's budget is spent for military purposes. We are in the midst of galloping inflation, reduced are health services, construction, social services and expenditures for culture. The economic and social crisis deepens. And, as a result of such politics the threat of fascism increases in Israel and racism rears its head.

Short-Sighted Policy

The policy of the Israeli government is a very short-sighted one. It is staking everything on its alliance with U.S. imperialism. It has isolated itself in the world community. The world balance of forces is moving against U.S. imperialism. Therefore, it is becoming an unreliable, unstable senior partner. And, there is no guarantee the U.S. will not sell Israel down the river—when it suits the oil corporations. The U.S. imperialist interest in Mideast oil is much bigger than its interest in Israel. So far Israel has been useful to the U.S. oil monopolies.

But this situation could easily change. Israel could become an obstacle to U.S. access to Mideast oil, in which case the United States would have no compunctions about dropping it.

True National Interests

The true national interests and security of Israel lie in a completely different direction than the one Israel has been following. It lies in sitting down at the negotiating table with representatives of all parties who have a legitimate interest in the region—the Palestinian people and Israel's Arab neighbors, the Soviet Union and the United States.

It is not in the true national interests of Israel to continue opposing the legitimate aspirations of the Arab Palestinian people to a homeland and state. It is not in the true national interests of Israel to continue establishing settlements which greatly aggravate and complicate the situation. It is not in the true national interests and security of Israel to continue annexing territory seized through aggression and war.

The true national interests and security of Israel lie in agreeing to implement the many United Nations resolutions and returning all annexed territory to its rightful owners. It lies in Israel agreeing to return to its 1967 borders as a condition of peaceful coexistence with its Arab neighbors. Israel's security is not guaranteed by military aggression and the seizure of other countries' territory. In this day and age a little more or less territory has no real military significance.

What really counts is to establish boundaries recognized by all, guaranteed by all, especially the United Nations, the United States and the Soviet Union. For this, working out a just peace is absolutely necessary.

Concerning Jewish Americans, it is important not to give mechanical, uncritical support to the policies of the Israeli government. On the other hand, it is important to support what is in the best interests of Israel. Among the Israeli people themselves there are many who do not agree with the policies of the Israeli government, including a strong and growing peace movement of the people, a movement that has been increasingly taking to the streets in large demonstrations.

Private Selfish Interests

The sole purpose of the big lie of anti-communism, including the non-existent Soviet military threat and the lie about Soviet anti-Semitism—which is the dirtiest of all dirty tricks—is to ensnare people into support for the Reagan policies of war, of nuclear superiority, policies of U.S. corporate world domination.

The falsehood about Soviet anti-Semitism is specially designed to ensnare the Jewish people. It is natural that the Jewish people should have an emotional attachment to Israel and a special concern about anti-Semitism. But there are those who take advantage of this attachment for their own purposes: U.S. imperialism, which has huge corporate interests in the Mideast; the Israeli ruling class which has accepted the role of junior partner and surrogate, serving the interests of U.S. imperialism in the Mideast; the corporations and bankers in both countries. All these private interests justify their policies and actions on the basis that they are defending the national interests and security of Israel. The truth is that in the long run their policies and actions jeopardize the very existence of Israel.

In all this the ideas and policies of the Zionist groups play a special supporting role. From their special angle, they fully support all these reactionary policies and forces. They misuse and betray the very concerns and sentiments of the Jewish people. Some have been perverted by the Zionist leadership and turned into support for the policies of war and aggression in both Israel and the United States.

The big lie of anti-Communism and especially the falsehood of Soviet anti-Semitism have become the main ideological substance of Zionism. They have become the trumpeters of the big lie of anti-Communism. It is attached to the old backward concept that anti-Semitism is an incurable, eternal, inherited human characteristic of all who are not Jewish. For this reason, it is important not to equate Zionism with the Jewish people, their just aspirations and sentiments of national pride and their support for an Israel at peace with its neighbors and the world.

A Lasting Lesson

As the struggles sharpen and the questions become more difficult and complex, the clear thinking and contributions of such great personalities as Mike Gold, Hyman Lumer and Moshe Olgin become even more significant. And, as truth conquers the big lie, they will stand even taller.

There is a lasting lesson in Mike Gold's classic, working class novel, *Jews Without Money:* Reaganism, with its anti-labor, racist, warmaking policies, can be defeated by the unity of Jews without money, Catholics and Protestants without money, Afro-Americans, Puerto Ricans and Chicanos without money—all uniting with our multiracial, multinational working class without money. It is the people without money that will form a winning all people's front against Reaganism.

It is especially appropriate to end my remarks today with the very old, very famous Jewish greeting: *Sholom Aleichem!* Peace be with you!

Together with the great majority of Americans, I am sure we agree that the all-important Jewish affair today is the preservation of peace and the prevention of nuclear war.

11

ZIONISM IN THE SERVICE
OF THE ULTRA-RIGHT*

BY LEWIS M. MOROZE

The demonstration "for Soviet Jewry" at the UN Plaza, Sunday, May 11th, featuring the convicted U.S. spy, Anatole Scharansky, Reaganites and local politicos, exposes further the Zionist leadership in the United States as the most vocal and active ultra-right grouping promoting U.S. neo-globalism and U.S.-Israeli hegemony in the Middle East. The gathering was a deliberate pro-war rally aimed to wreck the Geneva peace process despite serious warnings from within Jewish organizations. Of singular significance is the warning by the President of the World Jewish Congress, Edgar Bronfman, at a recent session of that body.

Bronfman vigorously asserted that: "We reject any linkage between arms control and the Soviet Jewry issue," and he insisted that "the road to peace runs not only through Washington but also through Moscow" and called for the participation of the U.S.S.R. in the Middle East peace process.

Bronfman took sharp issue with Morris Abram, head of the U.S. Conference on Soviet Jewry, a leading member of the American Jewish Committee and a Reagan appointee on the U.S. Civil Rights Commission, where he serves Reagan by scuttling civil rights programs and legislation. Bronfman attacked Abram for threatening to call for demonstrations of Jews against arms negotiations between the U.S. and the U.S.S.R. if the Soviet government does not open its doors for "Jewish emigration."

For the demonstration at the UN Plaza the Zionist leaders corralled school children enrolled in Hebrew parochial schools and large num-

*From *Jewish Affairs*, May/June 1986

bers of Jewish-American profoundly moved by the fascist perpetrated Holocaust into accepting the illusion that Zionism is a national liberation movement.

The key beneficiary of the chauvinism, bourgeois nationalism and jingoism generated by the Zionist leadership is the ultra-right and imperialist forces in the U.S. The Conference on Soviet Jewry, peddling the lie of "Soviet anti-Semitism," serves the Reagan military industrial complex in its drive for war against the U.S.S.R.

The Zionist dominated leadership invents anti-Semitism in the Soviet Union, but does not lift a finger to mobilize Americans to combat anti-Semitism in the United States. These leaders remained silent in the face of the anti-Semitic attack on the floor of Congress by the Reaganite Congressman, Robert Dorman. They take no steps to mobilize against the growing revanchism and anti-Semitism in the Federal Republic of Germany, nor have they mobilized for mass protests against the existence of active KKK elements in the U.S. Army and Marines.

A local Jewish committee for Soviet Jewry in the 11th and 12th Congressional Districts of New Jersey, gerrymandered to guarantee that the correct grouping of the wealthiest suburbs would select two ultra-conservative members of Congress, financed the Congressmen from the two districts, James Courter (Rep.) and Dean Gallo (Rep.) for a trip to the Soviet Union to meet with "dissidents" in order to whip up more anti-Soviet sentiment, not alone in the two congressional districts, but throughout New Jersey and in Congress.

Discontent with Zionist ideology and its alliance with the ultra-right in the U.S. is evidencing itself more and more in the U.S. In the U.S., at best, but 12% of Jewish-Americans are organized Zionists, that is participating members of the Zionist Organization of America.

"Breira," the Jewish committee established in the 1970's to call for a new policy in the Middle East was smashed by the Zionists in 1979. But the questioning of Zionist domination of Jewish Americans and the bureaucracy of the Jewish American organizations brought into being "New Jewish Agenda," which now has thousands of members in some 40 chapters throughout the U.S. New Jewish Agenda challenges the rigid positions of the Zionists, though many of its members consider themselves Zionist oriented.

The neo-conservatives in the Jewish American community are coming in for more and more criticism. Many members of the American Jewish Committee, sponsors of *Commentary* magazine, the ultra-right organ in the Jewish American community, are smarting from the criticism levelled at the magazine for its reactionary, pro-war positions.

Most recently, a combination of Jewish liberals, moderates and certain conservatives joined forces to combat the right wing in the Jewish American community. This group announced their sponsorship of a new quarterly magazine to make it crystal clear that: "The neo-conservatives don't speak for the Jews." They announced the publication of a new quarterly. *Tikkun* (from the Hebrew word *tikkhun* meaning to repair, heal and transform) stating that "Jews remain committed to the great liberal and progressive social movements of our time—for peace, nuclear disarmament, equality for women, anti-apartheid and for human rights and justice." Combatting narrow nationalism the sponsors of the new periodical assert that "*Tikkun* is not just for the Jewish world—its articles are addressed to all people who like to think deeply about politics, culture and society."

The World Jewish Congress, itself Zionist oriented, perforce finds itself differentiating from certain Zionist practices and from the ruling circles in Israel. Jews in the capitalist world outside of Israel are not being drawn to Zionism nor to Israel, accounting for this differentiating position of the World Jewish Congress. In England Zionists compose but 9% of the Jews; in Argentina but 4%. With the mass flight from Israel, some 500,000 Israelis now reside in the U.S. It is under these conditions that Zionist Organizations world-wide are trying to hold on in the face of growing differentiation and outright opposition. The World Zionist Organization is now even promoting a movement of "Zionist Christians."

Jewish Americans and all Americans concerned about anti-Semitism and seeking answers to the correct application of the national question and how best to combat anti-Semitism and racism would do well to win subscribers for *Jewish Affairs* and to become readers and subscribers to the new nationwide working class paper, *the People's Daily World*. Armed with this powerful working class voice, the democratic and peace forces in our land can embark on the road to peace and freedom for all peoples.

DECLARATION OF THE RIGHTS OF THE NATIONALITIES OF RUSSIA

The October Revolution of the workers and peasants started under the general slogan of freedom.

The peasants have been freed from the rule of the landlords, for large landownership no longer exists—the soil has become free. The soldiers and sailors have been freed from the power of the sovereign generals, for the generals are now elective and removable. The workers have been freed from the caprice and tyranny of the capitalists, for from now on the control of the enterprises and factories by the workers has been established. All that is living and vital has become freed from hated bondage.

Now there remain only the nationalities of Russia, who have suffered and still suffer from oppression and tryanny. Their freedom must immediately be worked for, and it must be brought about resolutely and irrevocably.

During the times of tsarism and nations of Russia were systematically instigated against each other. The results of this policy are known: massacres and pogroms on the one hand, the enslaving of nations on the other hand.

This hideous policy of rousing hatred must and will never return. From now on it will be replaced by the policy of voluntary and honest unions of nations.

In the period of imperialism, after the February Revolution, when political power passed into the hands of the bourgeoisie represented by the Constitutional-Democratic Party, the open policy of instigation was replaced by a policy of cowardly mistrust towards the nations of Russia, a policy of molestation and provocation which was covered with verbose declarations about the "freedom" and "equality" of nations. The results of this policy are known: the sharpening of national enmity, the undermining of mutual trust.

This unworthy policy of lies and mistrust, of molestation and provocation, must be ended. From now on it must be replaced by a frank and honest policy leading to complete mutual trust between the nations in Russia.

Only on the basis of such trust can an honest and firm union of the nations of Russia be formed.

Only on the basis of such a union can the workers and peasants of the nations of Russia be merged into a single revolutionary force, able to withstand all the attacks of the imperialist, annexationist bourgeoisie.

In June of this year the Congress of Soviets proclaimed the free right of self-determination of the nations of Russia.

The second Congress of Soviets, which met in October, even more resolutely and definitely established this inalienable right of the nations of Russia.

Acting on the decisions of this Congress, the Council of People's Commissars plans to base its actions in regard to the nationalities of Russia on the following principles:

1. The equality and sovereignty of the nations of Russia.

2. The right of the nations of Russia to free self-determination including separation and the formation of independent states.

3. The removal of every and any national and national-religious privilege and restriction.

4. The free development of the national minorities and ethnographic groups living within the confines of Russia.

Corresponding concrete provisions will be worked out as soon as the Commission of Nationalities is established.

In the name of the Russian Republic: *Chairman of the Council of People's Commissars,* V. ULYANOV (LENIN); *People's Commissar of Nationalities,* JOSEPH DJUGASHVILI (STALIN).

November 15, 1917.

APPENDIX II

RESOLUTION OF THE COUNCIL OF PEOPLE'S COMMISSARS ON THE UPROOTING OF THE ANTI-SEMITIC MOVEMENT

According to reports received by the Council of People's Commissars, the counter-revolutionaries are carrying on agitation for pogroms in many cities especially in the frontier zone, as a result of which there have been sporadic outrages against the toiling Jewish population. The bourgeois counter-revolution has taken up the weapon which has slipped from the hands of the Tsar.

The absolutist government, each time when the need arose, turned the wrath of the peoples directed at itself against the Jews, at the same time telling the uneducated masses that all their misery comes from the Jews. The rich Jews, however, always found a way to protect themselves; only the Jewish poor always suffered and perished from instigation and violence.

The counter-revolutionaries have now renewed hatred against the Jews, using hunger, exhaustion and also the backwardness of the most retarded masses as well as the remnants of that hatred against the Jews which was planted among the people by absolutism.

In the Russian Socialist Federated Soviet Republic, where the principle of self-determination of the toiling masses of all peoples has been proclaimed, there is no room for national oppression. The Jewish bourgeois are our enemies, not as Jews but as bourgeois. The Jewish worker is our brother.

Any kind of hatred against any nation is inadmissible and shameful.

The Council of People's Commissars declares that the anti-Semitic movement and pogroms against the Jews are fatal to the interests of the workers' and peasants' revolution and calls upon the toiling people of Socialist Russia to fight this evil with all the means at their disposal.

National hostility weakens the ranks of our revolutionaries, disrupts the united front of the toilers without distinctions of nationality and helps only our enemies.

The Council of People's Commissars instructs all Soviet deputies to take uncompromising measures to tear the anti-Semitic movement out by the roots. Pogromists and pogrom-agitators are to be placed outside the law.

Chairman of the Council of People's Commissars, ULYANOV (LENIN); *Administrator of Affairs of the Council of People's Commissars,* BONCHE-BUREVICH; *Secretary of the Council,* N. GORBUNOV. *July 27, 1918.*

230

APPENDIX III

FURTHER FLOURISHING AND DRAWING CLOSER TOGETHER
OF SOCIALIST NATIONS AND NATIONALITIES*

The CPSU takes full account in its activities of the multinational composition of Soviet society. The path that has been traversed provides convincing proof that **the nationalities question inherited from the past has been successfully solved in the Soviet Union.** Characteristic of the national relations in our country are both the continued flourishing of the nations and nationalities and the fact that they are steadily and voluntarily drawing closer together on the basis of equality and fraternal cooperation. Neither artificial prodding nor holding back of the objective trends of development is admissible here. In the long-term historical perspective this development will lead to complete unity of the nations.

The CPSU proceeds from the fact that in our socialist multinational state, in which more than one hundred nations and nationalities work and live together, there naturally arise **new tasks of improving national relations.** The Party has carried out, and will continue to carry out such tasks on the basis of the tested principles of the Leninist nationalities policy. It puts forward the following main tasks in this field:

—all-round strengthening and development of the integral, federal, multinational state. The CPSU will continue to struggle consistently against any manifestations of parochialism and national narrow-mindedness, while at the same time showing constant concern for further increasing the role of the republics, autonomous regions and autonomous areas in carrying out countrywide tasks and for promoting the active involvement of working people of all nationalities in the work of government and administrative bodies. Through creative application of the Leninist principles of socialist federalism and democratic centralism, the forms of inter-nation relations will be enriched in the interests of the Soviet people as a whole and of each nation and nationality;

—a buildup of the material and intellectual potential of each re-

*The Challenges of our Time, International Publishers, New York, (1986), pp. 189–190.

public within the framework of the integral national economic complex. Combining the initiative of the Union and autonomous republics, autonomous regions and autonomous areas with central administration at the countrywide level will make possible the more rational use of the country's resources and of local natural and other features. It is necessary consistently to deepen the division of labour between the republics, even out the conditions of economic management, encourage active participation by the republics in the economic development of new regions, promote inter-republican exchanges of workers and specialists, and broaden and improve the training of qualified personnel from among citizens of all the nations and nationalities inhabiting the republics;

—development of the Soviet people's integral culture, which is socialist in content, diverse in its national forms and internationalist in spirit, on the basis of the greatest achievements and original progressive traditions of the peoples of the USSR. The advancement and drawing together of the national cultures and the consolidation of their interrelationships make mutual enrichment more fruitful and open up the broadest possibilities for the Soviet people to enjoy everything valuable that has been created by the talent of each of the peoples of our country.

The equal right of all citizens of the USSR to use their native languages and the free development of these languages will be ensured in the future as well. At the same time learning the Russian language, which has been voluntarily accepted by the Soviet people as a medium of communication between different nationalities, besides the language of one's nationality, broadens one's access to the achievements of science and technology and of Soviet and world culture.

The Party proceeds from the belief that consistent implementation of the Leninist nationalities policy and a strengthening in every way of the friendship of the peoples are part of the effort to perfect socialism and a way that has been tested in social practice of ensuring the further flourishing of our multinational socialist homeland.

NOTES for pp. 36–81.

[1] *Posledniye Izvestia (News)*—a periodical bulletin issued by the Foreign Committee of the Bund from 1901 to 1906.

[2] *The Bund* (The General Jewish Workers' Union of Lithuania, Poland, and Russia) came into being in 1897 at the Inaugural Congress of Jewish Social-Democratic groups in Vilna. It consisted mainly of semi-proletarian Jewish artisans of Western Russia. At the First Congress of the R.S.D.L.P. in 1898 the Bund joined the latter "as an autonomous organization, independent only in respect of questions affecting the Jewish proletariat specifically." (*The C.P.S.U. in Resolutions and Decisions of Congresses, Conferences and Plenary Meetings of the Central Committee*, Russ.ed,. Part I, 1954, p. 14)

The Bund was a vehicle of nationalist and separatist ideas in Russia's working-class movement. In April 1901 the Bund's Fourth Congress resolved to alter the organizational ties with the R.S.D.L.P. as established by the latter's First Congress. In its resolution, the Bund Congress declared that it regarded the R.S.D.L.P. as a federation of national organizations, of which the Bund was a federal member.

Following the rejection by the Second Congress of the R.S.D.L.P. of the Bund's demand for recognition as the sole representative of the Jewish proletariat, the Bund left the Party, but rejoined it in 1906 on the basis of a decision of the Fourth (Unity) Congress.

Within the R.S.D.L.P. the Bund constantly supported the Party's opportunist wing (the Economists, Mensheviks, the liquidators), and waged a struggle against the Bolsheviks and Bolshevism To the Bolsheviks' programmatic demand for the right of nations to self-determination the Bund contraposed the demand for autonomy of national culture. During the years of the Stolypin reaction and the new revolutionary upsurge, the Bund adopted a liquidationist stand and played an active part in the formation of the August anti-Party bloc. During the First World War (1914–18), the Bundists took a social-chauvinist stand. In 1917 the Bund supported the bourgeois Provisional Government and sided with the enemies of the Great October Socialist Revolution. During the foreign military intervention and the Civil War, the Bundist leaders made common cause with the forces of counter-revolution. At the same time a tendency towards cooperation with the Soviets became apparent among the Bund rank and file. In March 1921 the Bund dissolved itself, part of the membership joining the Russian Communist Party (Bolsheviks) in accordance with the general rules of admission.

[3] The reference is to a Yiddish translation of Karl Kautsky's pamphlet, *Social Revolution.*

[4] *Black Hundreds*—a reactionary, monarchist, pogrom-making organization set up by the tsarist police to combat the revolutionary movement. They murdered

revolutionaries, assulted progressive intellectuals, and organized anti-Jewish pogroms.

5 The document is an editorial preface to the pamphlet *Report on the Third Congress of the R.S.D.L.P.*, published in Yiddish in 1905.

6 The decisions here referred to were Draft Terms for the Union of the Bund with the R.S.D.L.P. (adopted at the Fourth [Unity] Congress of the R.S.D.L.P. in 1906) and the resolution on "The Unity of National Organizations in the Localities" (adopted at the Fifth [All Russian] Conference of the R.S.D.L.P. in 1908).

7 *Nasha Zarya (Our Dawn)*—A Menshevik liquidator monthly published legally in St. Petersbury from 1910 to 1914. It served as a rallying center for the liquidationist forces in Russia.

8 These theses were written by Lenin for his lectures on the national question delivered on July 9, 10, 11 and 13 (new style), 1913 in the Swiss towns of Zurich, Geneva, Lausanne and Berne.

9 The decisions of the Prague Conference (1912) called the relations that the national Social-Democratic organizations had with the R.S.D.L.P. from 1907 to 1911 *"federation of the worst type."* Although the Social-Democratic organizations of Poland, Lithuania and the Latvian Area, and also the Bund, belonged to the R.S.D.L.P., they actually held themselves aloof. Their representatives did not take part in guiding all-Russian Party work; directly or indirectly they promoted the anti-Party activities of the liquidators. (See *Collected Works*, Vol. 17, pp. 464–65 and Vol. 18, pp. 411–12.)

10 *Russkaya Molva (Russian Tidings)*—a bourgeois daily, organ of the Progressists, founded in 1912. Lenin called the Progressists a mixture of Octobrists and Cadets. The paper appeared in St. Petersburg in 1912 and 1913.

11 *Narodowa Demokracja (National Democracy)*—a reactionary, chauvinist party of the Polish bourgeoisie, founded in 1897. Afraid of the growing revolutionary movement, the party changed its original demand for Polish independence to one for limited autonomy within the framework of the autocracy. During the 1905–07 Revolution, Narodowa Demokracia was the main party of Polish counter-revolution, the Polish Black Hundreds, to use Lenin's expression. They supported the Octobrists in the State Duma.

In 1919 the party changed its name to Zwiazek Ludowa-Narodowy (National-Popular Union) and from 1928 it became the Stronnictwo Narodowe (National Party). After the Second World War, individuals from this party, having no longer any party of their own, attached themselves to Mikolajczyk's reactionary party, the Polske Stronnictwo Ludowe (Polish Popular Party).

12 This refers to the segregation of the schools according to nationality, one of the basic demands of the bourgeois-nationalist program for "cultural-national autonomy."

[13] The *Joint Conference of the Central Committee of the R.S.D.L.P. and Party Officials* (for purposes of secrecy it was known as the "Summer" or "August" Conference) was held from September 23 to October 1 (October 6–14), 1913 in the village of Poronin (near Cracow) where Lenin spent the summer months. The Conference was attended by 22 delegates (17 with a vote and 5 with a voice but no vote). Sixteen delegates represented local Party organizations: St. Petersburg—Inessa Armand, A. E. Badayev and A. V. Shotman; Moscow and the Central Industrial Area—F. A. Balashov, Y. T. Novozhilov, R. V. Milinovsky and A. I. Lobov (the two last-named were found to be provocateurs); Ekaterinoslav—G. I. Petrovsky; Kharkov—M. K. Muranov; Kostroma—N. R. Shagov; Kiev—Y. F. Rozmirovich ("Galina"); Urals—S. I. Deryabina ("Sima," "Elena"). Lenin, Krupskaya, Troyanovsky and others represented the Central Committee Bureau Abroad, the central organ of the Party *Sotsial-Demokrat* and the magazine *Prosveshcheniye*. The Bolshevik deputies to the Fourth Duma also represented the Party organizations in the constituencies and towns that elected them to the Duma. Representatives of the Left wing of the Polish Social-Democratic Party, J. S. Hanecky, G. Kamenski ("Domski") and others attended; these delegates had a voice but no vote.

The Conference discussed the following questions: (1) reports from the localities, report on the work of the Polish Social-Democrats, report on the work of the Central Committee; (2) the national question; (3) the work of Social-Democrats in the Duma; (4) the situation in the Social-Democratic Duma group; (5) the question of organization and the Party Congress; (6) the strike movement; (7) work in the legal associations; (8) the Narodniks; (9) the Party press; (10) the forthcoming International Socialist Congress in Vienna. The first two days were devoted to a private conference of the Duma deputies on questions of practical work in the Duma.

Lenin guided the work of the Conference; he opened the meeting with an introductory speech and delivered reports on the work of the Central Committee, the national question and the International Socialist Congress in Vienna; Lenin also spoke on almost all the points of the agenda, made proposals and compiled or edited the draft resolutions.

Reports from the localities told of the growth of the working-class movement. The Conference decided in favor of united All-Russian Party work to guide the actions of the working class on a country-wide scale.

Lenin's report on the Central Committee activity summarized what had been done since the Prague Conference in 1912. In his report on the Vienna International Socialist Congress Lenin proposed sending as many delegates as possible from both legal and illegal organizations, and suggested the holding of a Party congress at the same time as the International Congress. The Conference ended with Lenin's closing speech.

The minutes of the Conference at Poronin have not been found. The resolutions were published as a separate pamphlet under the title *Notification and Resolutions of the Summer, 1913, Joint Conference of the Central Committee of the R.S.D.L.P. and Party Officials,* issued abroad by the Central Committee. For reasons of secrecy some of the resolutions were not printed in full; omitted were point 6 of the resolution on the strike movements and points 1–5 of the resolution on the Party press. The full texts of the resolutions were published illegally in a mimeographed edition.

[14] The resolution refers here to the decision adopted by the liquidators' August Conference in 1912 to the effect that "cultural-national autonomy" was compatible with the Program of the R.S.D.L.P.

[15] *Pale of Settlement*—district in tsarist Russia where Jews were permitted permanent residence.

[16] *Numerus clausus*—the numerical restriction imposed in tsarist Russia on admission of Jews to the state secondary and higher educational establishments, to employment at factories and offices, and the professions.

[17] *The National Equality Bill* (official title of the "Bill for the Abolition of all Disabilities of the Jews and of all Restrictions on the Grounds of Origin or Nationality") was drafted by Lenin for the Russian Social-Democratic Labor group in the Fourth Duma, apparently in connection with the discussion of the Ministry of the Interior's budget.

In publishing this Bill of the R.S.D.L. group, Lenin considered it a point of honor on the part of the Russian workers to support it with tens of thousands of signatures and declarations. "This," said Lenin, "will be the best means of consolidating *complete* unity, amalgamating all the workers of Russia, irrespective of nationality."

[18] V. O.—author of the article "The Deterioration of School Education" published in *Severnaya Rabochaya Gazeta* No. 35, March 21, 1914.

[19] The *Lecture on the 1905 Revolution* was delivered in German on January 9 (22), 1917 at a meeting of young workers in the Zurich People's House. Lenin began working on the lecture in the closing days of 1916. He referred to the lecture in a letter to V. A. Karpinsky dated December 7 (20), asking for literature on the subject.

[20] The making of gramophone records of Lenin's speeches was organized by *Tsentropechat* (the central agency of the All-Russia Central Executive Committee for the Supply and Distribution of Periodicals). Between 1919 and 1921, 13 of Lenin's speeches were recorded.

Index

Abram, Morris, 7, 224
affirmative action, 5, 13, 142, 208, 211
Africa, Israeli ties with, 117–21; with South Africa, 122–26
Agnew, Spiro, 145
Algeria, 109, 167
Allon, Yigal, 107, 108
American Council for Judaism, 127
AFL-CIO, 121, 193
AFSC study on Mideast, 172
American-Israel Public Affairs Committee, 170
American Jewish Committee, 128, 141, 225; survey by, 135–36
American Jewish Congress, 160–61, 203
Amin, Idi, 119
anti-Communism, use of, 186–88, 216–17
anti-imperialism, Mideast, 166–71
anti-Semitism: CPUSA position on, 2–3, 4–5, 17–18, 144, 186, 219
—"Black anti-Semitism," 141–42, 144;
—equated with anti-Zionism, 35–6; 139–40; 192–93, 199
—and the "Left," 35–6, 139–40
—Marxism-Leninism on, 1, 8, 30–31, 38–40, 80–81, 134–35
—in the U.S., 18, 135–37, 212;
—see also Lenin, V.I., and Zionism
anti-Sovietism, 6–7, 18, 36, 122, 147, 158–61, 224–25
Arab countries, Soviet aid to, 168–69, 180
Arab people, see Palestinian Arabs; specific countries
Arafat, Yassir, 181
assimilation, 27, 29, 32, 127–28, 137–38
Ausubel, Nathan, 32
Avidar, Avraham, 160
Avneri, Shlomo, 101
Avneri, Uri, 90–91, 199

Baghdad Pact, 11, 167
Balfour Declaration, 106–07
Bandung Conference, 180
Barkai, Chaim, 102–03
Bar-Zohar, Michael, 90, 110
Bauer, Otto, 60
Begin, Menachim, 154, 200, 208, 210
Belostok pogrom, 47–8
Ben-Gurion, David, 85, 90, 109–11, 123, 159
Berg, Alan, 14
Berry, Winston, 119
Biltmore program, 107
Birobidjan, 28, 31
B'nai B'rith, 145: Anti-Defamation League of, 151, 186–87, 212
Boas, Evron, 204
Borochov, Ber, 99
"Breira," 201, 225
Brezhnev, Leonid, 28, 195
British imperialism, 87–8, 106, 108–09
British Mandate, 87, 108, 128
Bronfman, Edgar, 224
Broslawsky, Dr. Farrel, 136
Buckley, James L., 145, 183
Bund, The, and RSDLP, 37–41, 51–3
Bunting, Brian, 124
Bureau of Jewish Employment, 213

CENTO, 168
Cohen, Aaron, 128
Cohen, Steven M., 205
Commentary, 225
Communist Party of Israel: 94–5n; 199, 220:
—on the Jewish question, 134
—on Meir Kahane, 154–55;
—on Zionism, 195, 203
Council of Jewish Federations, 212–13
Courter, James, 225

237